P9-DXM-881

Choral Directing

Choral Directing

by Wilhelm Ehmann

translated by George D. Wiebe

AUGSBURG PUBLISHING HOUSE
Minneapolis, Minnesota

Choral Directing

Copyright © 1968 Augsburg Publishing House

All rights reserved

Library of Congress Catalog Card No. 67-29816

This book was originally published in Germany as Wilhelm Ehmann, *Die Chorführung, Band II Das künstlerische Singen* Bärenreiter-Verlag Karl Vötterle KG, 1949.

Manufactured in the United States of America
By Augsburg Publishing House
Minneapolis, Minnesota

MT
85
E4B

Introduction

The purpose of this book is to present a sound pedagogical and artistic basis for choral singing and to provide numerous suggestions and guides for dealing with various phases of training a choir. This book is the sequel to an earlier volume which is concerned with the art of leading informal singing, a custom which is probably more prevalent in Germany than in North America. The present volume bases many of its principles and methods on an earlier book which as yet is not available in an English translation.

Professor Ehmann's basic philosophies of choral music permeate every chapter. For him a company of singers, no matter how well-trained, can become a choir only after it has become a unique fellowship — a choral community. Singing must serve to enrich the personal life of the individual. The choral sound must not only be of a high musical standard, but it must also reflect the human and spiritual qualities of both composer and singers.

The various choral techniques, methods, exercises, and suggestions are to a large extent original with the author, who has tested them over several decades with numerous and varied choral organizations ranging from a musically illiterate male voice choir to first-rate concert choirs and internationally known solo singers. As a guest student at the *Westfälische Landeskirchenmusikschule* I have observed how, in three short months, Professor Ehmann was able to develop a first-rate student choir from a group of thirty organ and conducting majors, most of whom possessed no outstanding vocal talent. With this choir he achieved a vocal richness, a musicality and enthusiasm that is hard to surpass. Only by attending every rehearsal could one understand how this could be accomplished in such a short time. Many of the principles and techniques described in this book were used but it seemed that many pedagogical procedures and choral techniques were improvised on the spot to meet a specific musical or vocal need.

The North American reader should find much that is new and helpful particularly with regard to unison singing, performance practices in canon singing, and the cultivation of improvisational singing. Choir directors could be stimulated and encouraged to re-evaluate their own thinking about the purpose and place of choral music so that it might have the proper relevance

77-09894

to the world of art and to life itself. It is also hoped that some of the human warmth, artistic idealism, abounding enthusiasm, and vitality of the author may be conveyed in this English translation, for no amount of technical know-how can compensate for the qualities which make some directors outstanding in their work with choirs.

*Translator's note: Although an attempt has been made to substitute the original music for familiar or readily available examples for American readers, it was not always possible or even desirable to do so. It would be advisable for choral directors who are interested in the choral music of the sixteenth to the eighteenth centuries, to avail themselves of the two German collections of choral works to which reference has been frequently made, particularly in the first chapter:

    1) *Gesellige Zeit* — (*Liederbuch für gemischten Chor*) — by Walther Lipphardt — Bärenreiter-Verlag, Kassel, Germany.

    2) *Chorgesangbuch* — (*Geistliche Gesänge für 1 bis 5 Stimmen*) — Richard Gölz Bärenreiter-Verlag, Kassel, Germany.

The former contains 83 short secular settings by foremost sixteenth and seventeenth century composers. The *Chorgesangbuch* is an anthology of two- to five-voice settings of the most important German chorale tunes by the greatest sixteenth and seventeenth century composers of church music. These have been selected and arranged according to the church year.

About the Author

Wilhelm Ehmann grew up with the church and brass music of Westphalia. His first music teacher was the well-known champion of brass music, Johannes Kuhlo. In his youth Professor Ehmann was indebted to the then prevalent *Singbewegung* (singing movement) for much of his incentive and inspiration. He studied musicology, church music, history, literature, and art history in Freiburg and Leipzig. He was professor of musicology at the universities of Freiburg, Innsbruck, and Münster. After the Second World War he founded the *Westfälische Landeskirchenmusikschule* (Westphalian School of Church Music) in Herford, Germany and the *Westfälische Kantorei*. The *Westfälische Landeskirchenmusikschule* has become the largest institute of its kind and trains church musicians who come there to study from almost every part of the world.

In the performance of choral masterworks with the *Westfälische Kantorei,* Dr. Ehmann continually strives for interpretations which can be historically and musically justified on the basis of his own musicological research. This has thrown a surprising amount of new light on performance practices and the interpretation of well-known choral works.

The *Westfälische Kantorei* has toured almost all European countries as well as the Far and Near East. In 1961 Dr. Ehmann and his choir accepted the invitation for a tour in the United States as a part of his annual International Choral Directors' Workshops. An average of twelve countries have been represented each year. He has also conducted choral clinics in various countries. Dr. Ehmann is the founder and artistic director of the Cantata-Production, the first and largest German recording company devoted specifically to sacred music. His numerous musicological and pedagogical publications concentrate on sacred and secular choral music, brass music, folk songs, and research articles on the music of Heinrich Schuetz, Handel, and J. S. Bach.

Combined with his interest and ability in musicological research are Dr. Ehmann's unique pedagogical talents. Whether lecturing to his history class or rehearsing a new work, Professor Ehmann completely captivates the interest and wins the response of his students. He is an outstanding conductor and his choirs have become well-known for their excellent singing, their "plasticity" of phrasing, their rich, warm tone, and their obvious enthusiastic enjoyment of making music together.

Table of Contents

Chapter V — Choral Ear Training

The goals of ear training, gesture, movement and rhythmic training . . . listening as a means of self-control for the singer . . . the concept of *hören* (to listen) in the everyday usage of the German language . . . singing of a sung or played tone . . . singing of scales . . . singing of intervals . . . use of initial intervals of a tune . . . practice in rote singing . . . singing of canons . . . formation of chords . . . multivoiced choral improvisation . . . musical reasons for loss of intonation.

Chapter VI — Body Movement and Choral Singing

Music and movement . . . strong association of music with movement in the older Occidental music . . . lack of sufficient physical movement in our modern civilization . . . bodily activity outside of the choral rehearsal . . . physical exercises during the rehearsal: the musical phrase is concluded by gesture of the hand . . . the hand controls and guides the course of a tune . . . a musical motive is represented by a body movement . . . the singers conduct themselves . . . the basic musical movement is expressed by the entire body . . . the rhythm of a song expressed by movement of arms and feet . . . the group dances a country dance to a tune sung in unison . . . the singers step to a tune sung in unison . . . a unison sung tune is danced to in free steps . . . a tune within multivoiced improvisation is walked, marched, or danced to . . . a multivoiced composition is expressed by free-walking steps . . . the relationship of individual voice parts to each other is represented by physical motions . . . walking, stepping, and dancing to canons . . . the sovereignty of the artistic will in creative music making.

Chapter VII — Choral Rhythmic Training

Rhythm as order within movement and division of time . . . rhythm is not a logical process . . . working with freely improvised rhythmic entities in various groups . . . overlapping of time and rhythm . . . rhythmic improvisation . . . difficult rhythms of individual voice parts from different choral works . . . rhythmic comprehension of an extended song ending . . . division of a large vocal form into several rhythmic groups . . . rhythmicization of canons . . . rhythmic comprehension of the structure of a composition . . . the transition from rhythmization to the music and text.

Chapter VIII — Conducting Patterns and Choral Gestures

Translation of movement and rhythm into visible signs . . . time-beating technique and choral direction . . . historical forms and practices of directing musical groups . . . the close connection of informal song-leading methods to artistic choral writing . . . basic relationship between choir and director . . . the means of choral directing . . . importance of a good time-beating technique . . . modification of orchestral conducting for choral conducting . . . directing without the baton . . . a course in time-beating technique: basic posture . . . loosening-up exercises . . . initial bodily stance . . . attack (onset) . . . the basic beat patterns . . . practice of the various beat patterns . . . rhythmic training for conducting students . . . assignment of exercises in multivoiced improvisation for the conducting student . . . height level and size of the conducting movements . . . modifying and changing conducting patterns . . . curves of musical motion . . . directing with both hands . . . unceasing motion in music to be reflected by unceasing motion in the conducting movements . . . conducting signals should be given slightly ahead of the choir . . . simplification and modification of the beat patterns . . . the conducting line . . . change of meter within a song . . . the cutoff . . . singing while directing . . . conducting from memory . . . technical signals during singing . . . eye contact with the singers . . . necessity of a contemporary, standard, universal choral sound.

SECTION B

Chapter I — The Preparation by the Choral Director

The importance and meaning of preparation . . . the selection of the musical work: occasion . . . the text in relation to the singers . . . level of difficulty . . . pedagogical and artistic training values of the music . . . extent of reliance on the music . . . the physical arrangements and acoustics of the room . . . familiarization with the text through reading . . . familiarization with the music by playing it on an instrument . . . overcoming technical difficulties . . . learning the music . . . the conducting line . . . phrasing . . . ability to work through the problems encountered in a foreign language . . . performance practice . . . marking the score . . . the rehearsal plan.

Chapter II — Artistic Unison Singing

Unison and multivoiced singing . . . significance of unison singing . . . appropriate tunes for unison singing . . . examples for unison choral work . . . "So Did Once Three Angels," "In the midst of earthly life," O Jesus, King of Glory" . . . elaboration of unison singing through responsive and alternative singing.

Chapter III — Artistic Canon Singing

The canon as a symbol . . . various ways of presenting and performing canons . . . approaching the study of the canon as in unison singing . . . assignment of parts . . . the "birth" of the canon . . . deciding on how and where a canon is to be concluded . . . musical introductions and conclusions . . . use of soloists . . . conducting signals during canon singing . . . choir formation for canon singing.

Chapter IV — Multivoiced Choral Singing (Method of Rehearsing)

Rehearsing without an instrument . . . explanation of a musical work . . . an artistic view of the work . . . learning the tune . . . isolating difficult parts before the rehearsal . . . choral improvisation as a transition to the rehearsing of the entire composition . . . three possible methods of approach: proceeding from the words, mastering the music, artistic development of other works requiring similar kind of treatment . . . proceeding from the melodic aspects of the work . . . the addition of the text . . . treatment of imitation, canon, contrapuntal, melodic parts . . . other works requiring similar treatment . . . proceeding from the rhythmic elements of the work . . . addition of the melodic elements . . . acquisition of the text . . . sense and purpose of such procedures . . . merits of the work as a basis for a genuine performance . . . use of instruments.

Chapter V — The Choral Evening (Final Rehearsal and Performance)

Relative and absolute values of the rehearsal . . . striving for a wholistic approach . . . completeness to music making at rehearsals . . . the choral rehearsal as an evening of music making . . . the deportment of the choral director . . . repetition . . . singing from memory . . . choir formations in rehearsal . . . final (dress) rehearsal . . . the performance . . . the concert tour.

Section A

Chapter I

Choral Posture

If it were possible to place a human larynx in the throat of a Greek stone statue of a human being, and if it were possible to direct a stream of breath to this larynx, the resulting sound would be a toneless, whirring noise. The explanation for this is the lack of any resonance spaces in the statue and the fact that the solid body of stone is not capable of transmitting sympathetic vibrations that are so essential for rich resonance. If, on the other hand, one should take an ordinary violin, strew a little sand on the sound board and draw the bow over a string, one could observe how the grains of sand are hurled up from the surface. Wood is the most suitable resonating material, and since it is used for the resonating box, it is immediately set into sympathetic vibrations by the strings so that the quick, quaking movements on the sound board hurl the sand particles into the air.

The singer should imagine his body as having the full resonance possibilities of the sound box of the violin. Continuing with the above experiment, one could spread a little sand on a singer's head, chest, and midriff and observe the grains of sand being hurled into the air during singing. The body of the singer is not just a container for his tone-generating larynx, but it is the *instrument* of the singer. With this instrument he must make music. Head and body help the larynx produce the desired tone, for without the full cooperation of the body, the larynx would produce only a whirring, buzzing sound. The singer should cultivate a consciousness of his body, letting it become alive to music and, under all circumstances, allowing it to be flexible, buoyant, and responsive to resonance. His body should never resemble the stone sculpture but rather the resonating box of a good violin.

A sense of physical alertness is a prerequisite for every singer. In singing, the body comes into its own so to speak. In every born singer there lives something of the idea of the ancient, that for example, the chemical body fluids are attuned to each other, that the proportions of the golden section* (*sectio aura*) which — in their view — governed the proportions of the body, also determined the measurements of the body. Through music making the body is awakened and supported in its original proportions, its parts are harmoniously related to each other and consequently begins to sound. According to this, sickness is a musical dissonance in the human body which can be cured again through consonant music.

In the singing activities and choral work of our own time we should experience a freeing of the whole person through a harmonious body-soul relationship within ourselves. Man, in his total complexity, must become vibrant within himself and must find his "own tone." All mental and physical inhibitions, suppressions, and "cramped-in" feelings are to be dissolved in this harmony.

The singer uses his body both *to sustain life* and *to cultivate his art*. He can never escape from himself, for with his physical life he either furthers or hinders his artistic life. A good singing teacher and choir director will utilize activities from everyday life as well as natural and acquired capabilities of the body for the development of his artistic work. On the other hand, the experiences and demands of the artistic life will influence the everyday life of the singers, be it with regard to posture, breathing, clothing, protection from colds, type of diet and moderation in drinking and smoking.

Following are some of the aids which are at the choir director's disposal for the *training of his singers:*

. . . the use of *calisthenics*, e.g. jumping, shaking the different members of the body to loosen up physically,

. . . the application of *life-related functions*, such as activating the diaphragm through laughter,

. . . *stimulating the imagination*, e.g. instructing the singers to "sing out of your eyes" in order to achieve a higher focus of the voice,

. . . *the use of technical suggestions*, e.g. noting the position of the tongue and lips through the formation of different vowels and consonants,

. . . the effect of his *own personal example*, e.g. with regard to bodily deportment and his manner of speaking.

The choir director must pay careful attention to bodily deportment. His own posture should be such that his body becomes an instrument which permits all its resonances to come alive. The body should be held in a vertical line, the shoulders slightly drawn back, the whole body resting within the bone framework. In this way, all unnecessary muscular tensions can be dissolved. The tense, military posture is a hindrance in singing. A forward tilted

*The golden section referred to an ancient formula for dividing a straight line. The line was divided into two parts in such a way that the ratio of the shorter part to the longer part was equal to the ratio of the longer part to the entire line, e.g. in A_____x_____ $\dfrac{AX}{XB} = \dfrac{XB}{AB}$

body burdens the chest and abdomen and hinders the chest and diaphragm in the breathing activity; a backward tilted body burdens the back and stretches the abdomen and chest. The head should be revolved from the swivel which is located at the top of the vertebrae column. Tilting the head too far backward results in rigidity of the throat and tilting the head forward encumbers the larynx. Let the singer imagine that his body is suspended from his head. This can help him to attain the feeling of physical freedom and lightness.

The chin should be slightly drawn in to allow the larynx freedom to function properly. The heels should not be touching each other, the feet should be pointed out slightly and the body should rest firmly on both feet. This position gives the singer a steady foundation to sustain powerful tones, and the ability to withstand the various tensions to which singers are subjected. The arms should hang loosely at the sides whenever they are not used to hold the music and should not be crossed in front of or behind the singer. The whole body must be free and relaxed.

A child usually possesses such a physical stance. The adult, however, because of changes during puberty, growth difficulties, misdirected vocational training, wrong mode of living, and demands of civilization, frequently has acquired all kinds of inhibitions and tensions. Simple calisthenics can help to promote relaxation and good posture, e.g. rolling the head in a left to right circular motion, shaking the arms separately, then simultaneously, shaking the legs vigorously, etc. The impulse for these activities should come from the center of the body. Additional exercises, such as rolling shoulders forward and backward and even knee bending, can be employed to dissolve some of the physical rigidity. The raising and lowering of the heels and stretching of the arms as high as possible as in fruit picking and basketball playing may also be usefully employed as calisthenics.

Another life-related activity that could be used is the "bell ringing" exercise. After sufficiently loosening up, the singer should imagine himself to be a large church bell and begin to swing from his hips. While performing this exercise the awareness of both the so-called *longitudinal axis* and the *transverse axis* should be developed. The longitudinal axis runs in a vertical, straight line through the vertebrae. On should think of this axis as pointing upward. The upward motion is not only present in old forms of sketching and painting but it represents the basic direction of man's being, for all that which strives upward, according to Herder, belongs to the nature of man (in contrast to the earth-directed posture of animals). If the singer envisions his longitudinal axis extending in an upward direction, he will feel himself so inwardly stretched or lifted in every part of his body (as if he felt spaces between different parts of his body) that in his imagination he will almost begin to soar.

To think of the body as being earthbound — weighted down toward the earth — weighs the body down into its several parts, i.e. one part presses upon the other and the body is compressed within itself. The body should swing around the longitudinal axis. The feet should be firmly positioned at a slight distance from each other, and a sense of freedom should be felt in every joint. The body should be able to move around freely (play!) within its mobile framework. When swinging the body the actual curve of the backbone is shifted against the imaginary vertical plumb line. While concentrating on this line let the body swing back and forth from left to right, forward and backward, and finally in a circular motion around the imaginary axis. During this exercise the eyes are kept closed and the concentration is directed completely inward so that a keen feeling and clear sense of a free-soaring body is attained; the singer must be fully aware and in full control of his body. The activity just described should not be performed as if the body had just received a jolt from without, but it should emanate from the center of the body, beginning with very small oscillations which gradually increase until the whole body is vibrant with life and motion.

The longer (vertical) axis of the body is counterbalanced by the two transverse (horizontal) axes. The first of the transverse axes is situated at the hip level. A second transverse axis intercepts the long axis at the shoulders. Man's basic physical form is patterned after the form of the cross and the double cross. The singer should also develop his awareness of the transverse axes. While standing in an upright position he can swing in a pendulum motion from the lower axis. Both movements may appear the same outwardly, but in the mind of the singer they must be clearly differentiated. The point where the longitudinal axes and the lower transverse axis meet is the *center of the body*. It is from this center that the impulse to sing should originate.

The awareness of the lower axis is stimulated through deep breathing exercises (see A II, p. 17 ff.). An awareness of the upper transverse axis can be brought about by such exercises as rolling the shoulders, cultivating good posture, holding a real or imaginary weight in different positions of the outstretched arms, and exercising with arms stretched sideways. The sensation of a free, swinging, liberated body should become a part of all vocal music making.

One can hear whether a phrase in a song issues from the larynx alone, or whether the loosened, freed body that contains the larynx is vibrating sympathetically, allowing the music the necessary plasticity and fullness. When listening to a choir, one can tell whether he is listening to many vibrating larynxes or whether the total being of the singers has been reflected in the sound and a unified entity of body and soul has come to vibrate.

The point of departure for liberating the body and soul toward this kind of freedom is complete relaxation, a complete letting go of all unnecessary muscular and nervous tensions. Certain muscular and nervous tensions are necessary for singing, but these desirable tensions are best realized when all extraneous and undesirable tensions have been removed.

All organic processes can take place as a result of a polarity between tension and relaxation. This is certainly true of singing. The activity of the heart and the breathing processes combine both tension and relaxation. Relaxation is not to be confused with inertness; nor is rigidity to be mistaken for tension. It is not possible for every person who is driven by the modern tempo of living to achieve this necessary relaxation without special aids or exercises. We must devise exercises and techniques to help them. A useful exercise to achieve relaxation is the following: The singer lies on his back with a maximum area of his head, back, buttocks, and legs touching the floor. This exercise can be carried out at summer youth retreats, camps, and other more informal situations where people meet for singing and recreation. The singers play "dead" or "sleeping"; not a nerve is twitching. After thorough relaxation each lifts an arm or a leg up to a great height and lets it drop passively to the ground. The choir trainer walks among them and lifts an arm or a foot to test the degree of relaxation attained. It is notable that professional musicians find it most difficult to achieve this complete relaxation.

Out of this necessity for a relaxed, unencumbered posture which is so basic to a free, rich resonance, conclusions can be drawn with regard to the technical aspects of choral singing. The singer must stand while he sings, if possible also during rehearsals. When seated for a time during longer rehearsals, he should sit straight, and with a sense of freedom from the hips and shoulders. The singer should not slump in his chair and he should never cross his legs. This only encumbers the breathing and the ability to resonate freely. The singer should sit in such a position that he could, at any moment, with the help of a little bodily momentum, rise from his chair to a full standing position. When one section is rehearsing its part, the other singers may recline back into a comfortable position.

Anything that hinders the free upright stance and the bell-like swinging movement from the axis should be avoided. The holding of the music puts the arms in a rigid position, encumbers the body, and can lead to muscular rigidity. It is worthwhile for choirs, if they are not too large, to place their music on music stands (after the model of the old choirs of the sixteenth and seventeenth centuries) so that the singers may enjoy maximum physical freedom during singing. At any rate, the music sheets should be held in such a way as to prevent any unnecessary rigidity of the arms and shoulders. Each singer should stand so that he can easily see the choir director without having to stretch, or cramp himself. The distance between the singers should be great enough so that each singer can move about his axis without interference from his neighbor. The distance should, of course, not be so great as to prevent the musical "spark" from jumping the gap from one singer to another. The musical current should at all times circulate unhindered throughout the entire choral body. Any leaning on chairs, benches, walls, or supports is to be avoided as well as leaning on each other or crossing of each other's arms which some girls seemingly cannot abstain from even during rehearsal. This only "lames" the singers and seriously minimizes the resonance potential of the singers.

The attire of the singer should be such as will allow for maximum breathing and singing comfort. Tight-fitting clothing should not be worn, particularly the type that would prevent free movement of the chest or abdomen. The singer will need to reject some of the newest styles in clothing, particularly the type designed to "fit the figure." The choir director must exemplify these demands himself since the influence of his own example will have the most immediate and lasting effects on the singers.

He should stand in a position where every singer can see him without difficulty. He should not change his position during singing. Most often he will have to stand somewhat elevated. He should, however, take care not to stand so high that the singers must stretch their necks and so create tensions on the larynxes.

The individual's awareness of an animated, vibrant body should be transferred to the entire choir. We speak deliberately of a "choral body." The different sections should "grow together" to form this choral entity, becoming "members" of one body. The total choral body requires its own kind of corporate awareness, so that it can project the music with animation and vitality. The choirs of the sixteenth and seventeenth centuries, whose art is the model for all European choral music, created this corporate ideal as a prerequisite to their music making through communal living — living and eating together, working and playing together. The communal life formed a basis upon which they could develop their art. Even today certain boys' choirs are benefiting through communal living which is regulated according to a prescribed order of activities. Over a period of time they acquire a kind of corporate rhythm through such group activities as hiking, playing games, and dancing. This interplay of the breath-supported energies which regulate mind and body provides the spark and nourishment for choral singing. The relationship between physical and musical activity is very close. As a student the author took part in a collegium musicum which had to change a large part of its membership at the end of every semester. It was noticeable that the students who came from various sociological and geographical areas amalgamated much more easily whenever the semester commenced with a musical weekend in which musical activities were complemented with skiing and swimming. This aided the process of getting people attuned to each other. Choirs have their own rate and manner of breathing and body activity, their own "group feeling" which one notices, for example, in art circles, folk dance groups, and hiking groups. If choral and music societies in the cities cannot go hiking or camping, etc., they would do well to stay with the kind of exercise described in the section on breathing and on rhythmic activities. (A II and VI).

The placement of the various sections of the choir should be regulated in such a way that the choir's awareness of its corporateness is preserved. This is generally spoken of as the *choir formation*. The placement of the various sections should be thought of as a redistribution and a rearrangement of a total body-soul organism. According to descriptions and engravings, the singers in traditional choirs were placed in a circle or semicircle around a large music stand. The circle is a symbol of unending motion like the old unceasing motion of polyphony. The circle formation is also the best solution for ideal music making; all singers can hear and see each other constantly; the musical circuit is closed, and the body-soul activity can proceed without interruption. Even today street bands and army bands employ the circular formation. In Germany, choral societies have kept this concept alive by naming their singing societies *Singkreise*, which literally means "singing circles." Today it is common for the director to stand in the center of the circle of singers during rehearsal, or between two voice sections in the periphery of the circle. (See Figs. 1 and 2):

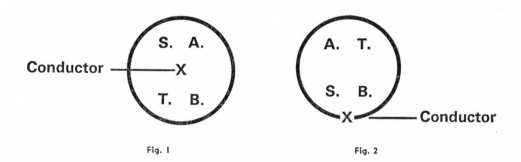

Fig. I   Fig. 2

To open this "closed circle" to a listening audience would have been inconceivable to early musicians. The liturgy of the Middle Ages, for instance, was conducted by those who acted, and all acting groups were considered to have direct access to God. The choir did not think of itself as singing to a listening audience, but as it took part in the various parts of the liturgy, the unending circle, the unending spiral of music which it produced, represented a direct link with eternity. In our day the ideal circular formation is preferred whenever a music society sings for itself, i.e. singing without an audience. This formation is also desirable for informal outdoor singing. Those who make the music build the circle, and all the rest gather around.

7

If the singing group is to face and sing to the listening group, the circle may be divided through the center, the one half constituting the singing group while the other half becomes the listening group. Thus the musical circuit is closed again. The listeners are drawn into this living stream of musical energy. The choir director stands where the circle has been broken, at the crossroad of musical emanations which he must control and direct. (Fig. 3). The advantages of the half-circle formation are realized in the closer contact of the singers with each other; it permits the director to be placed in line with the stream of sound and is conducive to the development of good sonority.

Fig. 3

The square formation seems to have been used in connection with eighteenth century opera productions. Such a rigid formation seemed to have had a negative effect on the concert life of the nineteenth century. This universally adopted "four corner" formation, so disadvantageous for both singers and director, can easily be changed into a semicircle formation by moving the wings forward and inward. (Figs. 4, 5, 6 and 7.)

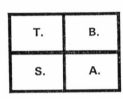

Fig. 4

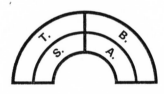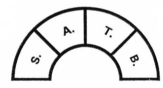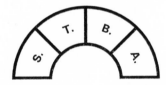

Fig. 5   Fig. 6   Fig. 7

The comparative size and strength of the sections help to determine the division of the choir formation. In a larger choir the male voices are placed behind the treble voices (Fig. 5) while in the case of a small choir with the same number of voices in each section, one can place the sections according to their normal order (Fig. 6). If the male voices are in a decided minority, they can be placed in the center (Fig. 7).

The formation of the choir should further be determined by the *structure of the music that is to be sung*. Arranging the singers in such a way, they represent the structure of the music in a visible, physical manner — they stand "right in the structure of the piece" as it were. All relationships to the

8

music and the unleashing of musical energies are represented in a visual and demonstrable form. Singing and listening are greatly facilitated by such formations. In homophonic music, where the soprano has the leading voice, the above order is most useful (Figs. 5, 6 and 7). A systematic breakdown of formation in keeping with the tonal and musical structure permits the following possibilities:

(1) Unison compositions: the choir stands in a circle or semicircle formation (Figs. 1, 2, 3);

(2) Two-voiced compositions in which the *first voice has the unrestricted lead* while the second voice moves along in a *faux bourdon* manner: the first voice stands in the first row and the second voice behind in the second row (Fig. 8).

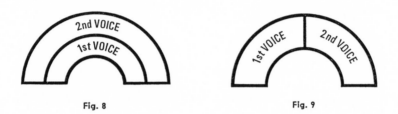

Fig. 8   Fig. 9

The same position is desirable in a cantus firmus piece, in which one voice sings the tune and the other voice sings a free, contrapuntal part against it, possibly in shorter note values. Even when the *cantus firmus part is sung by male voices in a low tessitura*, those singing it should be standing in the first row.

Johann Rudolf Ahle, 1662
Arr., Alexander Wagner, 1952

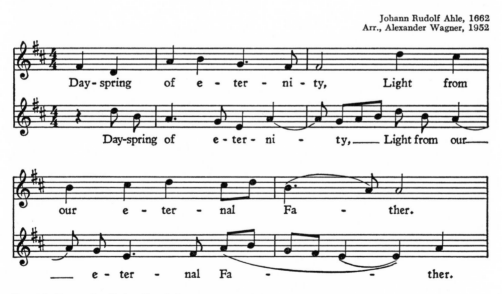

Copyright Baerenreiter-Verlag, Kassel, Germany.

In a two-voice arrangement where both voices move *alongside each other on equal terms* (possibly with more imitative interweavings): the singing groups stand next to each other and thus constitute a half-arc of the semicircle ("Erstanden ist der heilige Christ" by M. Praetorius, *Chorgesangbuch* p. 110, Baerenreiter 680, Fig. 9).

The numerous two-part songs in the form of bicinia by Lassus, Praetorius, Wannenmacher, and others, the new arrangements in the style of *Neuen deutschen Lieder* (New German Songs) by Fritz Joede and his followers are best performed in this formation. Also, two-part canons may be sung in this formation as an alternative to a complete circle formation.

(3) Three-voice compositions in which one voice has the undisputed prerogative throughout and where the other two voices follow along in a simple folk song harmony, note against note: the singers who sing the main voice stand in the front row and the singers on the other two parts stand behind the front row, (Fig. 10). An example of this type is a three-part setting of the familiar English air, "Drink to Me Only with Thine Eyes," *Sing Care Away*, Book III, Novello & Co.

This applies as well for cantus firmus compositions in which one of the three voices carries the tune and where the other voices form a *free counterpoint* against it, particularly if these two voices are similar, thus constituting a bicinium against the cantus firmus. This arrangement is useful regardless

Fig. 10

Fig. 11

of the tessitura of the leading part. (See "Vater unser im Himmelreich," p. 44, *Chorgesangbuch* by M. Praetorius and "Jesus Christus, unser Heiland, der von und den Gotteszorn wandt," p. 26, *Chorgesangbuch* by Johann Kugelmann). In any case, the singers who sing the leading part are always placed in the front. If the leading voice is written for the medium register and if the *subordinate voices have a direct relationship to it,* resulting in an even texture, it is advantageous to place the singers having the leading voice part into the center (Fig. 11), (e.g. "The Lord is my Shepherd," No. 210, *The Youth Hymnary*, Faith and Life Press).

For three-voice settings in which the voices are *almost of equal importance:* It is best to use the formation described above, by placing the singers in order of their voice parts, first, second, and third voice. Three-voice canons may also be sung in this formation if a complete circle formation cannot be achieved (See "Nun schein, du Glanz der Herrlichkeit," No. 9, *Gesellige Zeit*, Baerenreiter).

Three-voice settings in which *two voices have the unrestricted lead while the third voice forms a contrapuntal part against them:* both leading voices

10

are placed in front and the third behind them. This type of composition is frequently met with in German "Kantorei" practice of the late fifteenth century. The two main voices are often written canonically and a third voice is treated contrapuntally against them (e.g. J. Staden's setting of "Nun bitten wir den Heiligen Geist," p. 122, *Chorgesangbuch*). The voices may also be written in a free imitative style supported by a free-moving third voice. (e.g. "Wie schoen leutchtet der Morgenstern," p. 84, *Chorgesangbuch*, by Michael Praetorius). The second voice part in this example generally lies lower than the main voice so that instrumental support with optional *basso continuo* might be desirable.

Fig. 12

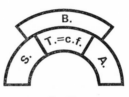

Fig. 13

(4) A four-voiced composition in which the *melody taken by the upper voice is supported by a simple note against note treatment,* (e.g. "Nun Komm der Heiden Heiland" by Lukas Osiander, p. 52, *Chorgesangbuch;* and "Feinslieb, du hast mich gfangen" by Hans L. Hassler, No. 56, *Gesellige Zeit),* or a setting in which no one voice is a pronounced leading voice but where the different voices are intertwined in motet-like fashion (e.g. "Ehre sei dem Vater" by Heinrich Schuetz, p. 47, *Chorgesangbuch* and "Nun fanget an!" by Hassler, No. 32, *Gesellige Zeit:)* it is advisable to use the formations illustrated in Figs. 5, 6, 7. This arrangement can also be used for three-voice canons and most madrigals.

Four-voice compositions in which the *leading voice is a cantus firmus in the tenor:* since the cantus firmus represents the central part and the backbone of a composition, the singers of the cantus firmus part should be placed in the middle. The bass, as the lowest contrapuntal voice, should stand behind the tenors. Sopranos (*Discantus*) and altos (*Contrapunctus altus*) are placed on each side of the cantus firmus as the two high contrapuntal voices and constitute the two wings of the semicircle formation ("Herr Christ, der einig Gotts Sohn" by Johann Walther, p. 78, *Chorgesangbuch;* and "Herzog Ull-richs Jagdlied" by Ludwig Senfl, No. 71, *Gesellige Zeit*).

Fig. 14

Fig. 15

11

If the cantus firmus is sung by the basses ("Christ ist erstanden" by Orlando di Lasso, p. 99, *Chorgesangbuch*), then one need only to switch the tenors with the basses. If the cantus firmus is in the soprano, ("Gelobet seist Du, Jesu Christ" by Adam Gumpelzhaimer, p. 60, *Chorgesangbuch;* and "Ach Eislein, liebes Eislein mein" by Ludwig Senfl, No. 58, *Gesellige Zeit*), it is best to place the sopranos in the front row and the other three voice sections behind them as in Fig. 14.

Four-voice compositions in which the tune is used *in canon*: the canon voices are placed in the center of the semicircle and the other two voices are placed as illustrated in Fig. 15. (e.g. "Entlaubet ist der Walde" by Ludwig Senfl, No. 65, *Gesellige Zeit;* and "Ach Gott, vom Himmel sieh darein" by Martin Agricola, p. 176, *Chorgesangbuch*).

In compositions with a "wandering" cantus firmus it is best to use the formations of Figs. 6 and 7.

Four-voice compositions in which the *two higher and the two lower voices are paired off against each other* in an imitative fashion, achieving a kind of double choir effect (e.g. "Lobt Gott ihr Christen, alle gleich" by Johann Herman, p. 70, *Chorgesangbuch;* and "Ich sag ade" by an unknown composer of the sixteenth century, No. 62, *Gesellige Zeit*): here it is best to use the half circle formations of Figs. 6 and 7.

(5) Formations for compositions written for five, six, and seven or more voice parts are developed according to the same principles. If, for example, in a five-voice setting the cantus firmus is treated canonically in the alto and tenor range, and if in addition to the high and low contrapuntal parts a descant voice *(Vaganstimme)* is used as the third contrapuntal voice which moves in between the two canon voices, "Nun bitten wir den Heiligen Geist" by Johann Walther, p. 124, *Chorgesangbuch),* then the formations illustrated in Figs. 16 and 17 are to be recommended.

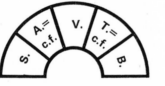

Fig. 16

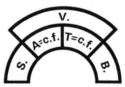

Fig. 17

(6) Eight-voice compositions which consist of two four-voice choirs, should be sung in two separate formations (e.g. the double choir motet, "Now thank we all our God" by Pachelbel, Concordia Publishing House). (See Figs. 18, 19, 20, 21):

Fig. 18

Fig. 19

12

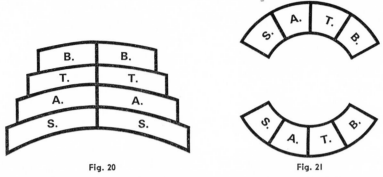

Fig. 20   Fig. 21

If choir members face each other, as is possible in churches with divided choir lofts, one should choose the old traditional formation illustrated in Fig. 21. In compositions for three, four, and more choirs, similar formations should be worked out.

Often the composer treats the second choir as an echo choir. Such a deliberate echo effect is made possible only when the second choir stands directly over against the first choir. Only after such a separation of the choirs can the necessary musical polarity and fine musical interplay be achieved between them. The choirs should imagine that they are throwing musical sounds to each other in the way they would throw hand balls to each other. In reality, they are playing a musical ball game with each other!

The entire room is set to music and the far ends become imaginary poles which create a musical tension across the space of the room. With no other choral formation can the space-creating effect be so well demonstrated.

If the choir is accompanied by an orchestra, either of the seating plans could be used. (Figs. 22 and 23.) Both have proven to be practical.

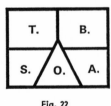

Fig. 22

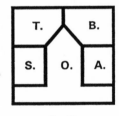

Fig. 23

A well-planned and meaningful formation is always the prerequisite for choral music making. Architecture as the "mother of the fine arts" is also the "mother of music." The musical form of the musical work determines the formation of the choir. Disorder in the seating arrangement brings about disorder in the music, and a stereotyped formation of the choir can result in stereotyped singing. A choir director who knows how to solve this problem intelligently has won half the battle in communicating the music to his audience.

In a concert with a succession of pieces of varying musical structures, it would be impractical to change the seating plan from one musical selection to another, since this would cause too much commotion. Yet, it is often possible to group together musical selections of similar structure so that only a minimum amount of reshuffling is required. This grouping of compositions of similar types illustrates an important principle of programming. If, in a religious or secular concert, a choir is required to sing only the occasional selection, there is generally no difficulty in arranging the singers to conform to the order and requirements of a work.

Some seemingly insignificant factors can also become important in changing the positions of voice sections: e.g. shorter singers should be placed as far forward as possible. Leading, solistically trained voices or otherwise brilliant and protruding voices should not be placed at the ends of rows, but should be placed centrally so that they support the total sound. If this is not desirable they should be placed farther back into the choir. In all this the choir director must often forge a quiet little battle with the all-too-human natures of his singers, particularly the female singers. However, this must and can be done through tact and a true sense of purpose.

Since singers must become accustomed to each other's breathing, it is important that the same singers always stand next to each other. Not every person can sing with every other person. New singers who may be somewhat hesitant and insecure should not be placed too far out but should be placed beside an experienced singer who will quickly help him become a part of the group both musically and socially. In smaller choirs a special sonority can occasionally be achieved through a heterogeneous arrangement of singers, but this is more often possible with vocally and musically mature singers in the singing of simpler homophonic choral selections. The formation of the choir should always represent a *sympathetic placement of singers*.

Chapter II

Choral Breath Training

If the human body, in relation to singing, is the vehicle both of art and life itself, then breathing fulfills a most important function because it sustains both life and song. All living and all singing is dependent on breathing. The first sign of life in an infant is the presence of respiratory activity, and from that moment breathing holds all vocal utterance including singing, concomitantly to the course and stream of life.

Most people breathe naturally and correctly in a lying position. Recognizing this principle the choir director or singing teacher should, whenever the occasion warrants it, have his singers perform breathing exercises when lying flat on their backs. It is possible to conduct these exercises at choral workshops, informal young people's gatherings, and in music schools. In other less ideal situations, the director may ask one of the more accomplished singers to demonstrate the breathing exercises and then encourage the other singers to practice them at home. The breathing exercises are performed as follows: the singer lies relaxed and unencumbered on the floor in a supine position. While inhaling easily, the chest and abdomen rise and the midriff section expands because the lower spaces of the lungs are filled up first. Meanwhile the shoulders remain relaxed and at ease without a trace of lifting. Inhalation is brought about by the action of the diaphragm — a wide, saucer-shaped muscle which divides the upper part of the torso from the lower part beneath the ribs. In a state of rest, the diaphragm is curved slightly upwards. During inhalation it flattens and spreads out somewhat, causing the ribs to expand. This permits the outside air to rush into the lungs. One may think of the diaphragm as functioning somewhat like a piston in a cylinder, in this case the cylinder being the lungs. The awareness of the breathing process must nevertheless be maintained in one's mind as an

15

"inner process," as a compression of the breath which results in the production of tone and not as control over some voluntary muscles.

In singing only full, deep breathing, i.e. the combination of diaphragmatic and intercostal breathing, should normally be employed. This kind of breathing helps the singer to become aware of the axis of the diaphragm, i.e. the lateral expansion of the waist in the region of the lower floating ribs. This awareness and control of a lateral expansion of the waist is of great importance to the singer because man's activities revolve around this center of the human body. The "slender hips" or the "tight waist" ideal is not conducive to good singing. Tight clothing is harmful both to singing and to physical health.

The Greeks regarded the body with broad hips as the ideal human form. Deep breathing expands the waist not only at the sides but also at the front and back. This develops the "breath ring" which the Greeks chose as one of the seven bodily graces, and its aesthetic appeal was held in sacred regard. Every youth strove to attain this physical ideal by means of mental contemplation and physical gymnastics. That the Greek concept of the ideal human form conformed most closely to the form which nature bestows upon man at birth appears to be evident, for even the infant has hips that are curved outward, and the rapid, sensitive respirations guarantee firm and full support to his crying!

To make possible the powerful development and unhindered work of the breath ring, the singer must avoid wearing tight-fitting clothes, stiff girdles, tight garters and suspenders. Deep breathing perfects the singer's posture and poise. The proper skeletal stance and the flexing of the right muscles and tendons prepare the posture externally, but only through inhalation is physical posture literally and inwardly "filled out" and completed. From this breath center the body is nurtured and built up; from the vital center of the breath-regulating diaphragm the singer acquires his posture and form. Every singer is in a sense an "inflated person," a rubber balloon as it were, a skeleton covered with a sack of skin which assumes its form when inhalation takes place (Fig. 24).

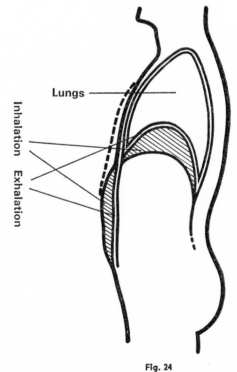

Lungs

Inhalation Exhalation

Fig. 24

16

Deep breathing is the only natural and genuinely effective means for the lungs, it promotes exchange of carbon and oxygen and renews the blood, it massages the inner organs, it stimulates circulation and invigorates the body, it regulates and aids digestion, it makes for greater freedom for the action of the heart. The diaphragm is the seat of the automatic nervous system. Proper diaphragmatic breathing invigorates the functions of the entire body, whereas insufficient or incorrect breathing interferes with these functions.

Deep breathing is beneficial to a variety of life's functions; it strengthens overcoming stage fright and the accompanying rapid heartbeat. Anxiety of this kind causes a drawing in of both shoulders and abdomen and results in nervous tension and congested breathing. Deep breathing fills the breath ring and shoulder girdle from within and is conducive to the relaxation of mind and body. The stimulated diaphragm activity allows the heart to beat more freely and steadily, and the body is flooded with breath, strength, and vitality. Emotional excitement can lead to a gasping or "fluttering" breath. Restlessness of spirit causes restlessness of breathing. Conversely, it is possible through steady breathing to control and reduce anxiety and tension. Even a marksman with a rifle is taught to inhale calmly before releasing the trigger. Every singer possesses a practical aid to overcome nervousness and stage fright through proper breathing habits.

Out of deep breathing issue physical and psychic energies. A deep breath is taken prior to a daring act. The weight lifter or furniture mover takes a deep breath before lifting a heavy object. A deep breath is taken after the command "heave," and the lift, pull, or push is then commenced on "ho." A wise athletic coach will allow his students to take up singing as an aid to strengthen the body and to achieve an easy, upright posture. Athletes often wear a supporting "power belt" to give greater support to the deep inhalations required by their strenuous activity. The biblical expression "let your loins be girded" most certainly draws its reference from strenuous activities of that time which required the support of a belt or strong cloth around the loins.

An eastern legend bears the account of a warrior whose sword disinte-grated as it touched the breath-filled body of a flute player. The author has met people with lung injuries who, through the wise council of their physi-cians, were encouraged to keep up their singing and the playing of wind instruments to strengthen their lungs. Whenever possible, deep breathing exercises should be performed out-of-doors, or at least before an open window.

From these considerations we can suggest a number of exercises for loosening up and strengthening the diaphragm. Many people have a rigid, inactive diaphragm which must first be stimulated to action. The singing teacher asks his student to lie down flat on his back. A heavy book or similar object is placed on his abdomen. The student takes a deep breath and lifts the object as high as possible. If it is not feasible to have all the choir members perform this exercise, distribute the singers so that they have ample space for exercising. Let them place the palms of their hands flat against the abdomen just beneath the ribs, the longest fingers touching each other in the solar plexus region just below the sternum. A deep breath should cause the hands to move away from each other. In a similar manner the breath ring may be completed towards the sides and the back by cupping the hands on the hips with fingers pointing towards the small of the back. Care should be taken that the movement of the hands is caused by the inhalation from within without the raising of shoulders or the manipulation of exterior voluntary muscles.

Frequently these exercises will be insufficient to achieve the desired results, and the choir trainer will have to resort to other nonmusical aids. He may make use of natural life-related bodily activities. Many age-old physical activities revolve around the center of the waist and hips, e.g. mowing with the scythe, sewing by hand, cutting by sickle, threshing by flail, pitching hay, shoveling, etc. These movements form a to-and-fro motion of bound and rebound, of tension and relaxation. In this movement of action and counteraction, of inhalation and exhalation, we must include the singing act. Also boxing, various forms of the folk dance, the balancing and carrying of objects on the head are dependent on the activity and strength of the hips. Whenever appropriate, these movements should be employed in choir training. Swinging, mowing, and sawing motions may be used to good advantage in any situation.

A more systematic approach would be the use of calisthenics. Running and hopping are valuable in promoting diaphragmatic activity. While running, the upper body should be relaxed and inhalations should be taken through the mouth. In addition to a variety of jumping exercises (on the spot, away from the spot, on one leg, on both legs simultaneously, etc.), rope-skipping exercises which are particularly conducive to activate the diaphragm, may also be included. Again, attention must be given to regular, deep breathing during these exercises, without a drawing in of the stomach walls which is a strong tendency in jumping and running exercises. Trunk exercises (e.g. twisting forward, sideways, backwards, rolling, bending, turning, etc.) also serve to stimulate deep diaphragmatic breathing. Systematic breathing gymnastics can be usefully employed between these exercises. Such breathing exercises can be performed in combination with stretching arms sideways or forward, heel-raising, trunk-bending, and knee-bending exercises. During these exercises the breath should be inhaled through the nose alone and exhalations should be made through the mouth.

Sighing, yawning, and laughing may be combined with deep breathing exercises. Such vocal expressions represent relief from tensions of body and spirit. While sighing the body should be permitted to slump forward, and upon completion of the sigh it is slowly erected during which a deep breath is inhaled. Yawning promotes the exchange of residue air in the lower lungs for fresh supplies of air. Yawning also encourages deep breathing and at the same time expands the pharynx (the spaces inside the throat) and so prepares for the possibility of proper, ideal vocal production.

The proverb "Laughter is healthy" also applies to healthy voice production. More than anything, laughter promotes good diaphragmatic activity. One hears people speak about "side-splitting laughter" or "holding one's sides with laughter." While laughing, the hands should be held on the solar plexus where the activity of the diaphragm is most noticeably felt and then try to control the activity of the diaphragm beginning with the light, small movements until it begins to shake. It is impossible to laugh with a drawn in abdomen (except for snickering). The explosive "ha, ha" eliminates a breathy tone which occurs when expelled breath has not been utilized to produce sound. Laughter exercises can be a good means for achieving the desired effect in singing. Tension, muscular rigidity, and residues of stagnant air are loosened up and shaken off by hearty laughter. The singing of "laughing canons" is most suitable to encourage this "laughter activity." An example of a good laughing canon is the following:

Three-part canon   Cherubini

Ha! ha! ha! ha! ha! ha! ha! ha! ha! Hear the ech - o hear the ech - o as we sing. Let us joy - ful,_ joy - ful_ be, for joy_ en - dures but for a _ day.

Such a canon must be sung in a cheerful frame of mind which is reflected in a happy facial expression. For the sake of promoting good breathing and voice production, a choir director should keep his rehearsals wholesome and happy. The choir director who is able to stimulate laughter in his choir is bound to be more successful in his work than an equally capable director who is unable to do this. A happy disposition influences the nervous system to prepare the larynx for ideal singing conditions. The imaginary inhaling

of the aroma of a beautiful flower or ripe fruit or breathing suddenly as if
pleasantly surprised are also excellent aids in promoting vocal readiness.
Try to perform these activities with drooped shoulders and drawn in abdomen and then with upright shoulders and expanded diaphragm; every
singer will soon discover which is the correct and best possible manner of
performing these breathing activities. The old instruction "Chest out, tummy
in" is precisely the wrong prescription for an ideal and proper singing posture. The relaxed but alerted and strengthened diaphragm gives the singer
confidence, power, and poise, and with the collaboration of the intercostal
muscles also lends him the much coveted "singer's support."

Because of this close organic relationship between breathing and life,
an approach to the healing of injuries to the body and soul may be made
through deep-breathing exercises. One need only recall some of the practices of the Oriental countries (e.g. the practice of the Yoga cults) where
systematic breathing exercises are employed to achieve tranquility of soul
and to induce deep meditation.

The impulse for breathing is stimulated by the need for more oxygen
in the blood. Inhalation follows exhalation, and so the undulating wave of
tension and relaxation within the body is again activated. The physiological
breathing process for singing is thus bound to an activity which at the same
time also undergirds the nature and essence of music itself, namely, the ebb
and flow of breath sustains the ebb and flow of music.

The immediate connection between a musical and poetic work of art
and the shape and duration of the breathing pattern has been recorded by
O. Rutz. He has observed three types of breathers among poets and composers. Rutz concludes that a song or poem should be performed as nearly
as possible in the breath rhythm of the composer if full justice is to be given
to the work of art. Whether this theory is tenable to the point where it can
be translated into practice remains to be investigated, but it is significant
that a composer's particular manner of breathing influences his work to the
extent that such experiments identifying various musical phenomena with
a composer's breathing habits have at least been possible to attempt. The
singer or choir director whose breathing rate belongs to the same type as
the composer's will undoubtedly do the better justice to the composer's work.

The singer's breath training does not begin with inhalation, but with
exhalation. It is the conscious, relaxed but carefully controlled, outgoing
breath stream upon which all good singing activity rests. Repeated inhalation, continual pumping in of air quickly results in stilted breathing. The
singer becomes cramped and the choral sound becomes tight and rigid. Since
most lay choir directors have not mastered breath support themselves, they
cannot retain the inhaled quantity of breath and so resort to applying
pressure to the larynx from beneath and allow the breath to be "puffed

away," thus dissipating the potential voice-producing energy of the breath. Some choir directors continually insist on inhalation, but well-meaning as it is, this can only produce the opposite results from the objective striven for.

Most choirs suffer from "overpressure" of breath. The choral director should commence his work with exhalation of breath. Most singers will be surprised to note how much "dead air" has been resident in their lungs, even when they prided themselves with having achieved complete exhalation. Permit the choir to exhale on a deep sigh and immediately proceed to use up the residue air by speaking on the syllable, yah, yah, yah. The singers will still be able to produce a long string of vocal "yahs!"

With this increased exhalation there is a slight falling in and contraction of the upper torso. Now slowly erect the upper body while inhaling through the nose. Inhalation should be regarded as a passive, completely automatic activity. The choir director would do well to insist on full exhalation also during singing; he should not permit singers to breathe in the middle of a phrase. There is no singer who, after completing a phrase on one breath, will not automatically inhale the necessary quantity of breath for the succeeding phrase. Inhalation therefore takes place as an automatic activity of the lungs, since outside air rushes in to fill the vacuum created by the exhaled air. Only after a consciously controlled and thoroughly utilized exhalation is the kind of inhalation which is beneficial to the tone made possible. The guiding principle should always be: "Develop the maximum tone with a minimum amount of breath."

With the help of such principles and some preparatory exercises, free, uninterrupted choral breathing can be quite easily attained. The singer stands upright as described above, with shoulders relaxed and slightly drawn back and down, while the chest is slightly lifted. This slight lifting of the chest represents an alert, prepared position.

In old traditional accounts a singer was said to have "lifted his voice to sing." Today one must only too often change this saying to read, "forced his voice to sing." The easy, free, lifted position of the chest promotes a voice production which is the result of a balance between inner and outer air pressures. While the breath is inhaled through the nose, the mouth assumes the "ah" position; the back of the tongue closes off the mouth space, thus allowing only for pure nasal breathing; the tip of the tongue is relaxed and loose against the lower front teeth: Conscious expression of wonder, surprise, or question opens the glottis of the larynx. By imagining that the breath rushes noiselessly into the lungs, the whole singing mechanism assumes the relaxed and open position which is so necessary for the moment of sound production. Breathing is a close union of passivity and activity. The kind of relaxed readiness exemplified by the athlete preparing to catch a light football, establishes the right conditions for a good vocal attack.

21

To obtain maximum resonating space in the pharynx some choir directors ask their singers to breathe through the mouth at all times while singing. The author prefers nasal breathing for the following reasons:

(1) Nasal breathing directs the breath directly *down to the breath circle*. The singer thereby gains the support of the diaphragm, the tone achieves its basis of support, its carrying power and amplitude. Mouth inhalation, which nevertheless must not be neglected, fills the upper area of the lungs first and as a result the tone may lack in color, intensity, and carrying power;

(2) Nasal breathing helps to give the tone the necessary *high focus* and correct position. The singer has the sensation that inhaling through the nose helps to get the tone to "spin" behind and above the nose. Mouth inhalation focuses the tone too deep in the throat with the result that the tone seems to slide still farther down while singing. Deep nasal breathing encourages the *low position of the larynx*, so absolutely essential to singing. Ask the singers to place their fingers on their Adam's apple and compare its varying positions as they experiment between nasal and mouth breathing;

(3) Nasal breathing *pre-warms the breath* to general body temperature which is essential for the activity and protection of the vocal cords. Nasal breathing also *pre-moistens the air* while mouth breathing tends to dry out the walls of the mouth and throat as well as the vocal cords. This can cause injury to the vocal cords and can also be the reason for brittle vocal attacks.

(4) Nasal breathing *filters the air*. Dust, bacteria, germs, and other foreign matter are caught up in the cilia and mucous lining of the nasal passages.

(5) Nasal breathing massages the *mucous lining* and *resonance chambers* of the nasal passages; circulation in these areas is stimulated and resonances are enhanced. A sense of well-being is generally experienced in the upper and frontal areas of the head — something which is not achieved by mouth breathing. "Mouth breathers" are often lazy people, and one associates them with the dull people who suffer from chronic catarrh.

(6) Nasal breathing helps the singer to *concentrate more keenly* when working for good choral attacks and clean entries.

Nasal breathing should take place as noiselessly as possible. This can be achieved by concentration and practice. With practice it is also possible to greatly increase the quantity of breath inhaled through the nose. Even so it will not always be possible to use only nasal breathing, for during singing some mouth breathing necessarily must take place. The function here takes care of itself if the mouth is kept open during inhalations. The beginning of a new phrase or any clearly defined musical section should always be preceded by a nasal breath.

To promote relaxed, steady, consciously-controlled exhalation, so important to vocal training and singing, the following exercises can be helpful:

(1) Ask the singers to exhale. To encourage relaxation it may be well to sigh on the breath and then permit breath to flow back into the lungs. The singers

22

can check the activity of the diaphragm with their hands as described earlier. The foregoing exercise, as well as those that follow, can be conducted by the director with the use of appropriate gestures.

(2) Exhale slowly and noiselessly through the mouth.

(3) Exhale while hissing a quiet, sustained *s, sh,* or *f*. Imagine that you have just punctured a bicycle tire with a needle.

(4) Now exhale and add voice to the consonants in Ex. 3 to simulate the sound of a hive of humming bees.

(5) Exhale while singing a soft *oo* in appropriate range of the voice; each singer selects his own comfortable pitch so that a multivoiced choir effect is produced. To achieve further relaxation and vocal flexibility have the singers slide up and down from their pitch as if they were raising a question with their voices. The director then gives a suitable pitch to the singers. They listen carefully and attack the tone easily and lightly without permitting the tone to waver.

(6) To train the singers to listen critically while singing tones, let them sing sustained vowels in two-, three- and four-parts.

(7) To stimulate greater awareness of breath control and to intensify breathing activity the choral director may direct the singers to *stop abruptly the outflowing breath stream* and then resume it again. This may also be done on a given rhythm, perhaps the rhythm of a familiar song. To guard against the so-called glottis attack (shock of the glottis) on such rhythmic exercises, the vowels may be preceded by *f's, k's,* or *p's.*

In all these exercises the duration of the sustained breath should be gradually increased. The choral music of the sixteenth and seventeenth centuries, which represents the ideal music for choral singing, contains unusually long passages to be sung on a single breath, a demand for which the singer needs some special training. Some of our more recent European and American choral compositions make similar demands on the singer. The famous singer Rubini is reputed to have been able to hold his breath for four minutes. The choir director encourages his singers to gradually extend the length of time used in sustaining the breath for the above exercises. Younger singers are quite ready to be challenged to a little breath endurance competition. The reading of poetic lines can serve the same purpose. Naturally it would be advisable to use a jolly, lively poem like, " 'Twas the Night Before Christmas." A serious, sacred, or philosophical text should not be used for such a purpose. Some singers will probably have taken a new breath by the time they reach the end of the first line, and they will automatically continue to take a breath after each line. Have the singers try to speak the lines on one breath and then try the same with the third and fourth lines. They should then be able to recite a four-line stanza with only one breath taken in the middle of the stanza. Finally, for the sake of practice, it may be possible to recite the entire verse with one breath without having to catch a breath anywhere in the verse. It is hazardous to utilize the last reserve of breath for singing because the larynx is under too much pressure from the lack of supporting breath. This results in a breathy, shallow tone.

To check whether they are emitting an even flow of air, singers can hold a piece of onionskin paper close to their mouths and observe the degree of uniformity of the vibrations which they can achieve with their controlled blowing.

Every rehearsal should begin with these and similar breathing exercises. Not only do they stimulate breathing itself, but to a large extent they also prepare the singer psychologically. Nervous tension which has accumulated from daily occupational stress is eased, the restlessness and distractions are forgotten, and the choir consisting of unique individuals from various backgrounds and vocations becomes relaxed and unified.

Breath training must become an integral part of choral practice. It cannot be left to the individual singer to deal with in his own private way — something which he will somehow acquire with time. With the help of proper breathing the singer can develop and perfect his ability to phrase artistically. Since the phrases are part of the musical structure or design, it follows that breathing must be regulated accordingly. The choir director then must be responsible for every breath which is taken. The preparatory breath is as important to singing as the initial preparatory run is to a broad or high jump. It should and must therefore become a concern of every choir member and must be controlled and guided under the leadership of the choir director. Not only should he give the choir enough time to take the necessary breath, but through proper gesture and reminder help the singers in their breathing, and whenever possible, he should breathe with the choir.

Corporate (simultaneous) breathing is one of the essential means toward achieving a vital, corporate unity within the choir. By inhaling together in the mood of the music, a psychological relationship is developed which welds individual singers together. This unity and sensitive mutual relationship of the singers to each other through unified breathing can, in smaller choirs, be developed to a point where entries, phrasing, tempo, and dynamics are so uniformly agreed upon that a director becomes dispensable. This also occurs in instrumental chamber groups of stringed and wind instruments.

In choral singing correct breathing should be cultivated — breathing at the beginning of a song and breathing during a song. The breath taken at the beginning of a song has a twofold significance: it unifies the choir into an animated, corporate unit right at the outset and thus helps to insure precise and tonally correct entries. The choir director breathes with the choir and accompanies this procedure with an appropriate gesture which leads directly into the first beat of the music.

This initial unification helps the choir to achieve the necessary physical and mental alertness. The choir director must be able to recognize when this alertness has reached a climax and then begin the music precisely at that moment. A director who does not consciously utilize this possibility relinquishes one of the most important means of securing control during the further course of the song. It is at this moment of preparation that the success of the work to be performed is to a great extent determined. A precise start is dependent on the unified manner in which the breath is taken at the beginning of a song. Without a unified preparatory breath, ask the singers to clap their hands in response to some kind of sign or gesture. The result will be an inexact entry with many "late clappers" coming in at different times. The experiment is then repeated, permitting the choir to inhale together. At the moment where the inhalation has reached its climax, a cue is given to the choir to clap their hands. The clapped entry will sound as if it were clapped by one person — so precise will be the reaction of the total group after a unified preparatory breath. The necessity of securing proper tonal placement through the preparatory breath has been dealt with earlier. Directors who come from a background of piano playing or orchestral directing should make sure that this principle is clearly understood.

The breath is the means by which the singer phrases his music, and therefore the choir director must not permit the individual to breathe according to his wishes and fancy. If the editor or publisher has not provided the music with sensible breath markings, then it is the director's responsibility to mark them in for every voice in accordance with phrase structure, and to make sure that these breath markings are carefully observed. Verbal instructions are inadequate. This method of marking in the breathing places is a recognition of the fact that breathing is regulated by the music, and that music is carried forward between the polarity of relaxation and tension — of inhalation and exhalation.

During singing, three different types of breathing may be differentiated: *deep breathing, snatch breathing,* and *staggered breathing.* Deep breaths should be taken at the end of well-defined phrases and after half-cadences and whole cadences. Strangely enough, musicians fail again and again to observe this elemental principle. Breaths are taken anywhere during the singing of a phrase resulting in a chopped phrase line. On the other hand, the breath is thoughtlessly carried over from one phrase to the next, which tends to rob the music of its clarity and weakens its very melodic life. One notices this same kind of carelessness in brass ensembles. If a choir director can prevent his choir from breathing during the middle of a phrase, and induce the singers to breathe deeply after phrase endings, the musical structure will be made clear and the music itself will begin to breathe and become embued with life and movement! The problems of overpressure and underpressure, of forced and husky voice production are, to a large degree, solved in the process.

When the music contains ornamentations (shakes, trills, cadenza notes) at cadences or other breathing places, very little time is left for a regular breath and the singer will have to snatch a breath. This kind of breath may also be spoken of as the catch breath or half breath. It is indicated by a quick, small movement of the stomach walls just beneath the solar plexus. The posture of the singer remains unchanged. While this catch breath clarifies the musical phrasing, it also promotes a diaphragm activity, strengthens breath support, and helps attain a firm, vital tone free from breathiness and tightness.

The original form of the song "Innsbruck, I Now Must Leave Thee" requires the regular deep breath after each phrase. The later form of this

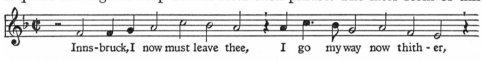

Example 1

song, "The duteous day now closeth," requires a short, snatch breath and allows for a full breath only at the middle of the song (*Example 2*).

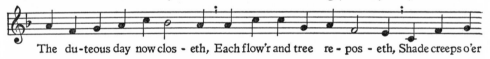

Translation by Robert Bridges, 1844-1930, from *The Yattendon Hymnal,* by permission of Oxford University Press.

Example 2

The deep breath and the half breath at the end of a phrase should in no event become a long pause or rest in the music if a pause or fermata has not been indicated. The free forward motion of the music must be preserved at all times. The singers should practice taking breaths as rapidly as possible, which is a particularly good exercise for mastering the snatch breath. The time used for inhalation should be taken from the time value of the last note of the phrase. A slight delay might be justified if the time lost is compensated by the organic breathing activity so that there is no cessation in the musical, physical, and emotional movement (*Example 3*).

26

Notation: Martin Luther, 1483-1546

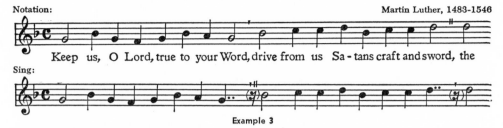

Keep us, O Lord, true to your Word, drive from us Sa - tans craft and sword, the

Sing:

Example 3

The breath simultaneously divides and joins the phrases; it severs and at the same time bridges them.

In the speech arts, breathing serves also to bring out the meaning or sentiment of the text. In the realm of choral art this is also true, particularly when the sense of the text coincides with the sense of the musical phrase. Some choir directors will give priority to the textual meaning by not permitting a breath between the phrases.

In a situation where the sense of the text is not completed at the end of the first phrase, some choir directors will give priority to the words by postponing the breath to a place somewhere in the middle of the succeeding phrase to coincide with the completion of the textual thought. Since music is not a verbal but an aural art, and since the musical form and structure must not be disrupted and the stream of musical energy cannot be halted, the author is inclined to give priority to musical considerations. Every congregation instinctively yields to the musical laws inherent in the song; where the spirit of a song has gained sway over the singers it is almost impossible to break the musical structure through an unusual textual sentence structure.

Observe the second line of the first stanza of "O sacred Head now wounded." No congregation would 'sing through' to "thorns" on one breath to preserve the textual thought, but in obedience to the musical structure and shape of the tune, the congregation would breathe after "surrounded." Organists and choir directors should not confuse the congregation by the literal observation of punctuation marks (See Ex. 4).

Ascribed to St. Bernard of Clairvaux, 1091-1153
Paul Gerhardt, 1607-76
Tr., J. W. Alexander, 1804-59a. Hans Leo Hassler, 1564-1612

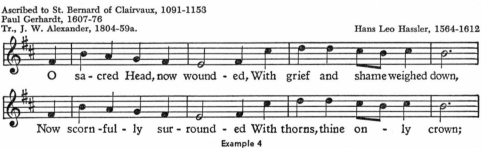

O sa - cred Head, now wound - ed, With grief and shame weighed down,

Now scorn -ful - ly sur - round - ed With thorns, thine on - ly crown;

Example 4

Certainly one would not call for a complete deep breath (ᛁ) but for a quick, light catch breath (:). With a choir it would be advisable occasionally to experiment or compare these two types of breathing in such a situation.

Caution must be exercised when attempting to mark in the breathing places according to the meaning of the text. For example, the second line, "Ah! I long and languish" of the first chorus of the Bach motet "Jesu, Priceless Treasure" is sometimes interrupted by a breath of affectation after "Ah," which results in an unnatural and unnecessary interruption of the characteristic long musical line of Bach's vocal music.

With fugal and motet-like choral compositions, breathing serves to bring out the motivic structure. Special attention should be given to marking in breathing places so that the same musical motives contain the same textual division and that the division through the breath marks are consistent. Unfortunately, the standard choral editions are not always reliable in this respect, and the conscientious choir director will carefully check the score. Often the short catch breath can be employed (Ex. 5, 6, 7) where a series or sequence of motives are present.

Example 5

28

Example 5 is taken from the choral setting of "Allein auf Gottes Wort" (Only upon God's Word) by J. Walther. He employs a cantus firmus in the tenor. At the end of the cantus firmus the composition develops into a florid web of sequential, overlapping polyphonic parts. Without the use of the short snatch breath to indicate the phrasing and form of the piece, the whole vocal structure would fall apart. The same would apply to the setting by C. Othmayrs, Ex. 6.

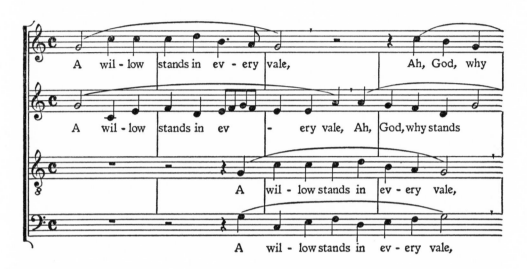

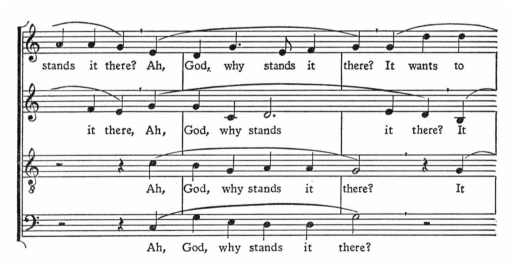

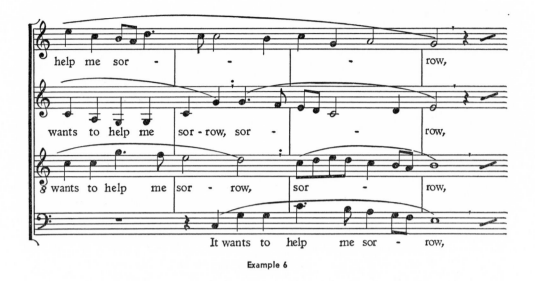

Example 6

Staggered breathing must be applied whenever the phrase is so long that the individual is unable to sing it in one breath. In such a situation the singers should help each other by breathing in turn in such a way that the whole phrase can be sustained without interruption and without any audible inhalation. The choir director should decide on the breathing places for the different sections; the mark (') can be used to indicate a quick snatch breath. If the singers cannot execute this kind of direction with the necessary concentration and dispatch, it might suffice to give the strict and yet somewhat general instruction, "Breathe wherever you like as long as the musical phrase isn't interrupted." Frequently this rule of thumb takes care of the musical demands and the breathing functions.

Instrumentalists, not only wind players, but particularly the string and keyboard players, should give more attention to the possibility of breathing at the beginning of a piece of music and at the end of phrases in the familiar way that singers do. The music would gain greatly in clarity, freedom, movement, and intensity.

In Leonhard Lechner's *Spruechen vom Leben und Tod* (Sayings on Life and Death), Ex. 7, the singer could give the instrumental player some helpful hints. The breathing places in the florid passages in music of this type are a good illustration of how instrumentalists could plot their breathing.

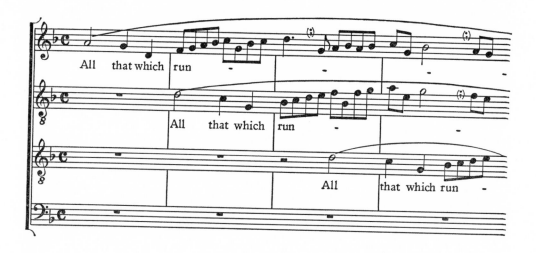

Example 7

In keeping with the old performance tradition of combining instruments and voices, the composer has prefaced the collection containing these
pieces with this direction: "New spiritual and secular German songs together
with two lively Latin songs which are not only to be sung, but are so composed that they can be conveniently performed to four or five parts with all
types of instruments . . . ." It was due to the narrow view of the nineteenth
century romantic ideal of a cappella singing that the instrumental world has
been estranged from the choral world and that a rift has been caused between
these two musical media. The historical events and instructions for combining these media can suggest new possibilities of combining voices and instruments. See the author's publication *Verwirklichung der Singbewegung* (Realization of the Singing Movement), Baerenreiter-Verlag, Kassel, Germany.

31

Chapter III

Choral Voice Training

"If the human body is the instrument of singing and the vessel of life, and if breathing is the prerequisite and the motivating force of all life and singing, uniting life and the choral art into the closest relationship, then this unity is perfected and fully realized through speech and language." Speech and language elevate man to the level of a human being; language is man's opportunity to express himself in speech and song; through language, singing becomes the expression of the very core of man's being. In voice and speech training the choral director deals with the noblest aspect of singing and the influence and development of human personality. Voice and speech training overlap — they are interrelated and inseparable.

In the German language the word "voice" *(Stimme)* is the etymon from which a long list of word combinations has been formed by the addition of different prefixes and suffixes. Most of these words represent dispositions and actions which indicate acquiescence or agreement. For example:

stimmen — tuning, voicing, agreeing

Stimmung — in music it refers to playing or singing in tune, but in everyday usage it refers to disposition, frame of mind

uebereinstimmen — agreement between all members of a group

es stimmt — it agrees

bestimmen — to decide or agree upon

abstimmen — to give your vote

unbestimmt — undecided

These examples illustrate the close relationship of the human voice with the central being of man. A thorough and proper training of the voice must take into account the whole web of man's attitudes and relationships so that his vocal endeavors will reflect and agree with the "tone" of his total inner life.

The vocal organs are an organic part of the body's physical functions. It has been pointed out that nature has lodged the vocal apparatus right at the juncture of the windpipe and the esophagus and that their use in speaking and singing is actually a secondary function — for the mouth cavity is the first part of the digestive tract, and the nose, functioning as the organ of smell, constitutes the entrance to the breathing canal. Whenever the speaking (eating) organs are set into motion, the walls of the stomach and intestines are also activated.

The voice production and speech habits which the choir director exemplifies are of far-reaching significance. The lay singer tends to acquire most of his singing habits by direct imitation. All of the choir director's instructions, well-meant and pertinent as they may be, are superfluous if he constantly speaks and sings incorrectly. The author knows a choir director who stuttered whenever he became excited. As a consequence, many of his singers began to stutter in their everyday conversation. The sensitive listener feels a pressure in his larynx when listening to a speaker with a hoarse throat. One may also observe how an entire audience begins to clear their throats when a speaker with a hoarse voice commences to speak.

Singing is a complex process; numerous physical and psychological energies must be harnessed in order to bring about that which we call "singing." This becomes particularly obvious in voice training. There are many different skills which the singer must acquire separately by conscious effort until he can finally coordinate and blend these individual skills on a higher level of uninhibited artistic activity. To achieve this goal one must always work from the whole to the whole; herein lies the essence of all artistic and human creative endeavor. This applies both to technical and to musical endeavors alike. A child does not first learn the grammar and then the language but he first begins to speak and only later does he become aware of the grammar of speech. To approach choir training on the basis of this principle presupposes that a choir director is in full possession of all artistic and pedagogical skills.

Just as relaxation is the prerequisite for exertion and tension, so relaxation and looseness of the vocal organs is essential for good vocal production. One should never interfere with the natural direction and activity of the voice through artificially produced tensions. In a sense the voice must seek its own way of functioning properly and find its own position and focus. One should never try to force a preconceived sound from a singer. If every pot, jar, or tumbler has its own unique timbre, then it is certainly true that every human body has its own unique timbre. To develop and realize the unique quality of the singing voice the following illustration may be useful: Imagine children singing in a spacious hall, under a large bridge, in a cave or tunnel. The sound begins to rise in volume and resonance and it fills the vaulted space with its own peculiar timbre. Similarly, a singer should think of his own voice as filling up the vaulted spaces of the chest, throat, and head resonators with rich, resonant sound. To assist the voice in finding its own natural resonance one could have the singer make light throat-clearing noises or moaning and grunting sounds. In doing so, the singer should imagine that the impulse for making any vocal sounds should come from above the head and that the sounds themselves originate behind the nose. Or, the singer may imitate the crying of an infant which, after several attempts, breaks out into a full resonant cry.

According to such presuppositions, any voice training should be undertaken with a consideration of *five basic principles* of voice production. These cannot be separated from each other and are always to be considered whenever any phase of voice or speech training is being touched on.

(1) The *pharnyx*, consisting of the spaces of the throat, nose, and mouth, and comprising the entire space from the vocal cords to the upper front teeth, must be opened as much as possible.
(2) The *larynx* (Adam's apple) should be maintained in a low but comfortable position at all times.
(3) The voice should be focused *high* and *forward* (between the eyes!)
(4) The *resonances* of the voice should be *stimulated*.
(5) *Vowels* and *consonants* should be formed in the *front part* of the mouth.

To help achieve these five aims, a series of everyday, life-related activities can be utilized. In addition, various vowels and consonants can be used as pathfinders to properly focus and place the vowels. Each vowel has its own position or spot and so the position and strength of one vowel can be utilized to equalize or overcome the disadvantage of another vowel. For example, the high focus of the *ee* vowel can help to bring forward the *ah* vowel which tends to stay back in the throat. The expansion of the resonators serves to unfold the sound and bring out the modulation of the vowels and the development of various vocal colors.

As an easy, natural exercise, yawning is one of the most conducive to expand and open the resonators. One should certainly not suppress the use of yawning exercises because of any social inhibitions! Further, the imitation of biting into ripe, juicy fruit can be useful, since the pleasures of taste and smell are combined here aiding both deep breathing and the opening of resonators. The eating of tasty fruit also stimulates the saliva flow which moistens the mucous lining of the resonators. Even the mimicking of the wide-open mouth position of a ravenous beast of prey may be helpful to induce widening of the resonators. The mere outward, downward pulling of the jaws is of course of much less significance than the intensive inner expansion of the spaces of the nose, throat, and pharynx.

34

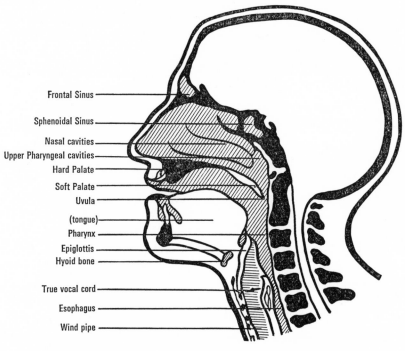

Frontal Sinus

Sphenoidal Sinus

Nasal cavities

Upper Pharyngeal cavities

Hard Palate

Soft Palate

Uvula

(tongue)

Pharynx

Epiglottis

Hyoid bone

True vocal cord

Esophagus

Wind pipe

Fig. 25

The *ah* vowel is most helpful in opening the way for this inner widening. Even here with the use of the *ah* vowel, it is not so much the exterior part of the face that should be expanded as the spaces inside the mouth. To help make the widening process a more conscious experience, let the singer begin with and gradually enlarge the opening over the vowel *oh* and then proceed to *ah*. It might be helpful and appropriate to precede the vowels with an *m* or *n* to prevent a click-like initial break of the tone, commonly known as the "glottis attack." In a similar manner, the *ah* may be arrived at by first singing *m-n-ng-ah*. This gives the *ah* a higher position and permits it to resonate freely behind the soft palate. This process of widening the resonators must be developed from a maximum state of closedness to a maximum state of expansion, using a step-by-step procedure. The choir director should accompany and support these exercises with appropriate head gestures.

The consonants which help to widen the resonators are the plosives *b*, *d*, and *g*. The common use of these consonants aids in the expansion because of the momentary stoppage of the breath and the subsequent build-up of air pressure required for their execution. At the same time they serve to massage the walls of the larynx. Appropriate musical exercises are given at the end of the chapter. For the correct pronunciation of the vowels, see A IV p. 49 ff.

A low position of the larynx is required to attain maximum relaxation and responsiveness. It is to be remembered that the vocal cords must be able to return to a maximum state of relaxation after strenuous tension. It is from this relaxed state that all its vocal activity has its point of departure. If the larynx rises, the throat becomes tight, the voice begins to sound guttural, hard, and cramped. Deep breathing should help to counteract this tendency. The practice of deep, lower breathing accompanied with good diaphragmatic support, and the habitual cultivation of a relaxed throat, can help to maintain the larynx in the desired low position.

The vowels *oo* and *oh* are useful aids for the low larynx position. For this reason it is good to begin with the dark vowels (see Chapter IV). The relative position of the larynx can be checked by placing your finger on it. Other vowels which have a natural tendency to lift the larynx to a high position should also be interpolated along with *oo* and *oh* such as *oo-ee-oo*; *oh-ah-oh*. This helps to keep the larynx in a lower position for the singing of the *ee* vowel. Again, it is advantageous in addition to *m* and *n* to use the plosives *p* and *b* as prefixes to *oo* and *oh*. Also in speaking the larynx should be loose and relaxed. Consonants cannot be used to help achieve a low position of the larynx. For appropriate exercises and correct enunciation, see A III, p. 38 ff. and A IV, p. 49 ff.

A high tonal focus helps the larynx to function with a maximum amount of freedom. The tone has to swell and to spread into all the resonators. The following suggestions to the singers can be of help to achieve this:
(1) telling the singers that the tone originates "behind the eyes," and (2) asking them to "sing through your eyes"; think of the tone as spinning behind the upper part of the nose, or imagine that the tone soars and circles above the head.
A slight raising of the upper lip with a completely relaxed lower jaw can also help to secure the high focus. The normal mouth and lip position should allow the upper teeth to be seen. The lower teeth remain covered of course. A natural activity which is conducive to head resonance is sniffing. Have the singers imitate a sneeze in "ha" and chiee" in various ways, prolonging the *ee* vowel for some length of time; proceed in a similar manner with "hatcheh," "hatchoh," etc.

The vowel *eh* (ay) can be very useful in achieving a high focus. It has somewhat of a nasal sound which vibrates instantly throughout the entire nasal passage. The *eh* should be produced with a slightly wide-mouthed position (formation as in a gentle smile and with a broad, somewhat thick and rich sound). Words beginning with the consonants *n* and *ng* are most useful for helping to obtain a high focus in singing; for example, in such words as nose, new, now. The high forward focus can be readily established and sensed. It is best to use *n* before and *ng* at the end of a syllable — e.g. "new song."

Even if used separately without a vowel, these consonants are an excellent means for achieving and maintaining a high, forward focus. The use of the French nasal syllables are a welcome aid, because the tongue must lie quite flat and loose, which makes for increased width in the mouth and nasal resonators. One can devise exercises with *bon* and *bien*. Whenever the *eh* is mixed with other vowels — *oo-we*; *oh-oe*; *a-ae*; it tends to direct these vowels to a higher focal position which results in a greater amount of head resonance. For further appropriate exercises and correct diction, see A III, p. 39 ff. and A IV, p. 49 ff.

The waking of the resonators of the voice gives it projection and power. Singing does not just happen because air rushes past the vocal cords causing them to vibrate. The process is a little more complex than that. Next to the stretching of the vocal cords, the thrust of the rising stream of breath against them and the proper alignment of the pharynx, the production of a rich resonant sound depends above all on the setting up of sympathetic waves of vibrations in all the resonators of the body — mouth and nasal passages, windpipe with its branching tubes, the bones, ligaments, and cartilages. One may compare the human resonating cavities to a radio set. The spaces within the set, as well as its different parts, must be filled with a maximum of resonance. These parts produce, as well as augment the sound. If it weren't possible to augment sound many times the strength of its original source, it would be impossible to conceive of two small vocal cords producing enough sound to fill a large auditorium.

The value of a gentle smile to promote resonance and enhance the beauty of the tone should not be ignored by the singer; it relaxes the resonating areas and widens the resonating spaces. The old Italian masters knew and practiced the singing rule "a slight smile while you sing." Now many choir singers put on a furrowed facial expression when they sing — as if singing were a most painful experience for them! Here is a good way to demonstrate the effect of facial expression on the quality and color of the tone: Begin to sing a long sustained note with a dark, scowling facial mien and gradually brighten the expression until it becomes an expression of sheer laughter. The sound will certainly brighten according to the brightening of the facial expression. The distension of the nostrils is an effective way of opening the resonators and the slight pulling up of the upper lip in this connection is of importance. Finally, the concept of "singing into the mask" is most conducive to the production of head resonance. While practicing these exercises, the singers can try out the effects of using their hands to form a megaphone around their mouths as if they were speaking into a large telephone mouthpiece. This exercise can help to make them more conscious of the resonance they are producing. As pathfinders for these high resonances, the same vowel sounds which were mentioned earlier in this chapter can be employed, but every

37

singer should check the particular vibrating areas by placing the hand on different parts of the head and face. When singing *n*, touch the temples and the forehead; *ng* — the back area of the top of the head; *eh* — the bony part of the nose. Keep changing to different sounds and let your hands find the different areas set to resonance by these changes. The chest resonances should not be forcefully "drawn out" from the chest, but instead one should think of these vibrations floating loosely upon the slightly raised chest. (For appropriate exercises, see A III, p. 39 ff. and A IV, p. 49 ff.)

The formation of consonants occurs in the front of the mouth, between the lips and the front teeth, at the tip of the tongue and the gums. This helps to free the larynx from any unnecessary strain, to prevent the tone from becoming blocked in the throat, and to help achieve a clear enunciation. To develop a keener consciousness and control over lip formations, ask the singers to form the embouchure of a flute player and to imitate a flute player as he varies the shape of his lips for different pitches and air pressures. This helps to attain a round and slightly forward protrusion of the lips which has a decided influence on the shape and color of vowel sounds. The tongue rests loosely and flat within the lower jaw and its tip is slightly projected forward between the upper and lower front teeth.

Let the singers whistle the music for a change. Whistling can heighten the enjoyment of music making if tactfully introduced, as for example in the rehearsing of a new tune or in connection with a multivoiced composition of improvisatory nature.

Exercises on quickly reiterated vowels while the tongue hangs loosely over the lower lip can also be beneficial. As an aid to keeping the tone securely focused between the lips and at the tip of the tongue, singers may "savor" the tone as when tasting a delicious dish.

If the imagination of relishing a sumptuous dish is accompanied by a wholehearted *hm* or *ah*, and perhaps a little pat on the stomach, then the activity of the diaphragm could be stimulated and coordinated with the vocal activity. Of the various consonants, *v, m,* and *z* are the best for stimulating activity and mobility of the lips. Of all common vowels, *ee* is most forward in its production. Exercises employing the forward consonants and vowels help to project the voice forward. Frequent change between *oo* and *ee* with energetic forward and backward drawing of the lips promotes sensitivity and strength of the lips. For further suitable exercises, see A III, p. 39 ff. and A IV, p. 49 ff.

By selecting and combining diverse individual exercises with their various functions, it is possible to realize several goals at once. For example, the syllable *nah* serves to widen the spaces of the laryngo and oropharynx to achieve high focus, and to develop a good head resonance. At the same time the *ah*, which has a tendency to "fall back" into the throat, is directed upward and forward. In the syllable *mö*, pronounced as in Goethe, the *oh* vowel keeps the larynx in a low position, the *eh* vowel pulls the tone upward and the *m* focuses it forward. The choir director can invent various combinations of vowels and syllables in accordance with the needs and aims of his choir.

These tone syllables can be utilized in the formation of systematic musical exercises. They should benefit the choral work during the rehearsal and can also serve as warm-up exercises prior to a choral concert. The following exercises are suggestions for the employment of consonants and syllables:

(1) *The sustaining of suitable consonants and syllables on a given pitch:* The result is an even, flowing stream. It is best to choose a common pitch in the middle part of the voice so that all singers will find it comfortable to perform this exercise. The famous choral singers of the sixteenth century commenced their rehearsals with a tone in the middle range which was sung with medium strength. From there the exercises are taken down in stepwise progression, and then up again in similar fashion. Altos and basses may sing a third or a fifth below the other voices in two-part harmony; three- and four-part harmony may also be employed. Some consonants and syllables which can be employed in this fashion are:

n, ng, m, v, g; noo, noh, nee, neh, nah; moo, moh, mee, meh, mah; zoo, zoh, zee, zeh, zah; boo, boh, bee, beh, bah; doo, doh, dee, deh, dah; bung, bong, bing, beng, bang; dung, dong, ding, deng, dang; dun, don, din, den, dan; bum, bom, bim, bem, bam, etc. The choir director should devise his own sequence of syllables to meet the particular vocal needs of his choir. In order to meet certain vocal needs one could form tone syllables with the umlauts ü, ö, and ä.

(2) *Constant repetition of suitable syllables on one pitch:* The tonal stream is constantly interrupted. At first this may occur at regular intervals, then in various rhythms, and finally in the rhythm of a song. The choir director indicates the repetitions of the syllables by a waving, circular hand motion. The syllables listed in the previous paragraph may be utilized here. In addition, syllables such as the following may be used: *bub, bob, bib, beb, bab; bug, bog, big, beg, bag; pif, päf, paf; diridiridon; simsalabim,* and other combinations of tone syllables such as are found in folk songs, Swiss yodels, and madrigals. First, repeat the individual syllable, e.g. *nanan, bobobob,* and then the entire sequence without interruption.

(3) *Appropriate words which aid vocal development may be repeated on a given pitch:* e.g. *bang, long, singing, sun, summer, zooming, zone, zing, zang, zebulon, bring, Minna, name, volvo, vowel, vulcanize.*

(4) *The singing of suitable vowels, syllables, and words to a simple musical exercise:*

39

Example 8

The exercise should be performed several times on the *ng* sound and then transposed to such two-syllable words as, singing, Minna, volume.

At first each syllable of the two-syllable words is sung to one note except when the word falls on the last three notes which are sung as illustrated in Example 8. Later the entire exercise can be sung on the vowel of the first syllable while the second syllable is sung on the last note. To guard against unnecessary tightness in the voice one should start with exercises consisting of descending scales or melodic passages. This exercise should be transposed to higher and lower keys to allow the entire tessitura of the voice to be exercised. The exercise should be completed with a beautiful, sustained legato tone on the final whole note. (See Ex. 9.)

Example 9

The tension in the ascending part of the tune is immediately relieved in the descending melodic passage of the second part of the exercise.

The musical tone must be produced with a twofold objective in mind: a long, even, musical stream, an arching, vibrant musical line which receives its strength and consistency in an unshakeably sure breath support. The two foregoing exercises can help to achieve this objective. On the other hand, the musical line also requires a certain amount of lightness and bounciness of sound; this can be encouraged by a relaxed voice production and by speaking the words of the passage in a lilting, flexible, speaking voice. The following two exercises can help to achieve this sound quality (Examples 10 and 11).

Example 10

40

At first this exercise should be sung on tone syllables, choosing the shortest ones, e.g. *dandandan, nununu, nanana, momomo*. Permit the consonants to shine through continuously and interrupt this musical stream only through short, "bright" vowels which brighten the tone between the consonants. Only then should the exercise be sung to a relaxed, hummed *n, ng, m,* and finally to entire words, whereby the first syllable is again sung to the entire sequence of notes, the last syllable falling on the last note. Particular attention must be given here to avoid separation of the individual tones of the *vocalize* by inserting *h's*, or by attacking each note with the stroke of the glottis. At first the first and fifth notes are emphasized, later only the first. This exercise can also be utilized with tone syllables and individual words.

Example II

Voice teachers generally divide the voice range into three *registers:* chest, middle, and head registers. Since their terms are frequently interpreted in different ways by different teachers, theoretical discussion of these terms may bring more confusion than help. The author prefers to forego a discussion of this phase of vocal pedagogy. The gist of the matter has been adequately discussed in the foregoing treatment. From a musical point of view, one should continually strive for a blending of the various registers so that out of the three registers we make one. Occasionally bright tones may be practiced in the low range and dark tones in the high range. The chest tones should be taken up as far as possible (not exceeding the point of undue tension or discomfort), and the head tones should be sung downward as far as possible. The singer imagines that the highest tones are drawn from the depths of the earth and the lowest tones drawn down from the sky! These opposing upward-downward forces are constantly employed to achieve the equalization of the registers. While singing descending scales, the singer inwardly erects himself and when he sings an ascending scale passage he thinks his tones downward.

In all of these exercises the ear of the singer must also be trained simultaneously with the voice and the singer should be challenged to exercise constant control over his own singing; the choir must not only be able to judge whether it is singing correct notes with good intonation, but also whether the tone "sits" right. (Compare A III, p. 34.) Throughout the singing of the various exercises the choir director must support, through appropriate gestures, the movement and direction of the exercise and at the same time seek to control the position of the tones. Certain choral societies tend to produce a big, impressive sound; in protest, other societies have adopted a practice of continual soft singing as a part of their choral creed. The one approach is as harmful to proper tonal development as the other. The exercises should begin with medium strength of voice — comfortably produced, and from here the director may help his singers to the right kind of *piano* and *forte* singing. The choir should be encouraged to practice this sound long enough to assure proper alignment of the larynx and tonal focus. A dynamic crescendo can be properly attempted only after the voice "sits" properly and when it functions with reasonable ease and freedom. Sufficient time for the preparatory breath must be given before every exercise. Every exercise must be attacked with relaxation and freedom, bounce and buoyancy!

The treatment of the most common voice production faults can be positively approached with the use of various exercises. First of all, any kind of forced tone must be relieved from overpressure of the breath by encouraging relaxed exhalation. Head and body should be relaxed and free. (Compare with A I, p. 1 ff. and A III, p. 36 ff.) The aids suggested for maintaining a low position of the larynx are helpful. (See A III, p. 36 ff.) Often a highly arched tongue can be the cause of a tight, throaty tone; think of letting the tongue relax into the concave shape of a spoon. In a breathy tone, not all of the breath is converted into tone; a portion of the breath escapes between the vocal cords whenever they are not closing properly. If one holds a burning candle in front of the mouth of a person who is singing with a breathy tone, the flame begins to flicker. With correct singing in which all the outgoing air is utilized in tone production, the candle flame will continue to burn without interruption, even when the person sings right into the flame. The necessary air pressure is best achieved by laughing exercises on syllables like *ho,ho,ho,* on repeated pitches. That this should be performed in a jovial and merry frame of mind is understood. This exercise may then be extended to stepwise exercise from the tonic to the fifth and back, and finally to a simple laughing canon, if desired. The diaphragm should work in light thrusts and can be felt and controlled by placing the hand on the solar plexus area. This hammer-like *martellato* singing has a compressing effect on the breath. Finally, from these laughing syllables, one should change into a full, round sound. The outflowing breath must now be so transformed into a full, resonant tone that a burning candle held in front of a singer's mouth would no longer flicker. In stubborn cases the syllables *piff, pöff, paff,* may be used as a basic exercise. These are first spoken in an almost toneless manner, then with vocal sound, and finally they are sung repeatedly on one note and on a short scale exercise from the tonic to the third and back in the range of *D* to *F♯* in the lower, middle voice range. The diaphragm must constantly operate with short, even thrusts which can be checked with the hand as described above.

42

Then the director may proceed to the use of exercises on repeated syllables like *ho,ho,ho,* and *ha,ha,ha.*

It is most expedient to do these exercises at the outset of the warm-up exercises prior to the choir rehearsal in order to achieve a clear, vigorous tone right from the start. The flickering tone stems from improper use of the breath. The tonal releases some singers give on fermatas and final chords remind one of the escape of the last bit of air from a balloon or tire tube. The suggestions and exercises in the chapter on choral breathing (A II, p. 15 ff.) may be applied here. If the flickering tone develops into a steady tremolo, these breathing exercises are not always adequate to remove the problems. Often some kind of physical tension can be the cause of tremolo singing and the quivering of the lower jaw which frequently accompanies it. In such a situation, yawning, swallowing, and other exercises which pull the larynx to a low position can help to strengthen the weak muscles of the larynx which may be the underlying cause (See A I, p. 3 ff.). If the tremolo stems from a nervous condition, the aids and exercises discussed so far would be inadequate to remedy it.

The improper use of the voice can easily lead to loss of pitch. To avoid faulty intonation, the choir director must be keenly aware of the causes. Often the source of the problem is found in a choral attack that is too hard and too low in the throat. In such an attack the tones are pulled up from beneath as it were, and like a diver, the singer emerges puffing and panting from the ongoing stream of music. The attack is not only focused too low, but the pressure on the larynx has harmful consequences, and a series of short, quick, grunt-like tones are generated before the actual tone begins to sound. This results in a poor, untidy vocal sound. To help remove this double fault see what has been said about the high focus (See A III, p. 36 ff.). The singer must always approach the onset of a new tone from above — like the landing of a parachute jumper who prepares to alight. It may also be helpful to compare the tones to light balls which one reaches up to catch. The choir can assist in making the image more realistic by using gestures and motions which suggest the landing of the parachute jumper or the catching of the balls; in certain situations the singers may perform these gestures with the director. Beyond this the choir should be disciplined to hear the tone it is to sing beforehand. This "inner" listening also gives the singers more control over the entire singing apparatus. The practice of first humming the first note or chord of a new entry promotes both a vivid tonal image and good intonation.

Sliding down from note to note can be as disturbing and harmful as the habit of scooping up from one note to the next. Singers often wish to produce a legato by this process, but in reality they achieve a "Schmierato!"

(*Schmier* is the German word for grease.) The temptation to slide or scoop is particularly strong when two vowels meet as in "I am the Way." In order to achieve a close-knit, flowing musical line, every tone must fit into its own spot in the area where head resonances are sensed. To overcome whining or sliding tones, the singers should think of the tones in the scale as a flight of stairs which are to be climbed by deliberately lifting the feet and then carefully placing them on one step at a time. Just as each step is clearly marked from the other, so the tones which he sings must be placed so that they are clearly recognizable from each other. The flickering and tremolant tone is also a common cause for poor intonation. Flatting can also be caused by singing the vowels with too dark a color. A deliberate "brightening up" of the vowels *ah* and *eh* may serve as the necessary remedy.

Problems of poor intonation which originate not in vocal problems but because of certain musical deficiencies can be approached with the help of ear-training exercises. Some causes for poor intonation are the following: frequent repetition of the same pitch, song, or voice part in an unfavorable tessitura requiring frequent changes from one register to another or from one kind of voice production to another; certain vocal compositions with B-flat tonalities seem to cause intonation trouble. The upward transposition by a half-tone can solve the problems remarkably well. Singing a rising major third too flat, a rising major second too sharp, a descending minor third too low, etc. are other reasons for bad intonation.

The choir director can be of considerable help in avoiding and correcting intonation problems through the use of appropriate signs and gestures, but the constant use of gestures to indicate heightening of pitch in an effort to restore flattened pitches to their original tonality finally leads to frustration and tension. Finally, extraneous factors like fatigue, poor ventilation, lack of concentration, poor facilities, and other personal conditions can be the causes of poor intonation, especially flatting. The exercises in A V, p. 74 ff. should be particularly useful in dealing with intonation problems.

Chapter IV

Choral Speech Training

Voice training and speech training are very closely related to each other. In the previous chapter, numerous speech sounds were listed as useful means for voice training. It is particularly the lay singer who is most often willing to accept help in the type of voice training which is based on resonant and expressive speech sounds. Voice and speech training must finally complement each other.

The choir director should cultivate a keen sense for the difficulties and problems which will be encountered in speech training. Speech inertia is common not only in many parts of Germany, but also in other parts of Europe as well as in North America. The reasons for this are not only to be attributed to negligence but more probably to the casual speech habits of the people living between the fiftieth and sixtieth degree of latitude. Many people, including choir singers, tend to turn all vowels into sounds resembling either *ah* or *ee*. These are formed with the same embouchure, and every expression of language, whether joyous or sad in character, is spoken with the same lack of facial expression. Such people wear one mask through which all words are drawled so thoughtlessly that mouth and heart often have no recollection or impression of the words which the lips have spoken. If this is typical of many people in North Germany, then one may note, on the other hand, with what lively and picturesque words, impressive articulation, mimic, and gesture the South Germans, the Italians, and the French speak.

The choir director should carefully study these differences in speech customs and then seek to dissolve these differences and fixed speech patterns by infusing the words with the true spirit of the textual, musical, and spiritual qualities of the work itself. The most difficult task in this process is in dealing with differences of temperament and character traits of people from various localities. These cultural and tribal characteristics are very closely related both to the individual and to his speech habits and therefore cannot be modified or changed by a general approach.

These differences are well illustrated in the regional dialects of North America. Whenever the choir consists of singers from such different regions, it is the responsibility of the director to strive for correct American English pronunciation. The dipthongized vowels of the Texas drawl, the broad-spoken *oh* in words like glory "glawry" of the northwestern region, the nasal vowel qualities in French speaking areas of Canada and such extremely localized speech phenomena as the Brooklyn dialect (goil for girl, boid for bird) must be made to conform to the neutral and clarified sounds of standard American English which has for some time been accepted as a norm for singers and actors.* The director will not always be able to achieve his goal here and will have to be satisfied with a partial solution. In addition to such variations of dialect one has to contend with unnatural tensions and nervousness which affect most public speakers and singers. Even the most simple and uncomplicated person who appears so natural and unsophisticated in his private and personal life begins to recite his words as soon as he has to speak or sing in public. Experiments have shown that people speak in a more relaxed manner and on a lower pitch when reading factual materials such as a list of figures. On the other hand, the reading of a poem or some other material with strong emotional content causes the pitch of the voice to rise. It rises even more with the reading of an unfamiliar text when concentration and excitement are most intense. The most devastating speech derangements occur in choral speaking which is commonly heard as an expressionless, sense-distorting declamation. The director needs to draw upon all his pedagogical skill (which demands far more than a good musical knowledge) to help his singers to achieve a relaxed and natural approach to singing.

Without scrupulous cultivation of correct enunciation no choral singing can fulfill its true purpose unless of course the singers are satisfied to regard an enthusiastic babble resembling a "speaking with tongues of fire" as the singer's noblest expression, or if a singing society deliberately seeks to evade artistic stimulation and is satisfied with musical mediocrity. It happens that both types of singing groups do exist. The listener must understand the words which the choir is singing. In a choral concert it is usually taken for granted that the words will not be recognized by the listener and for this reason he is handed a program containing the entire text. This visual aid should not be necessary. The choir should take particular care in the worship service to sing the words with utmost distinction because the congregation is expected to understand what is being proclaimed without the help of printed text. In a liturgical service where a musical response to the choir's singing is called for, lucid enunciation by the choir is mandatory.

In choral singing the language should not be treated analytically or melodramatically. Singers must learn the art of listening carefully for the inherent sounds of the words and let these sounds emerge in their singing.

*Translator's note: An excellent book on this subject is "The Singer's Manual of English Diction" by Madeleine Marshall, published by G. Schirmer, Inc.

It is then that the core and true meaning of the words come alive. Even the isolated sounds, when purely sung, contain a basic quality which reflects their meaning and character. The singers must waken and sharpen their senses for the different sound characteristics, so that the total sense of the sound may be grasped as they listen to the constant change of tonal color.

It is simplest to begin this kind of training by reciting poetic lines which are rich in alliteration. In the line, "In a summer season when soft was the sun," the "sense" of the line becomes alive by the frequent recurrence of the sibilant "s"; one can feel the warmth, see the brightness, and sense the nearness of the sun. Examples of alliteration which contain more than one image require a more intense listening for the sense of the word. In William Butler Yeats's line, "I hear lake water lapping with low sounds by the shore," the sensitive listener will have noted that the author paints a picture of sight and sound by contrasting the brighter vowels in the first part of the sentence with the darker vowels of the second part. The bright vowels *e, ay, a* conjure up a picture of dancing waves, reflecting bright flashes of sunlight, and the vowels *oh, ah-oo, uh* and *oh* represent with unmistakable clarity the gurgling, moaning, melancholy sounds of the waves. Furthermore, the poet has succeeded in making the listener feel that almost mystical, dichromatic mood which many people feel about the sea — it makes you gay and glad and yet it leaves you strangely sad. Many active verbs have captured the activity latent in the word, which in the course of animated, intensive speaking unleashes the energy and incentive to renewed action. This is particularly true of words that express activities which are associated with unique sounds, e.g. rustling, rumbling, tramping, hissing, clapping, ringing, rattling, etc. The words should be spoken with full participation of the imagination and with the constant desire to discover the central meaning and characteristic strength of the individual word. The decisive factor here is that the listener recognizes the corresponding activity directly from the forcefulness of the spoken word alone without having to reflect on what was said. Nouns, when spoken with clarity and imagination, help to make the intended object visible and real in the mind of the listener. For example, if we speak the word "hammer" with clarity and decisiveness, it is easy to visualize a hammer, or if the word "mountain" is spoken with sustained vocal energy on the first syllable, the rugged outlines and snow-capped peaks immediately begin to loom before the mind's eye. The essential character of the object is often characterized in the sound of the word. Take for example the word "eel" and note how naturally the roundness and the slimy smoothness of this sea creature are suggested; the word "fire" suggests crackling sound, red heat, and upward-reaching flames. The representation of essential meaning is also contained in the sounds of abstract nouns like love, hate, grief, ecstasy. The kind of speaking and enunciation which stirs the senses and conjures up an image in the listener's mind is of greater significance in the domain of choral art than has been recognized by musicians, for the sounds which best serve the words must, in the final analysis, originate and unfold from the basic character and meaning of the words themselves. In consideration of this basic relationship of sound and words, the singer should strive, not to put meaning into the words, but to draw as much meaning and significance as possible out of the words. The textual characteristics should be studied in detail with great fidelity, complete sympathy, and with intensive concentration so that every word, like a bell, begins to sound within itself. (For methods of choral speech in rehearsal see B II, p. 156 ff.)

The outward structure and the soul of the different languages vary so greatly that each language requires a unique treatment. Charles V was known to have said, "I speak with my God in Spanish, to women in Italian, to diplomats in French, to scholars in Latin, and to my hired men in German." Something to think about for choral musicians!

The vowel sounds can best be made to sound natural and vital by allowing the imagination to relate these sounds to experiences that are intimately associated with them. For example, the vowel *oo* is closely connected with fear. One has observed how children and even grownups, after listening to a horror story, will speak a long, drawn out *ooh* —. Perhaps this could be tried with the choir to achieve a desired vocal result.

In a similar fashion, the characteristic sound of *oh* could be evoked by feeling surprise or excited wonder, the *ah* from a sense of happiness and well being, the *ee* from a feeling of aversion or horror.

To render the inherent and peculiar characteristics of each vowel more clearly, sing a favorite tune, repeating it on each of the following: *noh, noo, nah, neh, nee*; with each repetition the tone character will be totally different and each syllable will require a complete change in the attitude of the singer.

It may be helpful to arrange the vowels within the framework of a pyramid in which the *ah* vowel may be arrived at through three series of vowels, each series originating from a different base: *oo, ü, ee*. Each sequence results in a different color of the vowel *ah*: the approach from the *oo* position encourages the low position of the larynx, the *ü* (umlaut) promotes richer head resonance, and the *ee* insures a more forward focused tone. (Fig. 26.) The diagram illustrates clearly the transition and development of the different vowel sequences: *ah, oo,* and *ee* are the cornerstones of the vowel structure, the other vowels are derived from the transitions.

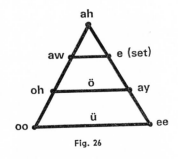

Fig. 26

48

The choir director should make certain that the singers consciously shape the appropiate mouth formation for each vowel. The following experiment may be tried: Speak a vowel and retain the mouth formation of that vowel for a moment while striking one cheek with the fingers; a fairly clear reproduction of the particular vowel should be discernible. Different pitches may also be achieved by altering the shape and size of the mouth spaces and then striking the cheek with the hand. This can be practiced to the point where scales and tunes can be produced and clearly recognized. The singers may occasionally be asked to try this exercise to realize for themselves the importance of mouth and throat positions in determining vowel sounds and in fixing pitches.

Correct vowel enunciation can be approached in three different ways: by illustrating the natural characteristic of the vowel in an animated, vivid manner, e.g. *ah* is related to happiness, joy; by creating an increasingly vivid concept of "joyousness" a purer, brighter *ah* sound is achieved. This kind of appeal to the imagination goes a long way to prepare the larynx and resonators for an ideal production of the desired vowel sound. The suggestion to the singer may be expressed in terms like "show a little more animation." Secondly, improvement of the vowel sound can be approached from the standpoint of what the musical ear demands in terms of purity, intensity, and color. The director may request a brighter *ah*, a more covered *ah*, etc. Finally, the director may meet the physiological requirements for correct vowel formations by purely mechanistic movements of lips, teeth, tongue and adjustment of mouth spaces; he may ask for a wider opening of the mouth, a flattened, more relaxed position of the tongue, greater projection of the lips, etc. The discreet director will employ and integrate all three approaches and emphasize one approach or the other in accordance with the age level, maturity, and composite ability of the choir. In working with young amateur singers it is best to use more of the first approach because of its closer connection with common experiences. All instructions and illustrations should be presented in a creative, dynamic manner, and any of these instructions should be followed by listening to the results and by giving mechanistic instructions with regard to proper phonetic production. Trained singers should be approached primarily with the third method: i.e. the mechanistic approach.

Before teaching the correct technical formation of vowels, it is important that the director should first practice them himself:

oo — with as much inner mouth and throat space (width) as possible, low relaxed tongue, very small, round mouth opening, slightly parted lips.

oh — somewhat larger mouth opening, *oh* formation of the lips, tongue remains relaxed.

ah — wide mouth opening but not so much a pulling of the lips as an expansion within the mouth and pharynx; the tongue remains flat but somewhat forward, the upper lip is slightly drawn up, the lower lip close to the lower teeth.

eh (ay) — the mouth closes slightly, the back of the tongue is slightly humped, the position of the lips remains as in *ah*, cheeks and nostrils slightly distended.

ee — mouth position very similar to that in the *eh* vowel; the back of the tongue is humped even more, the tip of the tongue remains in contact with the lower teeth.

Each vowel can be formed as a long or a short sound:

> *ā* as in day, shade
>
> *ă* as in hat, man
>
> *ä* as in far, march
>
> *ō* as in old, note, *ŏ* as in not, want
>
> *ī* as in ice, child, *ĭ* as in ill, pity
>
> *ōō* as in soon, food, *ŏŏ* as in foot, book
>
> *ē* as in eve, feet, *ě* as in end, pet.

In the four-voice canon "O Light, O Trinity" by M. Praetorius, the vowel "i" is sung twice to the same melisma — first in its short pronounced form and then in its long form (p. 4, *Nine Easy Canons*, Augsburg, 1333).

From Latin Hymn, VII cent.
Tr., composite, 1890

Christoph Praetorius, 1574

O Light, O Trin - i - ty most___ blest!

O God Al - might - y and best.

From "Nine Easy Canons," edited Riedel, copyright 1962 Augsburg Publishing House.

Example 12

Both the long and the short vowels are subject to a variety of modifications of sound and color, depending largely on the consonants which precede and follow the vowel. One may refer to any good dictionary or pronouncing gazette to illustrate the various forms of vowel pronunciation.

The short vowel is usually spoken quickly, while the long vowel sound is usually sustained much longer — e.g. "set it up," "please be seated." It has been correctly observed that words with short vowels express quick actions while words with long vowels represent the idea of sustenation. Compare the following words: quĭck, făst, hĭt, slăp, crăck, shŏt, flĭps, whĭp, with these long vowel words: sēa, strēam, nōōn, ēvening, wālk, brēathing, hēal, sōōthe. There are exceptions of course (short, rest).

It becomes somewhat of a problem to the singer when he has to sing a musical passage in which the short vowel sounds are placed on a long note or with melismatic passages and the short note values happen to fall on words with long vowels. In such a situation the short vowels must be sustained and lengthened and the long vowels must be shortened. The singer will achieve the desirable sound if he tries to make as clear a picture as he can of the meaning and sense of the particular word. In Johann Staden's "Now Shine, Thou Light of Glory," the words in the third line must under no circumstances be sung "Shĭne on ūs Thou clēar brĭght sūn." In spite of the seeming incompatibility of language and music, it should be sung as illustrated. (See Example 13.)

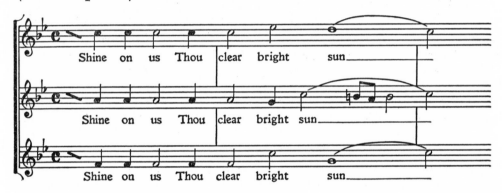

Example 13

In music with repeated notes or syllables, like the "fa-la-la" refrains in English ballets, one frequently hears a marked thickening or fattening of the *ah* on the final or semifinal note. This is due to the increased length of the note. The opening soprano line in J. Savile's "Here's a Health unto His Majesty" (p. 67, *Sing Care Away,* Book III, Novello) may serve as a typical example:

From *Sing Care Away,* Book III, Novello & Co., Ltd., London

Example 14

This tendency for vowels to become heavier and thicker when one note value is suddenly lengthened, or when the tempo is slowed, is always present and must be carefully controlled in order to maintain the desired tonal texture.

51

In the double chorus, "Have light'ning and thunder from heaven all vanished" in Bach's St. Matthew Passion, the basses sing a florid passage of twelve measures on the word "thunder" — a very realistic stretch of picturesque tone painting designed to give a musical description of rolling thunder. To achieve this the singer should imagine that the vocal and musical energy culminates on the *n* of thunder, meanwhile keeping alive a vivid mental image of a thunderstorm. In contrast to this example, let us examine the ascending florid sequence on the word "rage" in the fifth chorus of Bach's motet, "Jesu, Priceless Treasure." This passage should be sung on a greatly modified *ay* so that it approaches the *eh* — as in wretch — without permitting the sound to become breathy from inserting *h*'s between the vowels (which can occur so easily).

The vowels *oo, oh,* and *ah* can be transformed into the so-called German umlaut vowels by mixing in the *eh* (as in men). These umlaut vowels can be produced both in the long and the short form — e.g. long: as in grün or milieu; short as in the German "können"; long as in "Goethe," short as in the French "seul"; long ä as in "they" or "Väter," short as in "steppes" or the German "können." It has already been pointed out what resonance potential there is in a mixture of *eh* with *oo, ah,* and *oh* (See Fig. 26).

The diphthongs (double vowels) are *ah--ee* (thy, side, smile), *ah--oo* (how, mountain, sound), *oh--ee* (boy, toil), *ee--oo* (dew). A difficulty with diphthongs arises from the fact that they are pronounced differently than they appear to sound. All diphthongs should be approached by a clear formation of the first vowel. While sustaining the vowel, the singer keeps his mind on the mixing (vanishing) vowel as well as on the sense and meaning of the word, but postpones the addition of the vanishing vowel as long as possible, e.g. the word "shy" might be phonetically represented as *sh-ah-ah-ee* when sung on a half or whole note. The relationship of the length (duration) of the first note to the second note would be similar for all other diphthongs except for *ee--oo* as in "few," which could be represented as *f--ee-oo-oo-oo*. Only too often one hears the vanishing *ee* leap out like a jet flame in a word like light. The remedy for this is to try to coincide the vanishing *ee* with the final consonant; at the precise moment when the *t* is spoken, the light, vanishing *ee* is quickly inserted between *l* and *t*. In the five-part setting of the semifinal chorale movement in Bach's "Jesu, Priceless Treasure" (Measures 32 — 36), the word "life" is sung melismatically by the five voices on the vowel *ah* (as in far) for four measures during which the singers keenly visualize the sense of the word, and only after the fourth beat in measure 36 has been completed and the word is to be completed with the final consonant, do the singers insert a light, quick, vanishing *ee*. (See Example 15, next page.)

life ___
lah · · · · eef

life ___
lah · · · · eef

life ___
lah · · · · eef

life ___
lah · · · · eef

Example 15

A vowel acquires its particular shade of color from the consonants which enclose it. The consonant before the vowel serves as a starter, and the consonant following the vowel as the target; between these two, the vowel sound is suspended. This principle applies above all to coloratura passages; the listener should be able to tell from the first consonant what the word is going to be. Again, the singer can help himself and the listener only if he vividly holds in his mind the meaning and image of the word during the duration of the coloratura passage. The sound of *ah* for example, if started from the same consonant in two different words ending in unlike consonants, will be modified in color by the time the word or syllable is completed. The different final consonants will brighten or darken, expand or compress, mix or tinge the vowel. Compare the vowel qualities in the following pairs of words:

back — bad	bath — ban	tack — sack	pal — shall
bat — bang	bath — ball	call — wall	

Note that in each case the second word seems to have a somewhat darker, elongated *ah*.

In Examples 15 and 16 the long *ah* sound is initially sung with the same bright, round *ah* quality, but in spite of similar melismatic treatment, the colors of the vowels differ from each other because of the influence of the consonants which follow.

53

Ah - - gnus

From "Agnus Dei" from the Mass-Guillame Machaut (c. 1300-c.1377)

Example 16

It is common to practice the clear enunciation of vowels, umlauts, and diphthongs on such *freely improvised word sequences* as e.g. "Can Anna handle bananas;" ee: "Siegfreid flees to the sea to beat the heat." This, however, can end up as a dull, frivolous drill. The alert and resourceful choir director will invent suitable examples in the course of his work. Above all, he should draw his examples from the particular musical work that is being rehearsed. For example, instead of working on a dark *oh* sound by dull repetition of a line like, "O glorious note of hope, no thought of sorrow or gloom," it might be far more effective to achieve the desired sound and the proper mood or feeling by speaking the first line of Paul Gerhardt's hymn, "O sacred Head now wounded." The dark sound is obtained entirely from the darker vowels in "now" and "wounded." The occasion for vowel practice should arise from the work which is being rehearsed so that there is both a need and a context for such specialized practice. In such exercises the higher notes should be darkened somewhat, while the lower notes could be brightened a little. The mouth should not go through all kinds of cramped contortions during changes in tessitura. The mouth remains quite far open in all vowel changes and the lips should remain slightly projected as in pouting.

The attack of a word beginning on a vowel can at times be particularly difficult. In speaking words beginning on the aspirate *h* (Howard has hurried home), the vocal cords are opened by the *h* and the vowels are easily carried forward on the little puff of breath. When the sound is to begin softly on words beginning with a vowel, the aspirate is only imagined but not really sounded. The mere thought of an *h* helps to open the vocal cords a little in advance, permitting the vowel to be produced gently and softly.

The strong attack without the real or imaginary aspirate keeps the vocal cords locked until the moment when the vowel begins to sound, at which time the accumulated breath pressure suddenly sets the vocal cords vibrating. This results in a short, crackling sound (glottis stroke) before each vowel. The attack with the aspirate vowel should be employed only with those words which begin on an *h*. The ideal onset for the singer is the pliant, resilient attack. This kind of attack is inherent in the Italian, French, and English language, while the German language makes more use of the harder glottis attack. In singing, this vocally harmful and musically distasteful attack must be avoided. When confronted with a passage containing consecutive words beginning on a vowel, it might prove useful to first sing these words with a prefixed *h* and then "wipe" it out, allowing only the image of the *h* to remain: "(h)And (h)evermore (h)amongst (h)our mirth" or "(h)As (h)I sat (h)on (h)a sunny bank." Meanwhile, care must be taken so that the final sound does not retain a trace of the aspirated word. In the higher part of the voice it may be better to use a light *n* as the pathfinder for the vowel. The hard (glottis stroke) attack is warranted only in special, dramatic situations.

In long, melismatic sequences as in baroque coloratura, one often hears the singers insert an *h* before each note, presumably to increase the clarity of the work. This choral "coughing" and chopping of the tonal line is not only musically grotesque, but contradicts the basic principles of all singing. Such florid passages can be satisfied artistically and vocally only through deliberate mastery of *martellato* (meaning hammer-like) singing. This is by no means one of the easiest techniques to be learned by singers, but can and certainly must be mastered by every progressive choir. Mastery of this technique is based on the tone-supporting impulses of the diaphragm which can be felt by placing the hand on the solar plexus as was described earlier. (Compare with A III, p. 42 ff.) The simplest way of learning to sing *martellato* is to sing a series of *ah* tones (laughing syllables with sharp, strict staccato attacks in a comfortable range of the voice with carefully controlled impulses from the diaphragm). The individual hammer taps, i.e. the accents on the separate notes, should be "taken from above the head," as it were; the singer imagines each hammer-stroke attack as taking place not in his throat but above the head. When transparent clarity of the individual notes has been achieved and when every trace of breathiness has been overcome, the singer should then sustain the final *ah* syllable with support from the diaphragm. This sound on the final *ah* should be the norm for singing all the notes in the florid sequences. All new accents are articulated with the diaphragm, and may occasionally be accompanied with an affirmative gesture of the head. With this procedure it is also possible to achieve a very satisfactory legato by permitting the tones between the "hammer-strokes" to glide easily and escalator-like. In the musical example below (No. 17), the marked (X) target notes of the florid melodic lines are sung with a martellato attack, but the notes between these target notes are sung with a plastic, fluent legato. To gain this kind of control between the changes from martellato to legato singing, the following procedures should be helpful: Begin by singing longer florid passages on short tone syllables e.g. *don, dan, den, bam, nan*. To sing the short syllables musically, one should make sure that the phrasing is understood and that the phrase divisions are clearly marked. As the exercise is repeated, some or all of the final consonants may be left off, and finally consonants can be dropped and the entire musical passage is sung as a pure *vocalize*.

From *German Magnificat* by Heinrich Schuetz, 1585-1672.

Example 17

56

This vocal technique could be similarly applied to such polyphonic works as the motets by Schuetz and J. S. Bach. Before attempting to apply these exercises to syllables, the director should carefully work through the score and make the necessary markings.

The singing consonants *m, n,* and *ng* have been termed semivowels because the vocal cords vibrate in the singing of these consonants, just as they do when the vowels are sung. They give the German language particularly some of its unique characteristics; Richard Wagner even made an attempt to develop a unique system of German speech technique based on these singing consonants. The singing consonants form a bridge from consonant to consonant; they are rollers on which the words move forward; they are the backbone and the links of singing and give it the necessary bouyancy and flow. The life and passion of language are contained in the vibrant energies and the sustained and propellant strength of the singing consonants. For this reason they should be thoughtfully developed and utilized. The German term *Klinger* (literally "sounders") which is to describe singing consonants like *m, n, ng,* has been appropriately coined; these consonants must actually be made to "sound." The director should unite the consonants with a series of vowels and sing these series until each syllable has attained the same degree of fullness of sound. After an overemphasis on sheer sound and sonority in more recent choral traditions, our modern choral technique now very deliberately emphasizes linear dynamics. The change of concept of choral tone has its basis in the choral music of the sixteenth and seventeenth centuries and in the neorenaissance and new baroque music of the present. It is natural therefore that the singing consonants assume a central place in the vocal techniques used to achieve the desired choral results. These consonants constantly require special and careful treatment.

When the vowel resonance becomes so rich that the music is drowned in its own waves of sound, the singing consonants help to clarify the musical design of the composition. Without an easy mastery of their sustaining and propelling energies, their vibrant sounds, their clear delineations, no choir will be able to do justice to contemporary requirements. See A III, p. 34 ff. on the use of these consonants in voice training.

Here is a description of the proper formation for all the consonants of the alphabet:

m — lips loose and relaxed, lightly touching each other, mouth slightly pouted, no pressure applied — humming should give a slight tickling sensation.

n — tongue touches the upper front teeth loosely, upper lips and sides of nostrils slightly raised, wide space inside the mouth.

ng — tip of the tongue placed behind and above the upper front teeth, the back (hump) of the tongue is raised and moved forward as much as possible, mouth open; the forward moving of the back of the tongue can be practiced on the *i* or *ee* vowel — e.g. singing, sang, sung.

m, n, and ng — have also been described as nasal vowels, since nasal resonance is necessary for their production. To make the singers aware of this, have them suddenly clamp off the nasal passages during the singing of any of these vowels and the sound will be abruptly cut off.

l — tongue is arched right behind the upper front teeth, tongue should not be wide and flabby, but slender and agile so that air can pass by on either side of it; think of the tongue as being transparent, like glass!

r — there are three types in use: the burred, American "r," the flipped or British "r," rolled or trilled "r."

The burred *r* is the *r* most frequently used in American speech. It is produced by turning the tip of the tongue in the direction of the gum ridge behind the upper teeth but without touching it. (Madeleine Marshall, *The Singers' Manual of English Diction*, G. Schirmer.) The flipped *r* is sounded while the tongue flips against the upper tongue ridge. It should never "flip" more than once even when singing a word spelled with a double *r*, like sorry, morrow.*

The rolled or trilled *r* is sounded by increasing the number of flips of the tongue against the hard palate. It is used in certain British dialects and in the German language, but even where it is native to the dialect or language, the roll should never be executed too long. Many people have difficulty in executing it. The rapid repetition of *dddd* or the constant repetition of a word like "trigger," in which the *r* is substituted by several *d's* can be of help in learning to roll the *r*. Repeat until the tip of the tongue actually begins to vibrate and pulsate automatically and then try the rolled *r* sound. This technique can be used on other words like "Grab" (Gddab) whenever the *r* doesn't come through on the first try.

Similar exercises may be applied if anyone has difficulty flipping the *r* as in the English pronunciation of words like merry, sorry, very. Repeat meddy soddy, veddy several times as rapidly as possible and then try to "flip" the *r*.*
(Madeleine Marshall, op. cit.)

v — sounded by forming a small slip with the lips, the upper front teeth lightly touching lower lip, upper lip is slightly raised, and then vocalized.

---

*Based on Singer's Manual of English Diction. © 1953 by G. Schirmer, Inc. Reprinted by permission.

f, ph — the upper teeth are now set more firmly against the lower lip, all voiced sound from the vocal cords is cut out and breath is directed through the small slip with some degree of intensity. In the English and German languages there is no acoustical difference between *f* and *ph*.

s — teeth very close together, but not touching, lips slightly protruded, tongue relaxed with tip almost touching the gum of the upper front teeth, the breath should be emitted sharply in a narrow stream.

z — formed as above, but voiced.

y — as in yes; begin with an *ee* formation and hump the tongue so as to permit only a little space to the front part of the mouth; this brief obstruction gives the consonant its characteristic sound; it should be approached softly and emphasis should be given on the vowel which succeeds the y — y es.

ch — as in church: the sides of the tongue are placed firmly against the upper side teeth, the tip of the tongue touches the center of the upper gum. A vigorous puff of breath is quickly blown through this tongue and mouth formation.

sh — as in she: the tip of the tongue strives backward but upward into the mouth, upper front teeth close over without touching the bottom lower teeth, and lips are slightly turned inside out; blow a strong stream of breath. The vocalization of this sound produces the sound spelled by *s* in the word "measure," or by *z* in the word "azure" or by second *g* in the word "garage."*

h — this is produced against the soft palate by momentarily intensifying an exhalation to the point where it is audible; it is used most often as an initial consonant.

F, v, s, z, and sh are also classified as the fricative consonants because of the noise and friction caused by the movement of the air past the tongue, teeth, and lips. The consonant *h* is also called the aspirate or breath vowel.

Further, we have those consonants which, when vocalized, cannot be sustained and which do not have a determinate pitch. Let us first consider the so-called plosives:

p, b — the closure of the lips is exploded through a sharp buildup of air pressure; *b* is achieved by an accompanying vibration of the vocal cords.

t — the tip of the tongue is placed (not flattened) against the gums well above the teeth. As the tongue is quickly withdrawn from the position, a puff of air is blown.

---

*Based on Singer's Manual of English Diction. © 1953 by G. Schirmer, Inc. Reprinted by permission.

d — is formed by adding voice to this action. The frequent practice of adding an *h* after a *t* tends to make the sound breathy and can easily result in a distortion of the meaning of the text: e.g. sweet (h)and low sounds like sweet hand low, or a bright (h)airy room sounds like — a bright hairy room.

k, c — a puff of pressured breath explodes the high-vaulted position of the back of the tongue against the soft palate; the tip of the tongue remains close to or touching the lower front teeth; in singing through a *k*, or *g*, the position of the tongue should be moved forward as much as possible.

g — produced by vocalizing the *k* sound.

The two final consonants are unclassified: x — a combination of *k* and *s*, a consonantal diphthong; q — its sound is composed of *kwi* without voicing the *i* vowel.

It remains the task of speech training to attempt to make the nonsinging consonants (the consonants not having pitch) to sound as though they were singing consonants (having pitch). This is relatively easy to achieve in the case of such voiced consonants as *b*, *d*, and *g*. They must not be articulated too vigorously but spoken with a soft, relaxed attack accompanied by conscious vibrations of the vocal cords. The *b* may be associated with a light *m*, the *d* and *g* with a light *n*. In all other cases, the consonants should be closely tied to the preceding or succeeding vowels, even to the point where consonants and vowels seem to melt into each other, so that they (and this applies to all consonants because of their constant fricative, propelling, and directive energies) become the media for the enhancement and intensification of vocal sound. The consonants must actually "sound" along with the vowels. The two terms *singing consonants* and *nonsinging consonants* should not be regarded as opposite in terms of their influence on choral sound. With respect to their treatment in singing, the two types of consonants might best be characterized as singing consonants and sympathetic singing consonants.

If the consonants and vowels are compared respectively as framework and body, backbone and flesh, then one can observe the further relationship of consonants and vowels to rhythm and harmony. The vowels carry the harmonic element and the consonants help to uphold the rhythmic element. Neglect of consonants would weaken the rhythmic element. The singing tradition of the different epochs has treated the relationship of consonants and vowels in a variety of ways. The singing of one era has not always meant the same to people of another. In the Middle Ages, the nonvowel sounds were the means of realizing the ideal of a floating, linear, and rhythmically perfect sound. The Italian *bel canto*, on the other hand, achieves its rich and highly developed sonorous tone through the vowel sounds. The treatment of language has always been influenced by the character and style of the music. Since contemporary music is influenced by strong, new rhythmic impulses, the choral art of the present can meet the demands of this new development by recognizing the importance of consonants in the expression of the rhythmic idioms in contemporary choral writing.

Today, popular singers on radio, film, and television utilize singing consonants to produce, for sheer show, a colorful display of sound. The observant director could draw some important conclusions on the treatment of singing consonants in his own choral work.

With many singers the tongue bends to obstruct good diction; as a clumsy lobe of flesh, it causes a kind of blockade in the mouth. To acquire more deftness and facility, it is helpful to innovate special exercises which prevent the tongue from blocking the speech passage and which aid the tongue in carrying out its functions and in helping to form the various speech sounds. Whistling is helpful in obtaining the flat, relaxed position of the tongue, with tip touching lower teeth. The basic position is to be constantly guarded. The tip of the tongue never leaves contact with the front teeth and the surface of the hard gums of the lower and upper front teeth even when the back of the tongue assumes a somewhat humped position as in g and k. Some singing teachers have their students practice singing exercises with a piece of cork between their lips, during which time the tip of the tongue is in constant contact with the cork. To free the tongue from the roof of the mouth, it may be useful occasionally to let the singers hang their tongues out of their mouths in imitation of a panting dog and then perform a series of exercises, particularly those with *m, n, ng, f, v, g,* and *sh.* To stimulate all-around tongue sensations and to develop greater elasticity, move the tip of the tongue around the inner rim of the lips, over the rows of teeth and over the hard and soft palate. The tongue should feel slender and flexible during singing so that the tone can travel past on either side and above to the mouth opening. As a further exercise sustain the vowel *ah* for some length of time while describing various circular motions with the tip of the tongue. Finally, include some exercises with the flipped and rolled *r* and with *l: rov, roh, rah, blo, bla.* To stimulate agility and nimbleness have the singers trill (like in some western yodels) on one pitch while varying the rhythmic patterns. It hardly needs to be mentioned that there is great value in the singing of madrigals and folk songs which employ the "tra-la-la" or "fa-la-la" syllables in their refrains. Conversely it would be well to combine the practice of some of the earlier mentioned tongue exercises with the study of this type of song.

When singing in a choir, each member should exaggerate the clear enunciation of vowels and consonants. The size of the choir and the size of the room will weaken the exaggeration to the point where both the enunciation and the diction will seem quite normal to the listener. One should heed against too-sharp articulation which makes our speech instruments into cutting instruments (scissors) which snip up the words and so interrupt the steady tonal stream. The enunciation of the final consonants, *p, t,* and *k,* should, in particular, be watched.

To achieve an *uninterrupted musical and verbal line* in speech and in singing, syllables and words must glide into each other. In this activity of meshing and coupling words, the last consonants of the final syllable of a word is joined to the first consonant of the word that follows. This results in a sort of speech escalator or a moving conveyor belt. The unfurling of this speech belt would appear as illustrated in the following lines: "The morningstar beamsbrightly." "Inspring a youngman'sfancy lightly turnsto thoughts oflove." One should concentrate on soft, smooth, and unbroken transitions, except where punctuation marks or other pauses are necessary for bringing out the sense of the word. Cold and lifeless individual words are melted, so to speak, by the warm, sustained breath into a flowing stream of living speech.

If a word begins with a vowel, then the final consonant of the preceding word should not be drawn over next to it; this would only result in objectionable gliding of sounds and distortions of textual meaning. "Now let us in" could easily sound like "Now let us sin!" "Our house is old" could be understood as "Our house is sold!"

In everyday conversation, words beginning with vowels are separated from the preceding word by a light glottis attack. In singing, an imaginary *h* is inserted, and this results in a renewed, smooth attack. This also resolves the problem of achieving a proper balance between tying and separating individual words. "(h)In the beginning God created heaven (h)and (h)earth." The same procedure is followed when two vowels are adjacent to each other: "Of the day (h)and (h)of the night." "With all the (h)angel choir." If a word ends with the same consonant with which the next one begins, then the first consonant is cancelled (omitted) at the point where the preparation for speaking the consonant is complete; the singer refrains from exploding or voicing it: e.g. fond dreams would be sung, fon-dreams; the dog growls: the do-growls.

For solo singers and choral singers, the habit of listening to one's singing is highly recommended for checking and correcting one's own singing. However, since the singer's own body is also his instrument, the hearing of one's own singing as it is heard by someone else is possible only to a degree. The singer stands in the way of his own listening, and so he must imagine that he can step away from himself and listen critically. The old Italian masters used to place their singers before a cave or some other empty space to check their own singing by listening to the returning echo of their voice. Today with such easy access to tape recorders, the singing of an individual or a group can be recorded and played several times permitting critical comments and suggestions from the singing teacher or director. The author has experienced most valuable results with this method. Every singer and speaker is most surprised when he is confronted with the sound of his own voice; he doesn't recognize himself and thinks that he is listening to another person. The choir may be divided into groups which alternately sing and listen to each other and submit their own critical evaluations, which are then further supplemented by the director.

The problem of the relationship of language to music of the different periods and composers has been variously and diversely treated in the history and development of western music. H. Hoffman has drawn attention to the fact that this has various implications for our present choral practices. Performances based on sound, historical and stylistic studies were first given by the collegium musicum societies of the European universities. The resultant performance practices which have been transmitted to the populace at large are now being claimed as common cultural possessions of European choral life. The late Gothic Period which also encompasses the large multivoiced compositions of such German composers as A. Agricola, H. Finck, A. Fulda, exploit the use of the text as an ideological vehicle of the pure, freely flowing, musically inspired play of contrapuntal lines, which revolve around the augmented and abstract cantus firmus. The Reformation composers like J. Walther, B. Resinarius, C. Othmayr, and others also employ the methods of these composers. Hugo Distler maintains a similar relationship of word and music.

The florid and linear flow of the music which often runs contrary to the organic sense of the word should not be interfered with by attempting to give correct pronunciation to and clear enunciation of individual words. It is here where the singing consonants, because of their fricative and energizing qualities, can be fully utilized to promote the musical dynamics and rhythmic qualities of the work; the text of the cantus firmus is usually irrelevant and abstract in its relation to the music.

In the great works of the Renaissance composers, represented by the Flemish composers Josquin de Pres, Gombert, Willaert, the German composers Isaac, Lassus, L. Senfl, and others, the new importance of giving musical characterization to the inherent meaning and quality of the words, resulted in a more purposeful form and direction to the cursory and change-able contrapuntal web of earlier composers, and brought about a much closer relationship and balance between text and tune. Among contemporary composers of choral music, Ernst Pepping, in his approach to the relationship of words and music, could be regarded as standing somewhere in-between the possibilities described above. The music should be permitted to evolve from the text as a word-generated motivic process and supported by an enunciation which is freely flexible in accordance with the natural plastic qualities of the music. With the choral works of Heinrich Schuetz, the early baroque takes the text as a living organic entity and as a vehicle of emotional expression, right into the center of the work. The chief function of the music is to be music. In the late baroque music of J. S. Bach, G. F. Handel, Telemann, and others, word-inspired musical motives tend to be reduced to symbolic musical figures. Although these symbolic motives originate from the effect of the word, the music is in no way bound to the word but is completely self-contained; syllables only serve to give new impetus at the points where a new phrase or part of a phrase begins. Among contemporary composers, H. Kaminski and G. Raphael seem to use this approach as a starting point. One should strive to keep an equality of emphasis between speech and musical effect and utilize the speech syllables for a thorough working out of the musical properties of the composition. During the age of *Emfindsamkeit* (perceptivity) represented by composers like C. P. E. Bach and his successors, and the age of the musical folk-idiom, the intimate simplicity of the music was completely subordinated to the hallowed poetry, whose inner and outer rules of form were faithfully represented in syllabic musical treatment. In the Viennese Classical Period, W. A. Mozart reveals the type of his operatic characters through his musical treatment of language. From this inner, personal center the music sparks and flows with freedom and ease. In our own century, Paul Hindemith represents a similar approach to musical composition. And so, out of these changing basic relationships of music and language, there emerge for the choir director of discretion and insight, the essential and fundamental stimuli and incentives for creative work in the realm of choral music. Study the problems of relationship of music to text in connection with the rehearsal of a choral composition in B IV.

Chapter V

Choral Ear Training

The aspects of ear training, gesture and movement, and rhythmic training which will be discussed in the following chapters assume an important place in the total music education program. In this handbook on choral directing the possibilities of these three areas of training are deliberately treated from the standpoint of choral singing. The treatment given here will in no way treat rhythmic training as in independent artistic endeavor, nor attempt to develop a separate system of gesture and movement. The basic groundwork for rhythmic training (eurythmics) has been laid by Dolcroze, Orff, and their followers. G. Goetsch, in his school of music in Frankfurt has conducted some significant experiments on the subject of music and eurythmics. In spite of the results of all the research made in connection with the areas mentioned above, very little has been specifically utilized in the furtherance of choral singing. Within the framework of this book we may, however, set up the following goals in the areas of ear training, gesture and movement, and rhythmic training:

(1) to help the *individual singer* in the choir to relax and to stimulate and develop him musically;

(2) to blend the *members of the choir into* a well-tuned, thoroughly trained *musical unit*;

(3) to strengthen and support *the individual processes* through listening, gesture, movement and rhythm;

(4) to *provide practical guides* and approaches for grasping the musical structure of the works to be sung and to realize this structure in performance;

(5) to help the choir to discover and interpret the *character* and *essence* of the music which is being sung;

(6) to enable a choral society to find *fulfillment in music as a way of life*, quite apart from the virtuosic choral techniques of the director who happens to be responsible for its direction at the time.

When the breath-energized body through the activation of the voice begins to "sound," the ear is immediately confronted with its most important task. Through his own ear the singer exercises the necessary self-control over the attack, the color, and the purity of the tone. At the same time he must continually listen to the total sound of the choir. He must have the total choral sound in his ear. Not only must he hear how the singer in front, behind, or beside him sings, but he must also hear the sounds coming from the extreme ends of the choir. He must blend his voice into the *total sound of the choir* and learn to discern where and when he must add or diminish his own sounds; he must sense when he can permit his sound to be "carried along" or when he must sing out to help maintain the proper balance of sound. He should also listen for and assess the acoustical characteristics of the room. The ear is just as important to the singer as his voice. Some voice teachers do not permit their students to sing in a choir, for then their singing cannot be observed and controlled by the listening ear of the teacher. It is of great importance then for the singer to be able to listen to himself critically. No tone should be sung which is not immediately monitored by the ear. The choir singer, even more than the solo singer, must at all times be "all ears." Music is a listener's art. Every motion of the body and excitement of the imagination in reaction to music is determined and qualified by how and what one hears! This points up the importance to the singer of intensive, thorough ear training.

The significance of listening in daily life is expressed in the German language which has developed a long line of derivatives from the word *hören* (to listen); in these words it is the relationships between people and the nature of this relationship which is expressed in particular:

> *gehören* — to belong to, to be part of
> *umhören* — to listen around
> *zuhören* — to listen to
> *ungehörig* — unheard of, unseemly
> *Angehörige* — relatives, belonging to
> *Hörerschaft* — the listening audience
> *gehorchen* — to hear and obey
> *Verhör* — a hearing or a trial
> *erhören* — favorable answer to a request or prayer
> *ungehört* — unanswered

These derivatives reflect the integral and central role of listening in human relationships. Listening reaches deep into the very core and fabric of life. For example, the sense of hearing is of much greater importance for a human being than the sense of sight. Observations show that blind persons remain much more aware of the world about them and adjust themselves better to life than deaf persons. Our world outlook is influenced at least as much by what we hear as by what we see, and so one could speak not only of a world view but also of a "world hearing." Ear training should develop the ear for both the melodic and harmonic aspects of choral singing. Melodic listening should certainly receive precedence here, but we must not relinquish the rendering of clean, in-tune chord progressions in choral singing.

The singing of a tone which has been played or sung to the singers calls into play the easiest and simplest type of mimicking ability. Right at the outset the singer should be reminded to keep a clear head so he won't get lost in the swirling waves of choral sound. He must learn to listen with a certain sense of detachment. With a cool sense of direction the singer steers his musical barque through the labyrinths of choral sonorities. He first visualizes, i.e. "auralizes" the tone before he sings it; indeed he should sense the note so strongly with his inner ear that he can almost feel the tone, so to speak; this should insure an accurate and clear tonal attack. The director gives the pitch, which is then repeated by the choir. One should proceed from a pitch in a comfortable part of the vocal range. Next, chord members or any pitches within the scale are given, and finally the choir is asked to repeat tones which have no tonal relationship to each other. The author has repeatedly observed that some choirs as well as soloists respond less readily to a sung pitch than to a played pitch from an instrument. This may be attributed largely to a long-standing habit of slavishly leaning on a mechanical instrument, particularly the piano, for tonal support. Experimental psychology has drawn the conclusion that different types of singers respond quite differently to various tonal sources; the singers who find it easier to get their pitch and tonal support from a mechanical instrument are best represented. The choir director should therefore stress the importance of responding without hesitation to a sung tone. This ability is necessary even for a clean, in-tune attack on the first chord of a song.

When a group of people, irrespective of its average age, is called upon to repeat a tone which has been played or sung to them, they usually respond with a spontaneous *la*. The syllable *la*, however, particularly with beginners, is not without its dangers. First of all, the *l* is somewhat thick and gummy; and of all the vowels, *ah* still remains the most difficult one to sing properly because of its tendency to slide backward into the throat. It occupies more pharyngeal spaces than any other vowel and also possesses the greatest potential in terms of volume and fullness. When properly produced the *ah* sound "floods" the ear, making keen self-control over the tones even more difficult.

The director hums the notes to the choir and the choir hums them after him, preferably on *ng*. Next he should use syllables like *noo, moh,* which require small mouth openings, and then proceed to sing all other vowels: *zee, vay, moo*, ending with *nah* and *lah*. It is imperative of course that singers listen very keenly to their production of these syllables. If instrumentalists are present the pitches may be played by different instruments — i.e. pitches will be blown, bowed, and struck, and in each case hummed accordingly in various ways by the singers. The timbre of the instrumental tone can have an irritating influence on the singers' sense of pitch. A sufficient interval of time should be allowed between the giving of the pitch by the director and the response by the choir so as to give the individual singer enough time to obtain a clear aural image of the pitch to be sung. This interval may be gradually shortened to a minimum. Finally the note should be sustained on one pitch as long as possible to train the singer to maintain a clear aural image of the pitch over a longer period of time. This approach also applies to the exercises which are described in the following pages.

The singing of ascending and descending scale passages is beneficial to all singers including those who are not good note readers. The singer notes whether the music moves upward or downward and promptly sings the chain of ascending and descending tones. Visual sense comes to the assistance of the aural sense; the singer "sees" the tonal process. It follows then that the eye must be trained concurrently with the ear. Various aids can serve to illustrate this process: the person who has mastered the tonic sol-fa method has the advantage of not only visualizing the stepwise movement and direction of the notes, but he can also clearly indicate the inner pull and direction of each individual tone within the scale relationships by the use of various expressive gestures of the hand. A very simple system of hand gestures consists of extending the fingers forward and outward as much as possible, and then having the choir sing to the fingers! The hand is held in a perpendicular position, with its back turned to the choir. The small finger, being the lowest finger, represents *doh*. The position of the semitone can be identified by holding the respective fingers together; for example, the half-step between the third and fourth interval would be represented by placing the middle finger and index finger together. These reading sessions should commence with descending musical exercises; ascending exercises sometimes have an averse psychological effect upon singers by causing them to tense up vocally. The director points out the different "finger steps" and then completes the exercises by singing the pitches between the tonic and dominant.

The use of a small ladder can be of further help in teaching intervals. If such a ladder is not available, sketch one on the blackboard and sing the steps of the scales according to the rungs of the ladder which the director points out. The semitones can be designated by bringing two rungs closer together. The inner pull and tension of the different pitches in the scale could be represented by different colors of the rungs. This scale singing corresponds with the stepwise tonal structure of much of the music of the Ars Nova and the Renaissance. Singing from the ladder is not without its hazards since singers tend to tense their throats and tighten their larynxes when singing intervals for practice purposes. The exercises should not begin too high, and care should be taken to keep a proper balance between the descending and ascending vocal exercises. From the very beginning the choir director works deliberately and carefully to prevent these hazards. The exclusive practice of major and minor scales can also lead to undesirable consequences. One can achieve a balance by putting particular emphasis on the intervals between the tonic and dominant. The position of the half-tone can be systematically changed, thus creating the basic tonal relationships of the modal or so-called "church scales."

The singing by numbers which represent the various degrees of the scale may also be helpful. When first introduced they may be written on the steps of a ladder until the intervals can be sung to the numbers alone. The use of numbers is an easy way of learning to associate the correct numerical names for the various intervals — e.g. interval of a third, fifth, etc. Finally, to visualize the tonal relationships and the different sizes of the intervals, it may be helpful in certain situations, particularly with children, to have five or eight of them stand in line according to their height, each singer representing a different degree of the scale. Have these people form a scale by singing their respective pitches in the proper sequence, and so become a "singing ladder." Following this the choir director may ask for intervals in any order, or make up a tune in this manner. To alert the choir to new tonal relationships, transpose the musical ladder to a new key and continue to practice in the manner described. Eventually the singers should try to sing without the visual aid of ladders and numerals and learn to sing pitches represented by the higher or lower positions of the director's hands.

The singing of the various intervals improves the vocal execution of larger intervals, accuracy of pitch, and develops a stronger "intervallic consciousness." Even the person without a knowledge of notation can attempt to "hit" the different intervals as he begins to recognize them in the musical score. To master the intervals one may proceed from the ladder as before and sing each interval of the scale from the tone: 1-2, 1-3, 1-4, 1-5, 1-6, 1-7, 1-8, and then descend in a similar manner. The procedure should then be repeated without the ladder until the intervals are mastered. This exercise should be advanced, of course, by calling any intervals at random until the singers can sing them correctly and without hesitation.

The singing of the first two notes of a well-known song has proved to be of value in learning intervals. The members of the choir or singing class may look for examples of appropriate songs from folk song or hymnic repertoire. Then have them identify and sing the opening intervals. Here are the first lines of familiar hymns which may be useful for diatonic and intervallic training. The hymn numbers are taken from the *Service Book and Hymnal*. Folk song numbers are taken from *The Fireside Book of Favorite American Songs* (Simon and Schuster, New York) unless otherwise indicated. The folk songs are listed first in each case.

> "Chester," p. 242
> "Open Now Thy Gates of Beauty," No. 187

Major thirds:
> "The Crawdad," p. 106
> "Holy, Holy, Holy," No. 131

Minor thirds:
> "After the Ball," p. 35
> "What Child Is This" (Greensleeves), No. 47

Perfect fourths:
> "Pop! Goes the Weasel," p. 302
> "Hark, the Herald Angels Sing," No. 25

Perfect fifths:
> "Hush-You Bye," No. 37, *American Folk Songs,* Penguin Books, Baltimore, Maryland
> "How Brightly Beams the Morning Star," No. 404

Major sixths:
> The familiar ditty, "My Bonnie Lies Over the Ocean"
> "It Came Upon the Midnight Clear," No. 23

Descending intervals can be practiced by singing the ascending intervals (as in the examples above) in reverse. These may be practiced on syllables like *noo, nah*. The bass singers in particular must learn to sing descending intervals with confidence and accuracy, since these jumps occur so frequently in bass lines which support the harmonic structure. Songs like the following which begin with descending diatonic sequences and intervals constitute good musical exercises.

Descending scales:
> "Enraptured I Gaze," p. 244
> "Joy to the World," No. 15

Major third:
> "My Old Kentucky Home," p. 134
> "The Duteous Day Now Closeth," No. 228

Minor third:
> "When You and I Were Young, Maggie," p. 183
> "O God, Our Help in Ages Past," No. 168

Perfect fourth:
> "Mother Was a Lady," p. 26
> "All Things Bright and Beautiful" (Greystone)

Perfect fifths:
> "The Jam on Gerry's Rocks," p. 222
> "Out of the Depths I Cry to Thee," No. 372

Other examples too numerous to mention could be found. The half-step (semitone) should not be overlooked. Two of the many examples of the rising and falling semitone which could be found are: "Darling, I Am Growing Old" (p. 231, *Fireside Book of American Songs*), and "Spirit of God, Descend Upon My Heart" (No. 129, Morecambe) — for the rising semitone; and "March of the Men of Harlech" (p. 188, *Fireside Book of American Songs*) and "Holy God, We Praise Thy Name" (No. 167) — for the descending semitone. For a combination of rising semitones and return to tonic, there is the unique example in the main subject of the second Kyrie section in Bach's *B Minor Mass*. To sing the succession of three notes f♯, g, e♯ with complete accuracy is a challenge even to the experienced singer.

Singing a tune *by rote* trains the ear to grasp the melodic contour and the sequence of notes and helps to strengthen the musical memory. Such melodic dictation exercises are part of every music school entrance test. Choose an unfamiliar song or canon for this purpose or have the singers invent their own exercises. The exercise can be extended from four to eight and even to sixteen measures in length. It is important that the tune be first sung or played in its entirety before the singer or student attempts to reproduce it. The singer should develop his ear to hear the continuity of the entire tune, its inner divisions, the climax, and its shape and structure. The assignment should be made a little too difficult rather than too simple because notes which are missed on the first try can always be picked up after the second or third dictation; or the entire tune can be dictated and sung back by the students in sections if necessary. Here again the pedagogical principle of going from the whole to its parts is to be observed, not vice versa. The assignment can be made more difficult and challenging by including difficult rhythms and difficult intervals, and by using modal tunes.

In canon singing where harmonic relationships are formed by the canonic treatment of the tune, the ear is trained both melodically and harmonically. In the process of the melodic flow the singer listens harmonically and melodically. Furthermore, the singing of canons helps the choir member to become more self-reliant as a singer. He begins to discover the sensitive balance between strong, absolute self-reliance, and relaxed submission to the music in which the ear acts as the regulator. For the use of canons as ear training exercises, see A VII, p. 103 ff.; B III, and B V.

For ear training purposes, one should choose canons which have strong melodic interest. These will force the singer to think and listen melodically in the presence of strong dissonances as the different voice parts clash with each other at various points. From here one could proceed to two-part canons such as Carl Schalk's settings based on hymn and chorale tunes (Concordia 98-1762-4) or the two-voice canonic settings in *Nine Easy Canons* (Augsburg, 1333). Next one could select canons with strong harmonic interest in which each note of a voice agrees harmonically with the other notes above or below it. In these canons, which are mostly three-part canons, the first two voices usually move in parallel thirds, while the third voice forms a parallel fifth; these are intermittently interrupted by slight harmonic departures in different parts of the melody. The total sound consists of a series of triads or extended triads as in the following three-part canons: "Hail Thou Source," *Nine Easy Canons* (Augsburg, 1333); "O Lord of My Salvation," *Four Easy Canons* (Augsburg 1332); and "Hear the Echo," by Cherubini, *The Youth Hymnary* (Faith and Life Press, Newton, Kansas, 1956). In singing these canons the singers must always strive for the purest intonation possible. As an aid to listening, the words can occasionally be substituted by suitable tone syllables. The tempo should not be taken so fast that the singer does not have an opportunity to accurately hear and regulate the sound. In addition, the singer must be able to hear and evaluate the sound of the entire canonical network. Finally, one can practice singing larger canonical forms such as "Sing Ye to the Lord" (Praetorius), "Light From Above" (No. 295, *The Youth Hymnary*), and sections from the canonical mass by Palestrina. Chromatically constructed canons such as Joseph Haydn's *Ein einzig boeses Weib* (A singularly wicked woman!) could be particularly conducive to ear training.

To encourage the singers to rely solely on their ears when singing canons with tricky entrances, displaced accents, and harsh dissonances have them turn their backs to each other; this will prevent assistance from the director and eye contact among the choir members. To further stimulate self-reliance in this matter the first entry is to be given without assistance; only the time and place of concluding the canon is agreed upon beforehand. Not only does such an exercise stimulate and waken the ear, but it also greatly stimulates the singers' sensitivity for anticipating the course and progress of the music (and the sensitivity to the human element in the choir). So the singing of canons can, from a functional point of view, contribute considerably to creating a genuine musical fellowship within the choir. In a lively musical group the development of the ear and the ability to "pick up" music quickly, can be furthered to the point where canon singing, in the best classical sense, can become a skillful, creative social activity. The leader sings a part of the canon, and the choir immediately sings it after him in canon. A lively group of singers will not sing canons in a mechanical fashion but relate it to the structure and character of the rehearsal and to the musical life of the choir itself. For example, at the outset of the rehearsal one might sing a canon which expresses invitation or welcome, or one may close the rehearsal with the singing of a round song about evening or farewell. When someone has a birthday, a canon of congratulation (which is popular in the German language) is sung. (See also the discussion on canon singing in B III and B V.)

The building of chords contributes to better tuning and blending of voices. The singer in the choir must learn to fit his note of the chord into the total sound of the rest of the chord. One may then proceed to chords in which the given note is the root of the chord. The giving and the repeating of the pitches by the choir takes place as described earlier (See A V, p. 67 ff.). If the director sounds a "c" the choir sings in succession, *c,e,g,* or *c,e,g,c.* After the pitches have been repeated several times in this fashion, each section of the choir is given a note of the chord to remember which, after a by the other sections. Another procedure in this simple exercise would be to brief moment, they will be required to sing in harmony with the notes held let the singers choose and sing any chord member after the root of the chord has been given. The singer must be given sufficient time to form an aural image of the pitch he is about to sing; humming the pitch beforehand should not be permitted. The pitches should be reproduced only after the director gives a cue. Gradually the time interval between the assignment of the exercise and its execution should be shortened. Singers who have a knowledge of notation theory could sing the notes sung by the proper pitch name to strengthen the association of pitch sound with the pitch name.

The formation of chords in which the given pitch is the highest note in the chord presents a difficulty for most singers. For example, the pitch "a" is sounded and the singers try to find *f♯* and *d* to complete the triad. The pitch "a" may then be given as the middle member of a chord, and the choir is asked to find *c* and *f.* In these and other exercises the procedure described earlier — assignment, pause for fixing the tone aurally, singing of the tone — should be followed.

The finding of chord tones for a given key from a pitch which does not belong to that chord is a procedure which every director who uses a tuning fork must learn to master. This practice, however, is also extremely beneficial as an ear-training exercise for the choir. There are very few choirs which can promptly find the pitches of the initial chord when the director has sounded the "a" on his tuning fork. When proceeding from pitches which are not chord members it is helpful to build reliable bridges to the notes of the chord to be sung. Let us suppose that the choir is to sing the triad *g-b-d or g-bb-d* after "a" has been sounded. If the singers cannot easily and readily find the root "g" they may find it is fairly easy to move up to the *b* or *bb* and then proceed to find the other two notes of the chord. If a triad is to be built on *eb from* the "a" pitch, the singers proceed a half step upward to *bb* and then to the *g* and *eb*. These pitch-hunting exercises can be performed in a spirit of fun and entertainment by choirs and ear-training classes. The choir director should capitalize on the natural human delight of discovering that which has been sought after.

Choral improvisation is also extremely beneficial to aural training because it compels the singer to invent, with the use of his ear, a suitable countermelody against a given melody. The various types of choral improvisation can be briefly summarized as follows:

(1) *an open fifth (on the tonic) is sustained against a familiar tune.* Numerous shepherd tunes have been invented over an open "bagpipe" fifth. One could sing the familiar Bohemian Christmas carol, "Come, all ye shepherds, ye children of earth" in such a way that the majority of the singers would sustain the fifth *d - a* on the word "come" while the other singers carry the tune (which begins on "a").

(2) *an accompanying voice follows a given voice at a distance of a third* (in parallel thirds). This is possible only with diatonic tunes which do not modulate. Treble and male voices may each take a part, or the parts can be sung by two mixed groups of treble and male voices.

(3) *a familiar tune is treated as a cantus firmus to which free contrapuntal voice parts are invented.* At first one may use the same tunes in the two exercises described above, but then one should choose stricter song forms such as Luther's "From heav'n above to earth I come." Each section of the choir, in turn, sings the cantus firmus while the rest improvise counterparts. The tune could also be played by an instrument (string or wind) while all the singers sing contrapuntal parts. Numerous intervening stages between the simplest form of improvisation and the more complex contrapuntal improvisation could be devised. In any case, the ear must always function as the regulator or monitor of the musical proceedings.

Loss of intonation through flatting can be attributed to the ear, and to an extent this weakness can be overcome. Of decisive importance is the choir director's ability to recognize immediately the cause in a case of flatting and to provide a solution to overcome it. (The general and technical vocal reasons

74

for loss of intonation have been dealt with in Chapter III.) Sultry weather contributes to flatting because it affects people both physically and psycologically. In such a situation the director should be very careful in dealing with the problem by choosing the right tonal devices and by including a few ear-training exercises. Frequently the flatting of a choir occurs at the beginning of a rehearsal. In such a case it is better not to concentrate on correcting a particular fault, but rather to follow through decisively with a systematic rehearsal plan. After half an hour or so, when the vocal apparatus is warmed up, pure intonation and tone production will have been restored by itself. In structuring a rehearsal one must bear these problems in mind and not expect a choir to perform vocal feats which are possible only after a period of carefully planned vocal exercises. (See B V.) Loss of intonation can also be attributed to problems which have their source in the music itself. Flatting when singing in an unfavorable tessitura with frequent melodic turns in the area of the register change (*defg*, frequently referred to as the lift or break of the voice in North America), can be overcome by advanced voice training. If an unfavorable key is the cause for loss of pitch (as for example Bb), then the upward transposition of the music by a half step often solves the problem. The gradual flatting on a series of repeated notes can be overcome by thinking of walking up an inclined sidewalk. One can also think of slowly and inwardly lifting the body from the heels. The solo song "The Tone" by P. Cornelius, in which the voice part consists of a single repeated note, is certainly not easy to sing. Another example of this type is Schubert's *Der Tod und das Maedchen* (Death and the Maiden). Maintaining pure intonation is particularly problematic when note repetitions are followed by a series of falling melodic arches or descending sequences as in the following example:

A. Gumpelzhaimer

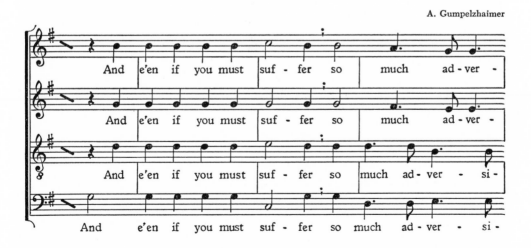

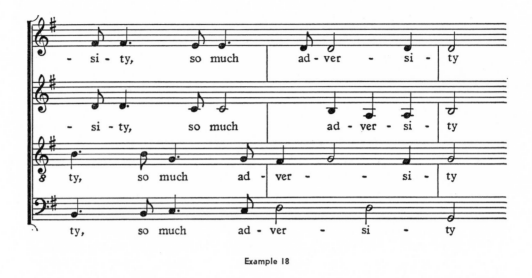

si - ty, so much   ad - ver - si - ty

si - ty, so much   ad - ver - si - ty

ty,   so much   ad - ver -   -   si - ty

ty,   so much   ad - ver -   si   -   ty

Example 18

Major thirds are easily sung too low. Particularly when the major third functions as a leading tone in an upward direction it must be sung high enough. A good "listening" choir does not sing with the tempered tuning of a mechanical keyboard instrument; between the *e* as the tonic of E major and the *e* as the leading note in the key of F and the *e* as the third of the key of C, there is a distinct difference which can be recognized by the ear. Here one must pay particular attention to proper enharmonic adjustments. Minor thirds are commonly sung too large, particularly in descending passages. Ascending major seconds tend to be sung too small. Descending scale passages tend to drop in pitch. Compositions based on the tune *Vom Himmel hoch* require particular care for maintaining good intonation. Special care is also required for the frequent leaps of a fourth or fifth in the bass.

Ascending intervals are often sung too high, while the descending intervals are sung too low. Most dangerous are those passages in which several or even all voice parts move downward in smaller or larger steps; this hazard is clearly illustrated at the end of the introduction of Hassler's popular *Lasst Instrument und Lauten auch erklingen* (Let instrument and lutes sound loudly). Long, sustained chords of final cadences easily tend to drop in pitch since the choir often does not have suffcent breath, mental concentration, and physical energy to support them. To prevent some of the numerous problems of intonation, one may occasionally have the choir hum the beginning of each new phrase and frequently resort to soft singing. At all times the ear must be as active as the vocal cords. In general, it may be said that an able director and an alert choir need not become the victims of flat singing or be defeated by the hazards of poor intonation!

76

Sharping is occasionally found in young, energetic musical groups. Here the "hushing up" quieting gesture of the choir director can be of assistance. On the whole, the conducting motions of the director are of great importance in maintaining good intonation. (Compare with A III, p. 122 ff.)

Chapter VI

Body Movement and Choral Singing

Since the beginning of Occidental culture, music has been conceived of as movement. The Greek thinkers expressed this concept in the adage, "Everything which sounds also moves." The chorus of the Greek tragedies exemplified in dance the original unity of the movement arts. Singing and dancing belong together. This intimate relationship between music and movement is realized to this day in native folk dances. Artistic choral singing of the present must be regarded as a late cultural form, and should be understood, in a sense, as "dancing on the spot." This concept of an "inner dancing" should continually be kept alive by the director as he directs his choir. He has a great advantage over the singer in that he is freer to express the movement of the music in terms of physical movement. The opera or stage singer regards the use of motions and gesture as a necessary and obvious part of singing. Even a concert choir should regard itself as being fundamentally a choir in motion and should be directed as such, even though the movements must be almost entirely transmited inwardly, and all visible movements consequently reduced to a minimum. The choir director should imagine himself as a leader of the dance. This minimum outward motion on the part of the choir must be present, even though the expression is limited to the stance which merely suggests a buoyant readiness to dance. The physical stance of the singers should suggest an inner readiness for moving into a toe dance, or engagement in a continuous pendulum-like motion from the central axis, diaphragm, and spine. Finally, the singer should feel that his total physical and spiritual response to the music is in complete harmony with the ceaseless to and fro rhythmic pulsation of the inhalation and exhalation of his own breathing. To the extent that movement cannot be expressed outwardly, it must be expressed inwardly as an intensive, bouncing, energetic movement; the less opportunity there is for manifesting the music in larger body movements, so much more must the music fill and animate the small movements with a strong propensity for outward expression. Thereby music is translated into and vividly illustrated in terms of body movements.

Occidental philosophies of music discuss music in terms of movement and activity, particularly in connection with the music of polyphonic and contrapuntal eras. The numerically regulated music of the Middle Ages symbolized the mathematical regularity of the movement of the suns and planets within the solar system. Pursuing this line of thought we could think of the continuous flow of the contrapuntal lines in polyphonic music as representing the endless orbits of the stars. Before beginning to sing or play music of this era, a performer should imagine himself surrounded by an inaudible cosmic musical stream, which, upon completion of his song, continues its soundless vibrations into the endless eons of time and infinite space. Through his instrument, the musician has, for a brief moment, translated the eternally present universal vibrations into audible sound. Before beginning each new phrase or section, the performer enters into a pre-existing, soaring spheric motion of cosmic rhythm and harmony which exists outside of and apart from the singer's own sphere of music making. A musically "right" attack, and, above all, a good ending can often be achieved only upon contemplation of this inaudible "music of the spheres." Even in Bach's time music was regarded as *imitatio naturae.*

Musicologists believe that characteristic melodic curves or typical patterns of musical motives can be found in the works of individual composers; according to this theory the personal style of the composer is to be understood by the recognition of such characteristic types of musical motives.

In the Baroque Period the visualization of the inner musical movement was expressed by describing the quality and tempo at the top of a composition with such words as *andante* (in a walking tempo), *largo* (slowly), *allegro* (fast), etc. All these instructions describe a quality of motion. These descriptions identify the essential nature of the piece and, at the same time, give the musician a rather accurate clue for its interpretation.

The era of the great church and court choirs whose admirable works remain essentially the most treasured possessions of our musical heritage maintained as the prerequisite and basis of their art the entire domain of man's normal life activities. Frequent secular and sacred dramas and processions, folk and professional dancing, competitive games and sports, the life of hunting and agriculture, long-standing traditional activities associated with agricultural and artisan occupations, travel by foot and horseback, literally kept life in constant motion. The representatives of this way of life could therefore also become the champions of the kind of music which is characterized by tremendous musical energies and a continuous variety of musical motion. The close interdependence and relationship between the mode of life and music has been clearly revealed in each great musical era. The so-called "technical era" of the eighteenth century was characterized by a profusion of mechanical movement and the hitherto natural way of life with its crude, unsophisticated activities began to disappear. The communal form of living where work, possessions, and recreation are shared freely was exchanged for living in secluded apartments or separate, individually owned homes. Folk dancing disappeared and the social dance, which included folk dances with partner dancing, took its place. In our own day, urbanization has to some extent thwarted spontaneous natural body movements; the machine-conditioned factory worker does not perform any physical movement which originally was native to such occupational handicrafts or trades as carving, weaving, and mowing, but performs the same isolated motion thousands of times a day as he stands in his place in the assembly line. The workman does not need to transport himself to his place of work with his own energies, but travels by car or bus. Modern civilization has brought the musical concert, the theatre, and the drama right into his home, where he can enjoy them from the comforts of his easy chair: he does not have to come into contact with society if he wants to experience pleasure and entertainment. The study (science) of human types ascertains that the active type of individual is decreasing with the increase of culture and modern conveniences; in a future era of civilization there will, according to experts in this field, be a dearth of physically active people as well as a dearth of forms of physical movement. In contrast to the lack of physical responsiveness to music on the part of adults, children readily respond to music in terms of physical movements.

Our life as well as much of our music making has become static. Today one speaks of a piece of music as being written in ¾ time, when we should really be saying that it moves in ¾ time. In Germany, it is common to say *es steht* (it stands) in ¾ time.

It is our task to work creatively toward artistic goals with people who have been deprived of many natural and life-related activities. The lack of such natural activities among singers has sometimes led to the most grotesque musical results and misinterpretations of musical works. As a result of this situation, after the Second World War various attempts have been made in Europe to compensate for the lack of natural activity: renewed interest in sports, outdoor living — hiking and camping, revived interest in dancing and other rhythmic activities, and finally revived interest in singing. In a variety of ways the making of music, as well as the sheer joy of living are expressed in physical movements. Insofar as it is sensible, feasible, and of service to the singer, it should be of prime interest and concern to utilize and realize the knowledge, skills, and approaches achieved through such activities.

Whenever feasible the entire choir should participate in some kind of physical activity outside of the rehearsal. This could take the form of a Sunday afternoon outing. Hiking, swimming, ball games, skiing, dancing, gymnastics, and rhythmic training exercises are excellent for promoting good music making; each exercise or sport prepares for a special unique function of the singing act. For example, skiing stimulates deep rhythmic breathing in which the supporting muscles of the lower back are brought into active play; swimming and running develop lung power and strengthen the diaphragm and intercostal muscles. The "singer's instrument," the human physique (body), is kept fit, fresh, strong, and alert. The music teacher in a public school should, whenever possible, collaborate with physical education teachers. If the music teacher is also capable of instructing physical education and sports, so much the better! Exercises certainly are not to be limited to outdoor or gymnasium events, but should be incorporated into the rehearsal period in the form of running on the spot, arm swinging, head rolling, etc. A choral selection in a waltz-like rhythm will sound more alive and convincing after the singers have tried to waltz some steps. As the string player continually checks and tunes his instrument, as the brass player constantly overhauls and cleans his instrument, so the singer should seek to keep his instrument, his own body, fit and alert so it will be responsive to the production of full, vibrant sounds (See A I, p. 1 ff.).

The author recalls from his own student years how the first few days of the semester for the collegium musicum classes were spent in hiking, swimming, skiing, and other sports during the day, and with music making in the evenings. This helped the student body, which always included some new students each semester, to amalgamate very quickly.

The inward and outward liberating effect of these activities provided the basis for further musical activities in the new semester. In the week prior to a concert tour, the author has often begun the day's rehearsal activities with a period of rhythmic training in which both singers and instrumentalists participated. The "lost" time from the rehearsal of the music was later more than compensated for in terms of increased alertness and efficiency. In Germany most directors of choral clinics begin their day's work with calisthenics, tumbling, breathing exercises, and rhythmic training. These activities should, whenever possible, be somehow directly related to the choral work which follows.

If such activities are not feasible, then one must limit oneself to activities which can be incorporated into every choral rehearsal. Some suggestions have been given in a preceding paragraph and elsewhere, but above all the exercise in the training of rhythm and gesture, as outlined in this and the following chapter, should be incorporated into the training programs of choir directors as they are offered in special courses, music schools, and conservatories.

The energy and intensity in a sustained chord or musical phrase can be relaxed in tonal intensity by means of a simple hand gesture. This applies particularly to final cadences where the music becomes very emphatic and intense, and where the sound as a result tends to become too loud, strident, and lacking in quality and intonation. To overcome this it may be quite helpful for everyone to make a few quick "rabbit paw" motions, with relaxed upper arms, raising forearms in an angle close to the body, and hands hanging down completely limp like grape bunches from a vine.

As a contrasting example the passage could be sung while maintaining a tense, rigid arm and balled fist. The music will immediately become rigid and dull, and the notes, instead of blending, will clash with each other. Only after a relaxed position like the "rabbit paw gesture" will the tone again begin to blend into a resonant, resilient sound. The final chord of a cadence is not forced into a fixed position, but it is suspended as it were in time and space, where the sound can vibrate and resonate to its full potential. Such an approach to *forte* singing relaxes the singers and frees them both physically and psychologically. The rhythmic momentum of the composition must not be "frozen" in the final cadential chords. This is particularly important to observe in some of the closing sections of Bach's works, as, for example, the last four measures of the dramatic "thunder and lightning" and the "crucify" choruses of the *St. Matthew Passion*.

This simple gesture of relaxing arms and hands could prevent a shattering, oversung *forte* in the following example taken from the *Hamburger Mottetenbuch* (see Ex. 19).

Example 19

82

Final cadences of the Netherlandish style, in which the undulating voice parts gradually come to rest over the subdominant, can also acquire the necessary looseness and freedom with the help of such a gesture; a good example is the final cadence of Adrian Willaert's cantus firmus motet, "Victorae paschali laudus" (No. 113, *Harvard's Anthology of Music Vol. 1*). Finally, this gesture can be used to prevent or relieve tension or rigidity anywhere in the course of the composition.

The movement and direction of a melody or voice part can be controlled with a hand gesture. This gives the melodic movement real direction, momentum, and plasticity. It is easiest and simplest to practice this with a song which employs the major scale, like the familiar tune, "Duke Street." The hand indicates a supporting gesture as it moves up and down with the ascending and descending melodic line. It is of decisive importance that the director thinks of his hands as leading and controlling the melodic flow through every beat of the music. He should never think of his hands as following the music, but always maintain the awareness that there is an indissoluble unity between hand and music and that the director in reality holds every tone "in his hand." The same kind of concentrated control applies also to the conducting of musical high points in supporting voice parts, i.e., wherever the voice leading or melodic line becomes most important in a given voice part, e.g. the tenor part in the last three measures of the final chorus of Schuetz's *St. Matthew Passion*. The musical character of a chant or chorale melody can be indicated before the initial attack of the music by a strong, clear gesture; the descending Phrygian fifth which constitutes the beginning of the second tune to Luther's hymn, "Out of the Depths," would require an upward sweeping gesture to suggest the span of tension from *b* to *e*.

A musical motive can be represented in a bodily movement. In an effort to emphasize a series of four eighth notes of a cadential formula, the choir director often resorts to all kinds of desperate motions: he may mark the tempo by counting or stamping his feet, he may have the passage sung staccato, which would probably result in chopping the music, or he may emphasize certain notes as focal points, etc. None of these attempts brings the desired result. If such a group of notes is regarded as one continuous surge of musical energy with a slight upsurge counterbalanced by an equivalent resurge, and as such is represented by an appropriate physical gesture, then the tempo, accentuation, clarity, and dynamics of the motive will fall into place and the musical outcome will be satisfying. The impulse of the body movements should not come from "without" but should originate from an imaginary vertical line through the center of the body (plumb line). The particular musical section could first be sung to "gliding" syllables: *n, doh, don.*

The body may gently swing forward and backward in keeping with the movement of the phrase — as if one were making little bows to an audience! This can also be performed while sitting, since all forward and lateral movements ought to be made from the hips. The culmination of a body movement should coincide with the culmination of a musical entity. A simple illustration of a motivic surge and its relaxation within a musical phrase is found in the concluding measures of the four-voice setting of the "Hildebrand song" by Melchior Franck (Ex. 20).

Example 20

The melodic course in the bass line of the four-voice cantus firmus composition of L. Senfl's *Entlaubet ist der Wald* (Now fallen are the leaves) can be treated in a similar manner (Ex. 21).

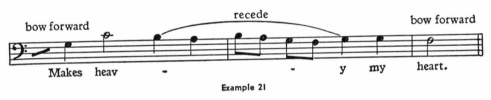

Example 21

The cadential formula can be treated in several or all voice parts simultaneously with one combined unified gesture. Such a gesture can insure a clean, precise cadence provided it is conditioned by a clear, auditorial concept of the sound. Bach's chorale harmonizations furnish numerous examples of this type of cadence, as for instance this excerpt from *Nun danket alle Gott* (Now thank we all our God) (Ex. 22).

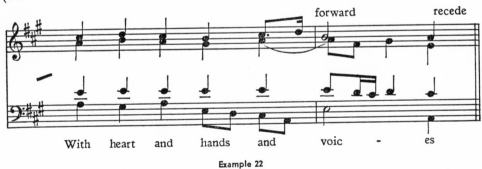

Example 22

Here it is the alto and tenor parts, in particular, which could be controlled by body movements. Numerous other examples where gesture in the form of body movements can be applied could be cited from the bicinium compositions of Rhaw, Walther, Othmayr, and many others who, after the compositional practices of their time, often let each line end with a changing note motive at the cadence.

The singers in the choir may on occasion "conduct" themselves as they sing. Any form of "time beating" is to be avoided since this would hinder the flow of the music and tend to make it rigid. Instead, the directional movement of the music should be represented by free-flowing, outward directed diagonal curves which take the form of the letter S. This helps the singer to identify with the basic pulse and flow of the music. It should also be obvious that the singer refrains from mechanical counting during the rests, but that he moves through with a keen sense of the sound frequencies which he has just heard. The singer does not make a new attack into the next phrase but rather "enters into it" on the wave of the frequency of the sound oscillations which have not ceased to vibrate during the rest. The singers begin by conducting with one hand at a time, and later with both hands. At first this may be attempted with simple canons written in a gentle rocking duple time, as in "Row, Row, Row Your Boat" in which the pulse and flow of the music is quite regular and unabating, but which has a half note pause before the new attack in the middle of the canon. However, this exercise may be applied to compositions with shorter or longer rests, e.g. polyphonic motets of Heinrich Schuetz and Melchior Franck, in which the singer must find his own way of giving support to the musical flow by means of gesture.

The basic pulse and movement of the music may also be expressed by movements of the entire body. The body now picks up similar movements which were made by the hands in the exercises described above. This results in a protraction and enlargement of the exercise, but the purpose remains the same as before. A good point of departure for learning to sway the entire body during singing can best be realized by imitating a swinging bell or by imagining that one is rocking an infant to sleep while holding it in one's arms. The round, "O How Lovely Is the Evening," which ends on a series of "ding dongs" in the last line, would be a simple but most effective song in which to practice the swinging bell motion; the trunk of the body sways from the central axis (waist) sideways to the left and then over to the right; the feet point outward at a slight angle and the arms hang loosely by the sides (See A I, p. 3). The rocking movement is assumed quite unconsciously whenever a cradle song is sung. Cradle carols like "Joseph, Dearest Joseph Mine" or "He Smiles Within His Cradle" lend themselves very well to such larger motions of the body during singing. In certain communities it may be necessary and helpful to use familiar dance tunes to stimulate the necessary rhythmic freedom and bodily response to the music. The director must decide for himself the type of dance music he must choose to bring about the desired response. These rhythmic activities and swaying movements may further be applied to simple polyphonic settings such as those written on the tune *In dulci jubilo* or to the ballet madrigals like Morley's "Sing we and chaunt it." The pastoral symphonies in Handel's *Messiah* and Bach's *Christmas Oratorio* strongly reflect the dance characteristics of slow peasant dances, which can be re-enacted through gesture and body movement by singers as the music is played or sung.

The rhythm of a song may be represented in movements of both arms and feet. The movement in the arms and the trunk is transmitted to the legs. This is not possible without simultaneously rhythmicizing the rhythm of the song. (See next chapter for detailed description.) Dance tunes and roundelays lend themselves particularly well to this kind of activity. In the song, "We sing of the polar bear," (p. 42, *Let's All Sing*, American Camping Association, Martinsville, Indiana) (Ex. 23), the rhythm could first of all be clapped with the hands and then stamped with the feet. Next, the rhythm could be simultaneously clapped and stepped. The basic rhythmic scheme could then be distributed to the hands and feet so that the feet mark the heavier down beat while the hands clap the following lighter beats. The strong beat may be alternated between the right and left foot as indicated in the diagram. After several successful attempts, the participants should sense the rhythm rippling up and down and back and forth throughout the entire body.

This exercise may be performed both in standing and in sitting positions. The tune can be sung, whistled, or played. Supplementations and variations can be made by selecting other types of dance songs. The director may make his own applications of this kind of rhythmic treatment when choosing part songs, but he should choose settings which have a fairly simple harmonic setting, such as Gastoldi's *A lieta vita* also used in some American hymnals with the text, "In thee is gladness" (p. 69, *Gesellige Zeit*, Baerenreiter). Such settings are most effective in obtaining a maximum rhythmic freedom and clarity. For further elaboration of this topic see the next chapter.

The activities on the spot are now extended to activities away from the spot; stationary activities now become mobile activities. The suggested aids and exercises which have been given thus far can be carried out by the convinced and energetic choral trainer with any choir in any rehearsal room. However, in the suggestions and exercises which are to follow there will no doubt be some divided opinions among different choir directors and singers. Singers of amateur or rural community choirs may not be inclined to participate in the following exercises. However, if the choir director succeeds in convincing his choir of the value of such exercises, he will have opened up a new field of opportunities for creative music making which would otherwise have remained inaccessible to him and the choir. The suggestions which follow should certainly be investigated and utilized for courses in choral training, in music schools, and other institutions where music constitutes a vital part of the total program.

(1) *The group dances in slow country dance style to a tune sung in unison:* A unison or part song is selected. One could simply proceed by marching and clapping to a song like "We sing of the polar bear" (Ex. 23). This

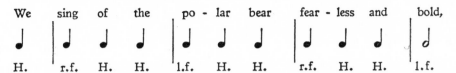

From *Twice 55 Community Songs*, copyright 1957 Summy-Birchard Company, Evanston, Illinois. All rights reserved. Used by permission.

Example 23

could be followed by dancing to an actual waltz tune. To stress the aspect of the choral community, one could next form a large circle and continue the waltz step. Finally, the waltz could be danced by couples while singing, or whistling the tune. If the large size of the choir or the small size of the room do not permit all the singers to dance at the same time, then have one section of the choir dance while the singers of other sections stand around the dancers and support the music with stepping, hand clapping, and singing or playing. Further variations and innovations could be devised as opportunity permits. A large variety of simple folk songs could be performed in this manner.

(2) *The singers step (walk) to a tune sung in unison:* For example, "The Herdsman Is Merry" (No. 1, *Let's All Sing*) is sung while the singers step to it rhythmically, first in a regular circular formation, and then freely without any particular formation. In these activities the posture should be upright and breathing free and unhindered; arms, shoulders, and head are also "in step." The steps should not be taken in a jerky manner. This rhythmic stepping can be substantiated by clapping the "Ho-le-a, Ho-le-e-e-e-e-a" refrain, and later the singers should attempt to make a few jumps in the exact rhythm of the song. Other suitable songs with further possibilities for variation should be selected. With tunes in which a 3/4 time refrain follows a 4/4 time verse the stepping activity may be combined with dancing. For example, in the ballet madrigal "All Ye Who Music Love," by Balthazar Donato (p. 3, *Six Easy Madrigals*, Western Music Co., Vancouver, Canada), everyone steps to a 4/4 rhythm in one of the ways described above and at the 3/4 refrain the group forms into couples and dances the "Fa-la-la" rhythm in the form of a country waltz. This is a good exercise for changing from one gait or pace to another. According to old dance traditions,

such songs could be stepped to 4/4 time and the refrain danced in a hop-skip manner. On festive, merry-making occasions such possibilities can be extensively utilized.

(3) *A unison tune may also be danced to in free step style:*

A unique illustration is the Polish folk song, *Steh auf hohem Berge* (Standing on a high mountain). The same rhythmic motives of two quarter plus four eighth notes are repeated eight times in a varied form (See example 32). This basic pattern should first be clapped; following this, the heavier quarter notes are stepped and the lighter eighth notes are clapped. It might also be useful to reverse the procedure. The entire song may then be sung or whistled while the rhythm is stepped and clapped. When the song has been completely absorbed by the body as well as by the ear, the choir should be permitted to respond to it in free movements. At first, a specific direction like "circular formation — walk in a counter-clockwise direction" could be given, but later, the singers could move in free confusion! The stepping, clapping, and dancing activities may be substituted by simulated movements. Two long forward steps are taken, followed by four shorter steps. The feet remain close to the floor so that they appear to glide as in skating, the arms swing easily as they help to balance the body in this act. As a further modification, clap the quarter notes while standing and skate the eighth notes and vice versa. Or, one may move in a forward direction while marching or skating on the quarter notes and in a reverse direction on the eighth notes and vice versa. This sudden change between stationary and mobile positions, and between forward and reverse directions is of tremendous value in developing a feeling for active body participation and movement as it relates to music making.

(4) *A tune which is sung or improvised to several parts is stepped or danced to:*

The suggestions which the author makes for choral ear training (A V, p. 65 ff.) should be combined with the various body movements described in this chapter. Let us take for our example the Bohemian Christmas carol "Come All Ye Shepherds." A simple Christmas roundelay (round dance) could be improvised as follows: The performers who sing and play the open "bagpipe" fifths (as given in many editions of this carol) stand in front; the singers who drone out the fifths remain standing while the people responsible for the tune, now divided into two groups according to the lines of the song, step forward and backward, outward (sideways) and inward, within the half-circle and away from it.

A sensible representation of the song in movement and gesture can be made as circumstances permit. On the basis of what has been suggested thus far, there are possibilities for improvisatory stepping and dancing in connection with the innumerable folk and dance songs. In all attempts the director should take certain precautions to prevent these activities from deteriorating into irresponsible and rampant musical dilettantism, and should keep his musical goals clearly in mind.

(5) *A tune with a harmonic setting can be danced, stepped, or marched to according to the rhythm of the tune and the other voice parts:*

The same activities and procedures described in connection with unison tunes may be applied to a harmonized tune. The harmony should be predominantly note against note, and the accents and stresses should occur at the same place in all voice parts. It should be a prerequisite that the singers know their parts by memory. Here are some suitable examples of such songs: "Now Is the Month of Maying" by Thomas Morley, "The Ash Grove," and "Waltzing Matilda." Have the singers dance to the song in the form of a large, circular group, and then as individual couples. With these musical settings, the movements of all singers in the different voice parts are uniformly performed. In settings where accents and rhythms differ from other voice parts, the movements are of course performed accordingly. If a setting begins with only the two upper parts, the singers in the two upper sections begin to sing and move about to the rhythm of the piece, and the lower voices perform some steps while remaining stationary until it is time to take up their own parts. (Compare with A I, p. 7 ff.). In this way the choir gives the rhythmic structure of the music a visual and bodily expression. Through such exercises the singers get a visual concept of the structure of the piece, of the movement, and relationships of the parts to each other; the singers literally experience the musical composition in their own bodies, and the acquisition of new concepts and a new grasp of the music is now absorbed and translated into the singing act itself with the result that the music has become more animated and alive. The suite-like change between 3/4 and 4/4 which has been discussed in connection with unison singing can also be used in part music. For example, one could perform the same madrigal, "All Ye Who Music Love" with all its parts in such a manner that the singers would stand during the singing of the stanza which is written in 4/4 time, while the 3/4 time "fa-la-la" refrain could be danced in the form of a light waltz step. Such activities need not be limited to use as preludes or interludes to choral singing; the author has frequently used this as an exercise "in praise of music" at the conclusion of a choral festival. While the stanzas

89

are sung either in unison or parts the choir stands or walks in a circle, the female singers forming an inner circle within the circle formed by the male singers. As soon as the waltz-like refrain appears, couples are formed. For each new repetition of the refrain, the partners are exchanged.

(6) *A multivoiced composition is represented by free-walking movements which are not directly related to the rhythm of the tune and its accompanying parts*:

This is what gives such music a weightless, soaring quality. The character of such music is graphically and effectively transmitted to the singer when he attempts to move to the music in a free, relaxed manner and when the overlapping of his own steps with the accents and stresses of the music are absorbed within himself and expressed in bodily motions. The constant attempt to express the ever varying and dynamic fluctuations of the music in appropriate physical movement helps the singers to grasp quickly the nature and character of the polyphonic art. Walking and stepping to the mensural time (time signature) is also a possibility. This method or approach may be tried in connection with the four-part setting of Thomas Morley's "It Was a Lover and His Lass" (p. 53, *European Madrigals*).

The structure of a cantus firmus composition may also be instructively represented by movement in this manner. In such a compositional form the cantus firmus, according to old traditional compositional practices, constitutes the kernel or the musical framework which is surrounded by a lacework of faster-moving polyphonic parts. Luther speaks about "celestial dance rows" when referring to florid contrapuntal parts which move around and about the cantus firmus as the planets move around the sun. The singers who sing the cantus firmus are placed accordingly in the center of the rehearsal room from where they do not move, while the other accompanying voices surround them like rows of dancers. Particularly suitable for this type of arrangement are settings in which the cantus firmus is emphasized by introducing it in the form of an "intonatio," i.e. long-sustained note values found in such works as the opening chorus of Bach's cantata, *Sleepers Wake* and *Now Come Our Dear Redeemer*. The singers who sing the accompanying polyphonic parts may move in around the cantus firmus singers in a closed circle or form into smaller concentric circles according to voice parts. It is important that the singers who represent the accompanying voice parts think of their singing and the accompanying physical movements as originating from and relating back to the cantus firmus group in the center of the room.

90

The relationship of individual voice parts to each other in terms of parallel and contrary motion may also be represented by physical movement. Contrary motion is a special harmonic device and numerous cadential endings apply this harmonic principle to the outside voice parts. To help the singers develop a keener physical awareness of contrary motion, the sopranos and basses may be placed so that they face each other as sections, and as the musical parts move toward each other the singers themselves also move toward each other at the rate of one step per note. The inner voice parts which might appear to be mere filler parts at such points may fulfill their function by remaining stationary. Some examples where this procedure may be applied are: Morley's "Fire, Fire" (p. 47, *European Madrigal Book*, Ed. 2601), and his well-known madrigal ballet, "Now Is the Month of Maying," and Purcell's "In These Delightful Pleasant Groves."

If a longer passage of parallel thirds occurs, have those who sing these parts walk and hold hands or interlock elbows with each other. Meanwhile the accompanying voices actually accompany them in walking at a little distance from them. See the madrigal, "Hark, All Ye Lovely Saints" by Thomas Weelkes (p. 60, *European Madrigal Book*), or the chorus, "For Unto Us a Child Is Born" from Handel's *Messiah*.

The director may look for other types of voice relationships which could be represented and clarified through physical motion. Often a great deal is achieved in choral singing if the singers of the respective parallel or contrary voice parts establish the necessary rapport toward each other through eye contact from their respective places in the choir.*

A canon may also be represented by walking or dancing. The choir director can develop the various possibilities on the basis of the foregoing discussion, e.g. through social games, round dances and stately step dances. Each voice part constitutes a movement group (action group). Each group is initiated in turn by singing — accompanied by stepping or dancing, and moves in parallel, contrary, and interweaving patterns with each of the others in accordance with the movement within the music. The canon may be concluded together, leaving each group at a different spot from where it started, or each group may in turn sing the canon to its conclusion, thus permitting each group to return to its original starting point.

At this point it should be emphasized once more that the suggestions in this chapter are aids and exercises which have frequently proved their usefulness in choral singing, but in themselves are without any musical value whatsoever. If the songs lend themselves to the creation of a suitable game, a skit, a festive dance or other similar activities which could become a natural part of a social or informal evening, then the purpose for suggesting the exercises and activities in this chapter has in part been fulfilled. As important

*Translator's note: This is possible only in a divided chancel or a circular or semicircular formation.

as it may be to achieve a harmony between musical and body activity and to rediscover this relationship in its original unity, it is also necessary, particularly at the conclusion of such a treatment within the confines of a book on creative music making, to emphasize that all physical energies reflected in constant movements and functions must in the final analysis be transferred back into the music itself. Music can then enter into its own kingdom in a renewed way and maintain its own laws of being which ultimately belong to the realm of the spirit. The freedom of music's own laws of motion cannot be adequately expressed or represented by the limited motions of the human body. Music therefore may, can, and must move in its own sphere of motion beyond these limitations of physical motion. Therefore we must conclude that the search for unity between music and body movements can exist only in theory, or, as the unresolved tension of a dialectical argument.

If, for example, during the rehearsal of a song like Morley's "Sing We and Chaunt It" *(The A cappella Singer,* E. C. Schirmer), the choir has actually danced to the music, then it should, from this bodily demonstration, have caught the feeling for the uninterrupted moving line, become aware of the rhythmic structure and a concept of a corporate plasticity of sound; these experiences should then be translated into the singing act. However, when this has taken place, the whole realm of creative music making is relegated to the intellectual and artistic control of the performer. A choral composition cannot be exhausted through a visual representation like dancing, for the musical art form must, in the final analysis, obtain its form from the mind and spirit which controls the elements of sound and movement. Often the musical mind operates above the active organic plane and occasionally even against it, as with Beethoven.

It is precisely at such moments that it is important to interpolate physical activities to avoid being overcome by tension. This applies to artistic music making—but in informal singing situations, music and physical movements should also be kept in continual balance.

A by-product of the element of movement is its influence on the sonority of the music. With systematic application of such exercises the choral sound loses its rigidity and forced qualities, its spread and lack of focus, but gains in freedom, focus, resonance, power, and beauty.

Chapter VII

Choral Rhythmic Training

Every action or motion is subdivided into further movements arising from and conditioned by the nature of the impulse of the action. This takes place rhythmically. The gait of man and beast, the flight of birds, the circulation of the blood, and the breathing process are rhythmicized. The mechanical movement of an automobile or a pullman coach is supported by rhythmic pulsations. Movement and rhythm cannot be separated from each other. Just as speech training becomes simultaneous with voice training, so training in movement and gesture reach into the area of rhythmic training. That which is rhythmically active is the basis for everything in music. "In the beginning was rhythm," said Hans von Bülow. It is noteworthy that a musical riddle is most difficult to solve when the rhythm of the music to be identified has been changed. Rhythm is the unifying, binding element and the governing principle in music. Rhythm is a stronger factor than sheer sound in unifying individual singers into a close-knit choral unit. Therefore there is no means which is so suitable for thoroughly fusing a group of individualists into a unified musical group as rhythmic training. Rhythm becomes a governing principle in the movement of the music, and since music is an art in time, rhythm also represents the division of time. We speak of "time signature" or "musical measure"; rhythm measures time. All of life is spanned between the rhythmic alternation of day and night, the rotation of the seasons, between activity and rest.

The older music was constructed upon principles of rhythm in motion. We may refer here to the system of rhythmic modes in the Middle Ages, or the division of longer musical compositions into dance suite movements in the Renaissance and Baroque Periods. Here the rhythmic element is decidedly predominant. The rhythm holds the performers to a fulfillment of the music's own demands. We sometimes speak of "rhythm which sweeps one along." At the point where the rhythm is caught or mastered the musician experiences a kind of delightful abandonment to the music. Bach's school rector, reporting on one of the Leipzig rehearsals, describes the Thomas cantor as possessing "rhythm in all of his members." Contemporary music, and particularly choral music, is characterized by strong, new rhythmic impulses.

Choir singers in general, as well as all music students, are encouraged to "keep time" through counting. The metrical organization in music is a means of mechanical time measurement, and counting is a logical procedure. However, in music we are concerned with achieving a unity of being; singing and playing are not logical musical phenomena, and so it is possible that in spite of "correct counting" one can most certainly "count oneself right out of time!" Every piano teacher has observed how his students, in spite of their ability to count correctly, continually tend to vary their tempo by playing faster here or slower there. This results in a departure from the path of musical motion and a disturbance of the music as a whole. It is not the mechanical counting of successive beats, however logical this may be, but the grasping of a rhythmic entity which permits the musician to perform the music with freedom and certainty. Herein we must train our singers. Through direct and immediate absorption of longer rhythmic entities the musician soon learns to take in at a glance and to master larger musical relationships; he is then less "glued" to the music than when he resorts to the very limited method of "counting off" the individual notes.

A choir which has gone through a program of rhythmic training will also attain a discipline and firmness in its music making which will make the singers immune to false emotion of any kind.

Rhythmic training may commence with freely invented rhythmic exercises or with the rhythmic patterns selected from choral compositions. A few rhythmic activities of a general nature may serve as preliminary exercises. For example, the choir director claps his hands eight times with even strength and spacing of the claps. Without any explanatory comment he asks the singers to repeat what they have heard. The large majority of singers will give an accurate reproduction and only a few will "clap late." The late clappers are usually those who have secretly attempted to count. Most people are unable to recall how many beats were clapped; the eight beats have been grasped and reproduced as a complete rhythmic unit, and this is the way it ought to be. Only later, after a short interval, the actual number of beats may be ascertained by mechanical counting.

One may use a few moments to stimulate this faculty within the choir. This, fortunately, is a natural gift for most people, but which, unfortunately, is often disrupted by mechanical music teaching. The above exercise of eight beats (claps) can be extended and the singers can be tested as to the number of beats which they can grasp and reproduce after one hearing. This should be followed immediately by varying the pattern for the purpose of expanding the exercise and making it more challenging. Secret counting must be strictly forbidden! Recently a method of music teaching has been introduced which aims to develop the ability to grasp longer rhythmic units through the eye. A rhythmic unit is written on the blackboard, and after a brief glance at the exercise, it is erased, whereupon the class reproduces the exercise by clapping. Even here, most students are able to grasp and repeat the entire exercise at once.

With reference to the above exercise, the singers could be questioned as to the time in which the eight notes were clapped. They will no doubt suggest that these eight claps (beats) can be interpreted as four measures in 2/4 time or two measures in 4/4 time. Upon further examination it will be seen that in the duple time the first beat is the heavy beat and the second beat is the light beat and that in the quadruple measure the light beats fall on 2 and 4 but the strongest emphasis goes to the first beat. This review of the relative stress within the meter should serve to show the difference between metrical time and rhythm and should be elucidated and established before commencing with actual time-beating exercises and conducting pattern drills. The hands should not be clapped loudly or roughly. Both arms and hands should move with an elastic bounce which is emoted from within. All rhythmic movements should be thought of as originating and emanating from the center of breathing which, once activated, continues the activity and keeps it spontaneous and alive. The entire body must participate in and become part of every clapping exercise. The same holds true, of course, for stepping or marching exercises.

The two 4/4 measures of quarter notes may now be treated rhythmically. The director divides his choir into two groups in a variety of ways — ladies and gentlemen members on the right and left side of the choir, front rows and back rows, upper voices and lower voices. This variation in the make-up of the groups encourages a thorough rhythmic workout for the entire choir. In the following two-measure exercises for the two groups, it is important to maintain an even, pulsating rhythmic flow, so that the moment of change from rest to clapping and vice versa occurs without a "break" or lull and that the transmission of the exercise from one group to the next is smooth and "seamless." Late clapping must be avoided; the entire group should clap as one person. Here are some possibilities of working out rhythmically the two measures of eight quarter notes with two groups of people:

(1) the first group claps the first measure while the second group claps the second measure and vice versa;

(2) the first group claps the first and third beats (accented) and the second group claps the second and fourth beats (unaccented) and vice versa.

The latter exercise can be further utilized by dividing the choir into four groups (e.g. according to voice sections) and having each section in turn clap one of the beats in a measure. Group 1 claps the first beat, group 2 the second beat, etc. This could be done for four measures, after which the groups are assigned to clap a different beat in the measure. The resulting rhythm should sound and feel like the rhythmic hum of a grain harvester in full operation! These exercises induce inner and outer relaxation, alertness, and develop a keen sense for blending the rhythmic actions into the rhythmic momentum within one's own being as well as into the rhythmic momentum of the entire group.

These innervating rhythmic impulses should be transferred to the entire body and could also be performed with separate parts of the body, e.g. nodding the head forward and backward and from side to side, or jerking or nudging the right and left shoulders alternately, or moving the hips in a similar fashion, etc.

Finally, this lilting activity should flow over into the legs and feet: To begin, the first measure may be clapped and the second measure marked with the feet by stepping and vice versa. Next the accented beats are stepped, the unaccented beats clapped and vice versa. (See Ex. 24.)

The unaccented beats may be further divided as illustrated in Example 24.

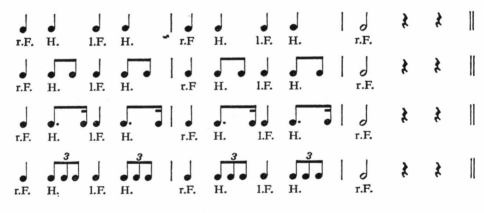

Example 24

All exercises are first patterned by the director and then repeated by the choir without hesitation and without counting. The notation of the exercise could be ascertained after it has been correctly executed, perhaps by writing it on the board.

The choir is again divided into two groups in any of the combinations described above and the following two measures of 4/4 time are performed as indicated. (Note that the second measure is a variation of the first.)

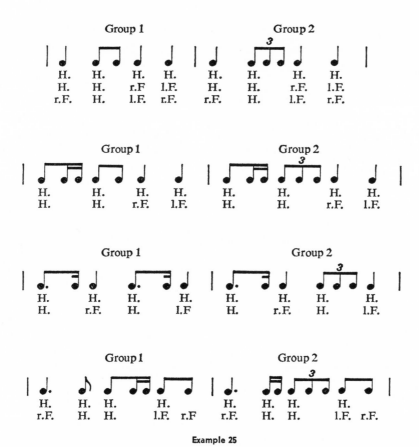

Example 25

The first group rhythmicizes the basic rhythmic pattern (theme) and the second group performs the variations of it and vice versa. This may be done several times in succession.

Choir directors or individual singers may devise other useful exercises of this kind. One should vary these exercises by performing them with three, four, or more groups and by varying the rhythmic units in relation to each other.

The entire choir may form a rhythmicizing group and may be asked to grasp and reproduce longer and more difficult rhythmic exercises.

Example 26

The choir director and singer should devise new rhythms, which of course ought always to be related to the nature and style of the music which is being rehearsed.

The choir director should include a similar procedure of rhythmic training in duple and triple time.

As an exercise to stimulate the ear to grasp a complete rhythmic entity with its subdivisions, one could clap twelve evenly accented quarter notes to the choir and ask individual singers as to how they heard the time divisions. A traveler on a passenger train, while listening to the regular turning rhythms of the wheels on the rails, may recognize different meters. The twelve quarter notes may be organized into the following meters, each of which may be clapped accordingly by the choir:

3 x 4/4 measures; 4 x 3/4 measures; 2 x 6/4 measures.

Every singer should master the skill of reading rhythms in the framework of a given meter. In multivoiced choir singing the basic beat pulsates throughout the piece within the framework of a constant metrical beat. Supported by the constant pulsations, the singer organizes his own rhythmic groupings according to the prescriptions of the score. Beyond this movement he may further create his own image of free, varying rhythmic patterns not contained in the score! The singer should therefore develop a keen awareness of and feeling for the regulating pulse prescribed by the tempo and meter of the music and carry this pulse within himself so that he might be free to sing the musical rhythms in relation to it. To train the choir in this musical skill, the director should divide his singers into various two-group formations (See p. 95 of this chapter) for the performance of the

Example 27

exercises given in Ex. 27. The first group claps an even beat while the second group claps the rhythmic pattern above the repeated quarter note scheme of the first group and vice versa.

Not only must the corporate body of singers be able to recognize simultaneously the varying relationships in movement between the time and rhythm, but each individual singer should experience this in his own body. Each singer must be able to feel the movement of the two strands of motion within himself. To help the individual singer to develop an awareness of this, the time may be indicated with the tapping of the foot while the rhythm is clapped with the hands. The time-beating level of motions is relegated to the legs and lower part of the body so to speak, while the rhythmic level is transferred to the arms and upper body. In this connection the exercise in Example 25 should be worked through again whereby the rhythm of the first group is stepped, walked, and danced and the rhythm of the second group is clapped with the hands.

This exercise may also be applied to songs. The metrical beat is marked with the feet, while the hands clap the rhythm of the tune. This should be practiced with some familiar songs in 3/4 and 4/4 time e.g. "John Brown's Body," "Come All Ye Shepherds," "Jingle Bells," "March of the Men of Harlech."

If the number of singers isn't too large, and if there is sufficient space, the singers could represent the rhythm of the song through walking and dancing, whereby again the basic beat is indicated with the feet and the rhythm of the tune is clapped with the hands.

To give the choir an opportunity to go beyond these specified assignments one should encourage free rhythmic improvisation. To begin with, a basic pattern such as the one in Ex. 28 could be introduced.

Example 28

This two-measure pattern may serve as a recurring couplet and should be clapped by the entire choir. Meanwhile individual singers invent new variations which are also two measures in length. To regulate the sequence in which the individual singers take their turns at improvising, one might simply let them take their turns according to seating arrangement, or the director may appoint the next group of individuals for the improvisatory parts. The couplet and its variation should gradually be increased both in difficulty and length. Stamping and various types of clapping sounds may be included. Finally the singers should be encouraged to invent melodies to the given rhythmic couplet.

99

Difficult rhythmic passages may be singled out from individual voice parts of choral compositions. This is usually done while the particular work is being rehearsed. Many rhythms, as for example dotted eighth and sixteenth notes or syncopated notes, cannot be rendered with clarity and decisiveness in any other way than through such an aid. Here are some excerpts of rhythms from musical passages which require particular rhythmic precision.

Tune

Oh, my dar - ling,　oh, my dar - ling,　oh, my dar - ling Clem-en-tine

Accomp. voices

Clem-en-tine　Clem-en-tine　Oh, my　dar-ling Clem-en-tine

Ex - ul - ta - te De - o ad - ju-to vi - no - - stro.

"Praise the Lord, Jehovah" (Exultate Deo) by Giovanni Pierluigida Palestrina (1526-1594) edited by Arnold Payson, copyright 1965 Frank Music Corp. Used by permission.

throne　that sit-teth up-on　the　throne　up - on　the throne up - on　the throne

From "Worthy Is the Lamb" *Messiah*, Handel.

Ad-am lay i bound-en, bound-en in a bond　Four thou-sand win-ter　thought he not too long

A *Ceremony of Carols* by Benjamin Britten, copyright 1943 by Boosey and Co. Ltd. Reprinted by permission of Boosey and Hawkes, Inc.

Example 29

Such parts can, during the study of the work, be performed with both feet and hands as described earlier, or they may be selected as passages for rhythmic training prior to the rehearsal of the piece.

One should also select exercises with longer pauses. To prevent rhythmic stagnation during the rests and to keep up a sense of rhythmic pulsation, it is best to clap the beats "in the air" without the palms touching each other. This sweeping motion in the air is also helpful in keeping the pulse moving when singing long notes. This exercise could be performed by placing the fingertips of each hand against each other and then clapping the hands noiselessly together.

The rhythmical grasp of the conclusion of a song can often be a determining factor in recalling the music of the entire song from memory. It would then be profitable for the singer to clap the entire rhythmic scheme of, for example, the Scottish gypsy song, "The Wraggle Taggle Gypsies"

(No. 5, *One Hundred English Folk Songs*). As a further procedure have the singers step the three even quarter notes which conclude each line, while clapping all the other notes. A similar procedure may be followed with Billings' setting of an old English carol, "A Virgin Unspotted."

Some songs have the same basic rhythmic pattern for each line. Therefore it is important to animate this rhythmic motive with great clarity and precision. In the delightful American folk ditty "Skip to My Lou," the same rhythmic pattern appears four times in each stanza:

Example 30

In order to gain a thorough grasp of the basic rhythmic form of even such a simple ditty, clap the rhythm of the entire song. Then clap the sixteenth notes while stepping the eighth and quarter notes and vice versa. Finally, the choir is divided into four groups, each group producing the rhythm of one line in the manner just described. The validity of this exercise is greatly dependent on smooth, even transition from one line to the next. The singers may also "think the text" during the performance of the rhythmic exercises. The choir may also be divided into two groups, the first group clapping the sixteenth notes and the second clapping the eighth and quarter notes and vice versa. Another possibility is the clapping of the sixteenth notes by the first group and the stepping of the longer notes by the second group and vice versa.

The Easter tune *Gelobt sei Gott im hoechstem Thron* (Now God be praised in heav'n above), by Melchior Vulpius (E. C. Schirmer), makes use of two basic rhythmic patterns:

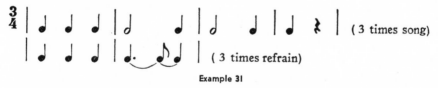

Example 31

The beginning of the lines of the refrain are a variation of the beginning of the song. The rhythmic work proceeds similarly, as described above for "Skip to My Lou" (Ex. 30).

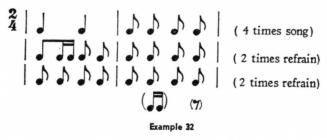

Example 32

101

The distribution of the total rhythmic scheme of a song among several groups serves to bring into relief the form and structure of the piece from the standpoint of the rhythmic construction. Certain dances written as the final dance number at social dances are written in AB(bb)A form. The rhythmic parts can again be distributed in a variety of ways to groups formed from the choir. One could, for instance, have two groups which could perform separately or together as illustrated in Ex. 33.

Example 33

One might divide the singers into four groups and have the A section clapped by the first, the first b section by the second, the second b section by the third and the final A section by the fourth group. The A section could be clapped while the B section is stepped rhythmically and vice versa. Different timbres of clapping sound can be obtained by clapping the hands in various ways, and the resultant differing sounds could be set in contrast, e.g. clapping with a flat hand results in a bright sound, clapping with cupped hands produces a heavier, sombre sound. For further variation, hands may be clapped on the chest and thighs, the backs of the hands could be struck together, or the fingers could be snapped in rhythm. In the above example of the concluding social dance, the A sections could possibly be clapped with cupped hands and the B section with flat hands. Other possibilities of sound effects by clapping hands should be tried out. Care must be exercised so that the sounds employed serve to clarify the rhythmic structure of the selection.

The children's nursery song, "Hop, hop, hop, Go and never stop," shows the same structure AB (bb) A. Since each A section begins with three quarter notes on the words "hop, hop, hop," there is further opportunity for developing the rhythmic sounds: the three quarter notes of each A section may accordingly be stepped with the feet and the rest of the song treated as before. Any detailed organization of rhythmic clapping should not be undertaken at the outset when the song is introduced but the rhythmic design should gradually emerge before the singer so that the unfolding of the form of the structure becomes a fascinating and impressive learning experience. At the outset the entire song may be clapped in any unprescribed manner, the first three notes may then be stepped and finally the various types of clapping sounds of the different groups may be set up against each other. One should look for other songs whose structure might require special rhythmic rehearsing.

The rhythmicizing of canons disciplines the singers to respond to each other rhythmically both in unison rhythm and in imitative rhythm. One might simply begin with a two-voice canon such as Carl Schalk's setting of Neander's tune to "Praise to the Lord, the Almighty" (Concordia Publishing House 98-1764). The choir is divided into two groups, the first group claps the first voice with flat hands for a bright tone, the second group claps the second voice with cupped hands for a darker tone. The division of the singers into groups and the type of clapping sound should be varied frequently. Three- and four-voice canons may be treated similarly. Canons with lively rhythms can be used most profitably, for instance, Cherubini's three-part canon, "Solfa ------ ing" and his laughing canon, "Hear the Echo" (p. 293, *The Youth Hymnary,* Faith and Life Press, Newton, Kansas).

The strong contrasts of individual canon parts in many canons demands a rhythmic treatment which will clarify these contrasts. In rehearsing a three-part canon like "The King Shall Come When Morning Dawns," by Joseph Haydn (Augsburg 1333), which is in ABC form, each of the three singing groups rhythmicizes the canon with a different clapping sound corresponding to the different musical textures of the three sections of the canon. For example, the A part may be clapped with cupped hands, B could be stamped and C clapped with flat hands. The transitions from one section to another should be made as smooth and "seamless" as possible. When the canon has been organized into suitable divisions according to clap-sound timbres, it is clapped through in its entirety. Finally each group rhythmicizes the canon with the clap sounds with which they began their respective sections to allow for further variation and contrast of rhythmic sounds.

With the increase of voice parts a richer and even greater variety and density of clap sounds is obtainable. A six-part canon like "Where is joyfulness" (Augsburg 1333) suggests the following possibilities of treatment (over which, however, the choir director must exercise control), clapping with cupped hands with varying intensity, clapping on the thighs, chest, chair, table, back of hand; stamping with a flat area of the foot, toe of the foot, heel of the foot, etc. In so doing, the canon should be developed systematically and with growing intensity and interest from its first unison appearance.

A grasp of the rhythmic structure of the entire musical framework is often indispensable for a clear rendition of the harmonic structure. In the repetition of the closing line of H. Isaac's "Innsbruck, I Now Must Leave Thee," the rhythmic pattern between the soprano and alto is identical. The tenor, though having the same basic pattern, is displaced at a distance of one quarter note. To obtain a sure grasp and a strong impression of the rhythmic web of this setting, it would be helpful to rhythmicize all four parts of this concluding section.

Reprinted by permission of G. Schirmer, Inc. American agents for the original publisher Pelikan Verlag, Zurin.

Example 34

In doing so one should attempt to bring out the character of the individual voice parts and their relationship to each other by appropriate rhythmic sounds. Since soprano and alto both move easily and smoothly to the same rhythm they could both be represented by the same sound color by clapping with flat hands. On the other hand, the tenor, with its displaced rhythmic pattern, could be clapped with cupped hands while the supporting bass notes are stepped. In this manner the texture of the entire setting is brought into relief by means of varying rhythmic clap sounds. If one should wish to give each voice part a characteristic clap-sound, have the sopranos clap with flat hands, the altos with cupped hands, the tenors clap on their thighs, and the basses mark the rhythm with their feet. A successful rendition of this section is dependent upon a relaxed but confident, rhythmically secure flow of all the voice parts, during which the singers must hear each other. Here again one should proceed systematically, building up the rhythmic structure from one voice part, making certain that each new voice part is thoroughly mastered by clapping activities and keen listening.

In ordinary situations this passage would undoubtedly be sung correctly at first sight by many choirs. Normally such a passage could be learned without such rhythmic aids. However, these exercises help the singers to sing this passage with reliability and faultless precision and give to the sound a body and depth which might not be attained in any other way. The individual voice parts are woven together as if they stemmed from *one* root and the individual singers are unified into *one* corporate singing body.

This approach can also be applied to a cantus firmus bicinium or to a three-voice polyphonic composition. The cantus firmus could be stamped with the feet or clapped with cupped hands while the contrapuntal line is clapped with flat hands, e.g., "The Agincourt Carol" (p. 62, *An English Song Book*, Doubleday & Co.).

In the four-voice setting of the fourth stanza of Bach's Cantata No. 4, "Christ Lay in Death's Dark Bonds," the cantus firmus appears first in the alto and is differentiated here from the other parts by its comparatively slow-moving quarter notes in contrast to the predominant sixteenth note

104

movement in the contrapuntal voices around it. In working through this section rhythmically, the cantus firmus should be stamped or firmly clapped with cupped hands while the lighter, quicker-moving contrapuntal voices should be represented by light, quick claps produced with flat hands. Should the cantus firmus appear in the form of a two-voice canon the principle of rhythmic treatment remains the same — main melodic (thematic) parts are clapped with cupped hands and the accompanying voices with flat hands. In a polyphonic composition in which all the parts are similar in character and of equal importance, the rhythmic clapping should be treated accordingly. The lively rhythms in the concluding "Fa-la-la" section of Thomas Weelkes's five-voice setting, "Hark, All Ye Lively Saints," dominate the entire relationship of the voices to each other. Here it would be most helpful to clap all five voice parts lightly with flat hands.

Reprinted by permission of G. Schirmer, Inc. American agents for the original publisher Pelikan Verlag, Zurin.

Example 35

Such rhythmic work has also proved to be a significant aid in the rehearsal of larger choral works. For example, in the fourteenth and fifteenth measures of the third chorus in Bach's motet, "Jesu Priceless Treasure," clarity can be quickly achieved in this way. The author has found it to be indispensable in rehearsing choral fugues like the one following the Verse 3, "They the Flesh No Longer Follow" from the same work. One should engage the singers in a relaxed but active clapping session in which a precise and instrumental-like clarity is achieved — the singers may imagine themselves to be members of a "clap orchestra." The strong emphasis on the rhythmic element in contemporary music likewise demands similar special rhythmic drills, e.g. the "Hallelujah" at the conclusion of Ernst Pepping's *Ich bin der Herr* (I am the Lord) (Ex. 36).

Copyright Baerenreiter Verlag, Kassel, Germany. (BA 1199)

Example 36

Here one should isolate the two rhythmic textures by a contrast of clapping sounds, viz., the upper voices with claps from flat hands and the lower voices with claps from cupped hands.

Rhythmic exercises are also an important help in the study of works for double choir. The singers throw imaginary balls of rhythmic clap sounds from one choir to the other. This strengthens and enhances the concept of concerto and antiphonal singing. Consequently each choir claps the rhythm of its music in varying timbres, during which the short rhythmic motives are clapped toward each other as it were until the rhythms are identical in both choirs, e.g. "Sing Ye a New Song" by J. S. Bach, or "Praise Ye the Lord" by Heinrich Schuetz.

The transition from rhythmic clapping exercises to the music and words should be a methodical one.

Normally the rhythmic exercises are introduced (interpolated) in the course of rehearsing the music, then after specialized rhythmic drill work of certain passages, the singers resume singing. The procedure of moving from music to rhythmic exercises and back may well consist of several intermittent steps. A thorough rhythmic workout might take the form of the following procedure:

(1) *Rhythmicization of the music* . . . For this a *short tone syllable* should be used, e.g. *don, dain, dan, tan, bam* (all a's as in far). Attention should be given to having the spoken (sung) tone syllable coincide precisely with the clapping or stepping of the rhythm. The rhythm must be instantly transferred from hands and feet to the larynx and mouth. Each singer articulates his words according to the rhythm in his larynx.

(2) In rhythmicizing the music by clapping, the *rhythm is also sung to a short syllable on a prescribed pitch whereby all sections maintain the same pitch.* This is followed by the rhythmic singing of each voice part on a different pitch in the form of a three-or-four-voice chord.

(3) *Next the music is sung to the syllables* in conjunction with the clapping exercises.

(4) If the work with tone syllables has been satisfactorily mastered up to this point, then the same exercises should *be carried out without the support of rhythmic clapping.* The rhythmic "pacemaker" is disconnected, as it were.

(5) *While clapping rhythmically* the singers now *think the text.* Into the rhythm which has been mastered by hand, foot, and mouth, we now fit the words. This is not only a physiological process, but the total word-orientated ability to think and imagine must, in a real sense, fit into the rhythmic flow of the music. Each singer *thinks in the rhythm of his larynx.*

(6) To the rhythmic clapping the singers next *speak the text.* The clapped rhythm and the spoken words should correspond precisely.

(7) To the rhythmic clapping the *tone syllables* are spoken to a predetermined pitch during which all *voices maintain the same pitch level.*

(8) To the rhythmic clapping the *text is spoken to a given pitch* whereby each part takes a different pitch to form a three-or-four-voice chord.

(9) To the rhythmic clapping the music is *sung with the words.*

If this step has been satisfactorily attained, the music can now be freely sung without the help of the rhythmic clapping.

107

In this process the rhythmic articulation of the words will not always correspond as closely with the clapped rhythm as might have been anticipated. Here the choir director must in particular be aware of the various changing relationships between words and music, and seek to relate the two in a satisfactory manner. (Compare with A IV, p. 63 ff.)

It would of course not be necessary, practical, or wise to go through all of these steps in such a methodical fashion with every choir. In fact, one could hardly think of any situation in which every step of this systematic treatment would actually be carried through. These exercises are recommended when the rhythm of the music appears to be somewhat foreign to the natural rhythmic flow of the words, particularly where the rhythm is the most prominent and important musical factor. The resourceful choir director will know how to choose and use these suggestions in accordance with the purpose and occasion of the music to be sung.

Chapter VIII

Conducting Patterns
and Choral Gestures

Choral conducting consists of translating the movement and rhythm of music into visible signs. That which the choral singer must frequently transmit inwardly and invisibly, the director must reveal and express outwardly. Just as a pianist, for example, can become a virtuoso on his instrument, so the director can be a virtuoso in his direction of the choir. To attain such virtuosity the whole domain of musical expression—phrasing, dynamics, and coloring—must become the language of gesture and expression for the director.

Contemporary musical activity which is largely dominated by instrumental music hardly recognizes a professional musical status for the choir director and cantor. It seems that many choir directors lack the realization that the choral art ought also to have professional and vocational status. Many music schools offer only one course in orchestral or choral conducting. There is a general tendency to regard choral directing as a supplementary skill which accompanies good piano playing as a matter of course whereby the student attempts to imitate, consciously or unconsciously, some outstanding orchestral director.

We must remember, however, that an essential property of orchestral directing is time beating, and its craft is conducting technique. This has its historical basis in the music of the Classical Period where the concept of musical measures of regular recurring patterns of strong and weak beats was fully established. It is from this music of the Classical Period that our present conducting practices have developed. Since it was natural that the heavy beat was represented by a downward motion, it is clear that our modern conducting practice bases its technique on the principle of the downbeat. The choir director must remember, however, that the great choral masterworks of the sixteenth, seventeenth, and eighteenth centuries which form the core of his musical and artistic efforts, and which historically speaking come before the orchestral music of the Classical Period were not conceived in terms of a regular recurring scheme of heavy and light beats. This music is based on a unit of measurement which was known as the *Taktus*.* To a wide extent contemporary choral music has been freed from the dominance of the metrical system of the Classical Era. The choir director who applies modern orchestral conducting techniques to choral music encounters the difficulty of trying to apply a method of directing which is often in complete contradiction to the basic character of the music being sung. The music in a sense is forced into a mold which it originally was never intended to fit.

The mere application of a time-beating technique to the choir can, metaphorically and musically speaking, "beat the music to pieces." With all the need for a sound conducting technique, we must do our best to free the choir and the music from a straight-jacketed conducting format and to allow the free unfolding of the essence and life of the music. This is recognized in the editing of some of the more recent editions of older scores as well as in some of the contemporary publications by omitting the regular bar lines and by indicating the divisions by the use of short strokes between the two-note systems — i.e. the stroke joins the top line of the bass clef with the first line of the treble clef.

To use meaningful gestures and signs in the process of training and directing a choir, it would be worthwhile to make a study of the gestures and signs used by choral groups since earliest times till the present. The choruses in Greek tragedies were directed by means of hand signals which imitated the melodic movement of the choral pieces. A rhythmic emphasis was added by clapping the soles of the sandals. We assume that chironomy was also practiced in a similar manner during the Middle Ages in connection with the singing of Gregorian chant. The art of chironomy has been transmitted to us in the chants written in the so-called *neume* notation. One may also conclude that the *neume* script approximately imitated the rise and fall of the hand movements which the cantor used as he conducted the chants.

The cantor of the later choir schools often used his own voice in guiding the choir as well as the congregation in their singing; and so the cantor was also the precentor who directed by means of the sung word. The frequent noisy rhythmization with the feet, hands, handkerchief, keys, paper roll, and walking cane were already criticized by writers and commentators of the day. The names of the cantors of some of the distinguished choirs of the sixteenth to eighteenth centuries who were instrumental in the brilliant performances of the multivoiced choral compositions of their time receded into anonymity.

*Translator's note: usually represented by a half note value.

They were not set apart from the singers by a podium or by a special conductor's spot, but they frequently stood with the singers, perhaps somewhere in the center of the choir. It is not even possible to identify the cantor in pictures and engravings of choirs of that time. The tempo of the pieces was indicated by an up and down movement of the hand which then became the even, regulating pulse. The cantor, who usually sang with the choir and was a vital part of the breathing and singing organism, became, so to speak, the heartbeat (vital force) of the choir.

The contemporary choir director must combine all the various approaches to choral directing because the works to be sung have represented within them all historical possibilities of style and interpretation. He must not only show preference for one approach or another in a given situation, but as a matter of principle he must have absorbed within himself the historical developments of choral directing and be able to realize these various approaches in actual performance. This can be achieved by combining the orchestral techniques with the older chorally orientated practices with a new contemporary art of choral directing which can meet the requirements demanded of the choirs of today. The basic forms and techniques of orchestral conducting which can help the director and the choir to achieve a high degree of reliability and precision from a technical and vocational point of view are combined with the following choral practices which have proceeded from the nature of choral singing itself:

(1) the actual imitation (chironomy) of the melodic line as practiced in the music of the Greek tragedy and Gregorian chant, leading with one's own voice which is possible only in an informal singing situation;

(2) speaking the text prior to singing (a practice of the older singing schools and church choirs) which can find application in artistic choral singing only if the words are mouthed silently;

(3) the simple down-and-up pendulum-like time-beating movement as practiced by the cantors of the great cathedral choirs which placed the initiative for creative music making with the choir itself, thus allowing the interpretive and artistic abilities of the individual singers to come into full play.

It follows then that the basic skills which are necessary for leading informal singing are a prerequisite to artistic choral directing. A director's knowledge and mastery of the different song types which are associated with marching, hiking, informal social singing, canon singing, and folk dance music, and his ability to lead informal community singing and congregational singing all serve to give him a special degree of confidence, directness, authority, and rapport with the singers. Without these abilities and experiences such authority and rapport might be difficult to achieve.

From these presuppositions there can emerge the basic relationship between choir and choir director in which the director feels himself to be an integral part of his choir. The leader must be a member of the choral body and should feel at one with it. He should be the central and driving force of his group but his control should be less of an imposition from without than an implicit controlling force originating from his own person. His distance from the choir and his elevation by the podium should never be greater than necessary to establish eye contact and rapport between himself and the singers. In accordance with the ideal traditional leader, the choir director should regard himself as a precentor or leading dancer who, as the best performer in his group, emerges from the group to give direction and leadership, but always withdraws again into and identifies himself with the group as *Primus inter pares*. He should cultivate and strengthen this feeling within himself. His ideal objective should be a gradual withdrawal from the choir to the point where he could on occasion be dispensable. Even if this idea might not be achieved in our own day, it is still a valid hypothesis and merits further consideration and discussion. According to historical reports, the papal choirs in Rome, at the end of the seventeenth century, sang complete masses without measured time-beating (conducting). Even today, English college choirs sing great traditional choral works in their evening services without direction from a conductor. The following advice, which applies after successful rehearsals, is suggested for orchestras by a critic of the late seventeenth century: "it then conducts itself, so to speak, as a watch after it has been wound" (J. M. Kraus). During the era of the emerging virtuosic podium Franz Liszt saw the real purpose of the conductor: to make himself indispensable and not to assume the "function of a windmill!" The actual and major portion of the training assignment of the choir director takes place before the so-called "performance." For intelligent and responsible choir directing the director must do even more than meet the various artistic demands or realize the various tonal and musical possibilities (in an efficient, almost play-like manner by means of virtuosic hand movements and graceful time-beating techniques). As important as the presence of an autonomous artistic will may be in shaping the musical performance, the question of letting the choral music become a way of life for a group of singers must remain a prime consideration. The director must know how to approach a particular choir and its music so that the choral art will be expressed in terms of the group's own grasp of and feeling for the music. To achieve this, much more is required than a good time-beating technique. What has been said earlier about posture, breathing, voice, speech, hearing, bodily movement, and rhythm can be helpful here. These attributes can also be consolidated and utilized as a means to aid the technical aspects of choir directing.

Now it is certainly possible for an orchestral director to achieve excellent rapport with his body of orchestral players, but because of the rhythm of simultaneous breathing, articulation of words, concentration on the same content, because of the similar posture and rhythmic movements which stem from common impulses, the bond between a choir and its director will be much more intimate. The guest orchestral director who is faced with a different group in each locality he visits has become a problematic phenomenon of our musical culture even though there may be some merit in hearing the interpretations of famous directors in different localities. The frequent change of choir directors becomes even more of a problem because of the closer and more personal bond which is necessary between director and choir for good singing. A professional choir director who seeks to make his living by directing a different choir each day of the week will hardly have experienced the reality of a close and genuine relationship that should be present between a choir and its director. The engagement of a substitute director to do most of the preparatory rehearsals seems to be just as questionable. After many laborious rehearsals of note drilling (for better or for worse), he hands over the choir to the regular conductor, who, in one or two dress rehearsals, shapes the work with a master's touch and astonishes the audience with what he as a master conductor has accomplished in one or two final rehearsals! The spirit of the choir and the music both must suffer under such an arrangement. It might require a great effort for the regular director to conduct all the researsals, but it pays off in the long run, not least in the artistic results achieved.

The use of signs and gestures in choral directing is only one among several other means. Since all singing is based on breathing and since corporate breathing unites the singers into a unified choral body, it also helps to unify them musically. This holds true particularly for unified phrasing and entries. The conductor directs his choir by the manner in which he breathes with them just prior to commencing and during the singing of the music (Compare with A II, p. 24 ff.). Singing is bound to the word. The ceaseless flow of the speech line binds the singers together as they move forward within the stream of the verbal sentence. Informal amateur singing groups are guided by the words as they pattern them after their leader, and as they sing with one another. The soundless mouthing of words in a demonstrative manner can be a helpful aid in choral directing. If this is done imaginatively and in good taste, the alert singer in the choir will want to "take the words out of the director's mouth!" (Compare with A IV, p. 45 ff.)

In the course of frequent repetition of the selections, which are for the most part much shorter than orchestral works, the choir and the director tend to memorize most of the music rather quickly. This permits the use of the eyes as an aid in directing to a much greater extent than is possible in

113

an orchestral situation. The choir and its director can develop a much closer and better "eye to eye" relationship than is possible between an orchestra and its director. In addition, singing evokes the use of gesture and mimic to a much greater extent and such use is heightened by the additional stimulus of the words. The rhythmic movement receives its impulse from the music itself; the choir director captures these impulses and absorbs them into his own movements and projects them back to the choir. In an orchestra the performers sit while their director stands, and whereas each of the different instrumental groups execute completely different movements on their various types of instruments, singers in a choir assume the same basic posture and stance as their director, and the rhythmic activity of the director is transmitted to them in such a manner that they begin to feel the same rhythm within them. In every choir which sings with vitality and animation there is present a rhythmic current which unifies and directs them. The presence of this rhythmic vitality is proof of its indispensability as well as its potential in choral leadership. (Compare with A VII, p. 93 ff.). The choir director therefore must not only have his choir "in hand" by means of good time-beating techniques and appropriate hand signals, but to an equal degree must hold the choir "in his eyes," "with his breathing," "with the words," "with gesture and mimic," and "with rhythmic impulse and movement."

Among the various possibilities of signaling and gesturing, the time-beating technique does not represent the basic form (means) for choral directors. The employment of a good time-beating technique has already become a complicated, highly developed form of choir directing. The patterning of the melodic line in the air, the use of finger and hand signals, the indication of various degrees of the scale by hand motions, and the system of metrical measurement have already been presented as natural and historical forms. The mastery of a time-beating technique is not a prerequisite for directing simple songs in informal singing situations. On the other hand, it is almost impossible to do artistic work of high caliber if the director hasn't thoroughly mastered a sound time-beating technique. This must be strongly emphasized in view of and precisely because of the limitations and the problematic aspects which have been indicated in connection with the application of orchestral time-beating to choral directing. If in actual practice the ideally prescribed conducting patterns are seldom used in a strict fashion and if in the larger choral works one should hold oneself merely to the conducting of the voice parts in a sequence in accordance with their importance, and to the free modeling of the melodic leading as it relates to the words (e.g. in motets), there still is no other device in choral work which offers the possibility of the same security, precision, thoroughness and economy of energy as the mastery of a sound time-beating technique. It is astonishing to observe

114

how time and time again many choir directors with many years of experience reveal an astonishing lack of knowledge and ability in this aspect of their work and because of this have to resort to a more casual or free-lance manner of directing their choirs. It would be most beneficial to the choir director if occasionally he were placed in front of an orchestra and were forced to learn thoroughly even the most basic and essential skills of a sound conducting technique!

A certain amount of modification of orchestral conducting technique when applied to choral work seems to be indispensable. Instrumental conducting technique of the angular and jerky type which is practiced in the military camps of all countries, when applied to singing, results in tight and throaty voice production and the consequent loss of pitch. Such abrupt time-beating also tends to fragment the music. It follows, then, that the orchestral beat patterns produced by forearm and stick movement when transferred to movements of the arms in choral directing must be rounded off and be made to swing more to the outside; and instead of the predominant vertical movements the director should strive for more horizontal movement. The director and singers should think of an imaginary horizontal plane at the level of the solar plexus, and imagine that the music moves back and forth on this plane. This concept should be constantly maintained by both director and choir. It remains to be one of the functions of the director's left hand to stimulate and support the awareness of this suspended horizontal plane by means of appropriate gestures. Each beat which is made with the right hand must be compensated for by an equivalent amount of sustained effort by the left hand; to stretch the point one could say: "What the right hand destroys (with its beats) the left hand must constantly sustain and support." The choir should carry the music through and beyond the imaginary suspended line, and the movements and gestures of the director should help the choir in doing this. The director may therefore not impose his beat on the choir or simply "beat at" the choir, but must, on the other hand, try to draw out and elicit everything which the choir is capable of rendering musically and artistically. His gestures are not so many predetermined movements which are imposed on the singers but rather they are gestures which grow out of and which are conditioned by their musical activity and response.

Among the modifications of orchestral conducting technique which the choir director should be ready to adopt is conducting without a baton, at least when the singing is not accompanied by orchestral instruments. It seems that the voluntary choral societies present an unusually favorable climate for promoting the use of this artificial vintage. The right hand which holds the baton is fixed into a more rigid position by its grip. The entire right side of the director becomes more or less useless for animated choral activity and the

115

entire activity tends to become mechanical. The choir director must never allow himself to become a mere metronome. To properly guide and modulate the tonal stress and vocal processes, every finger and finger joint must be free at his disposal. To establish good coordination between bodily movement and the measure and tempo of the music, the possibility of complete freedom of physical movement from the larger body members down to the smallest finger is necessary. In this respect the following relationships could be suggested:

complete measure — body	half measure — arm
rhythmic subdivisions — hands	word syllables — finger

Such free movement is particularly necessary for the numerous and different suggestions and aids which the choir director has to give in connection with breathing, enunciation, tone production, phrasing, shading, rhythm, etc. The choir director must feel somewhat like an extremely skilled glassblower, who with his highly trained hands and fingers forms with greatest dexterity, the stream of hot liquid glass while it is being poured into a work of art. The director who has mastered the primary forms in all its variations and possibilities in relation to choral singing will not want to lessen or hinder his creative work by resorting to the baton and so turn his sensitive creative fingers into a fist! An interpretive dancer who uses only the fleshy parts of his hands forfeits most of his possibilities for expression and interpretation. The baton is actually a recent device which came to be used as the size of the orchestra increased and is therefore, historically speaking, a tool foreign to choral work. The older schola cantorums (*Kantoreien*), who were the bearers of the great European choral traditions, apparently were not very well acquainted with the directing stick. If pictures of these times show the cantor using a stick, then it most likely was used as a teaching device or it may even have been used as a disciplinary measure! Perhaps it simply symbolized the director's dignity and authority. If Palestrina had actually directed his papal singers in Rome with a golden stick, then it could be implied that there were as many inherent symbolic values as practical values in this. A musical treatise of the sixteenth century speaks about "using the rod on the singers standing close by!" A further quote states that "a skillful cantor shrinks from this practice" (Schuenermann). Only with the origin of modern measures and time signatures in the field of classical instrumental music did time-beating with a baton as we know it today come into vogue. It is true that J. B. Lully introduced a large stick for disciplining his Parisian operatic orchestras. Historic accounts further report that on one occasion while Lully was pounding the floor with his stick he accidentally wounded his foot, which resulted in blood poisoning and eventual death.

The use of the small baton by a distinguished conductor who stood in front of his own podium facing the choir became a common practice in connection with the triumphant epoch of the Viennese classical music in Europe. This practice of leading a body of players by clear, sharp movements of a small stick was popularized by its enthusiasts at music festivals in the larger musical centers, e.g. J. F. Mosel in Berlin (ca. 1790), Ludwig von Hessen in Darmstadt (1801), J. F. Mosel in Vienna (1812), C. M. von Weber in Prague (1814) and Dresden (1817), L. Spohr in Frankfurt a.Main (1817) and London (1819), F. Mendelssohn in Leipzig (1835) and so on. Today choral directors are divided on the issue of whether or not to use a baton in choral directing. The use of the baton will remain indispensable for contemporary instrumental conducting, even though some open-minded contemporary conductors like the late Herman Scherchen dispensed with it entirely. If one is to direct a work which employs both choir and orchestra, one should decide upon the proportion of choral and instrumental participation. Where the program called for singers and instrumentalists the author has directed the choir without and the orchestra with a baton, and in works where both choir and orchestra performed the baton was used or dispensed with according to the particular situation or need.

Some choral directors feel that the so-called "born" choir directors find it exceedingly difficult or even impossible to master the forms and techniques of instrumental conducting. In view of the widespread notion that conducting cannot be taught or learned, let it be emphatically stated that a good conducting technique can be developed to a high degree by anyone who is willing to concentrate and practice. Even the cultivation of the proper basic body posture as required for conducting is of decisive importance here. It should be the same posture (stance) as one would look for in a singer (See A I, p. 2 ff.). In contrast to various other concepts which are commonly held, the author does not believe that the choir director should stand before his choir with a straight, "locked leg" position nor should he adopt an entirely informal "at ease" position. The example of the choir director's stance should be of help to the singers, for it is here in particular that "a poor example spoils good manners!" In assuming a stance with slightly separated feet in which the knees are free of any rigidity, the choir director possesses the sturdy footing which he needs to face and catch the stream of sound waves from the choir and to form and shape these sounds into an artistic result. He has to stand in such a way that he can work with the entire choir! The stance should be as firm and at the same time as relaxed and mobile as he is capable of assuming. Not every choir director brings with him an erect, alert, bile, and "relaxed to the fingertips" posture. Such a posture can, be developed to a high degree.

indispensable preparatory training for the choir is the use of rhythmic body movement exercises outlined in Chapters VI and VII. These exercises in particular should be worked through and developed in connection with choral conducting classes.

As special loosening-up exercises the following are helpful to the choir director: letting the arms fall from a stretched-out-sideways and upward extended position; letting the right or left forearm fall and vice versa; swinging the arms loosely in a floppy manner by turning right and left from the waist; all types of arm, head, shoulder, and hip rolling; arm and leg swinging; clapping the hands together behind the back; forward and backward trunk bending; turning and twisting with loosely hanging arms; running and jumping exercises. As preliminary exercises drawn from everyday activities the director may go through motions of bell rope pulling whereby one imagines the bells to be of various sizes and operated alternately with the right and left hands as well as with both hands simultaneously, the larger movements being supported with action from the waist and hips. Going through the motions of a blacksmith or a carpenter at work is a good conditioning exercise for the director. The iron in the fire can be handled with the right and left hand in turn while the hammer is swung with the other hand. This exercise prepares the director for the work of performing different movements with each arm. However, all these exercises are of little help if the student does not know how to fully relax his entire nervous system to the extent that all conducting movements unfold and proceed from this inner state of poise and relaxation.

The initial body stance of the choir director should suggest a readiness for the onset of the music and should awaken within the choir and the director himself a readiness to sing. By consciously assuming a certain kind of stance the choir director can influence the singers to assume the same kind of stance. The director then lets his eyes move from one side of the choir to the other to establish rapport with each singer. Meanwhile the singers assume the necessary singing position and the director can by a light gesture (if possible with the eyes alone) correct the position or posture of the singers where necessary. Only when the position or stance of each singer indicates a readiness to sing and only when the attention is completely focused in the direction of the director, and only when rapport between singers and director has been well established through eye contact, does the director raise his arms to conduct. With shoulders relaxed, the elbows are raised slightly sideways, the hands are held at chest level about 1½ times the width of a hand away from the body. The hands do not quite form a continuous straight line with

118

the forearm, but are raised at a slight angle and should appear as if they are in the process of releasing some muscular tension. Normally the hand is slightly opened and the position of the fingers should be as natural in appearance as possible, the fingertips should not be pressed together, and the back of the hand should face upward. Deviations from this normal position of the hands will be necessary in some instances, as for example in conducting a very large choir, when giving sharply accented entries. If the choir director is quite short in stature, he will have to raise his hands higher than the normal position. The opposite would hold true in the case of the taller-than-average director. A sharp and most precise entry can be delivered by placing the tip of the forefinger on the top of the thumb and forming a circular or oval closed formation, while a soft, flowing entry can best be indicated by slightly opening the hand with palms facing outward, but drawn close to the body. By raising the hands from the normal starting position the attention of the choir is heightened. By his own example the director imparts to the choir the necessary composure, self-confidence, and alertness. Every trace of nervousness, distraction, uncertainty and lack of preparation and purpose on the part of the director can have devastating results at this critical moment. Any unnecessary movements, any putting on of airs, is to be avoided.

It is of decisive importance for a good *attack* as well as for the successful continuity of the song that the choir director, through his body stance, his facial expression, and by the gesture of his hands convincingly transmits to the singers the basic mood or character of the work — which presupposes of course that the mood and meaning of the work has first come alive within him and is reflected in his own bodily deportment. Occasionally this process can be supported by a gesture or a whispered instruction. Even as the director walks up to face the choir he must be so immersed in the spirit of the work and have such a grasp of the details and exact nature of the attack that the basic character of the work is immediately and directly transmitted to the choir. He should not have to preoccupy himself with irrelevant details when he faces the choir. At the precise moment when concentration of the choir is at its keenest and at the point where the spirit of the work is unmistakably reflected by the singers (during which, incidentally, the reaction and rapport with the audience may be of no small significance), the director gives his initial beat. He must be careful to strike the "right" moment, for the attack can follow too early or too late and create a devastating effect on the music to follow. So, by the manner in which the director appears before his choir and in which he gives his cue he has either won or lost the effectiveness of the first half of his particular assignment.

The attack must not be delivered like a pistol shot but must be carefully prepared in keeping with the time signature and relative strength of the starting note. The attack requires its own kind of preparation. This occurs with the initial beat which moves directly into the beat on which the music starts. The beat most commonly employed as a preparatory beat is the beat in the measure which immediately precedes the note on which the music begins. If, for example, a song in 3/4 time begins on the first beat, the third beat in the measure would be employed as a preparatory beat or if a song in 4/4 time begins on the fourth beat, then the third beat is used as a preparatory beat for the attack of the song. The preparatory movement has an "upbeatish" character and must be given with absolute clarity. To practice this upward preparatory motion the conducting student should adhere closely to the conducting patterns, i.e. practicing the preliminary beats exactly in accordance with the directional lines in the pattern (See Fig. 27). Later he may modify the preparatory beat toward a more lateral or upward direction, depending on whether the music begins on the upbeat or the downbeat. To simplify any situation where an initial beat is required one could substitute the sweeping preparatory beat by a downward cutoff movement. However, this might easily lead to a schematic and mechanical treatment of the music. The proper execution of the initial beat is decisive for the proper launching and ongoing movement of the music for the following reasons:

(1) It *heightens the attention* of the choir to a maximum just before the actual singing commences and it indicates the command to start;

(2) in a slower tempo it unifies the choir through *simultaneous inhalation*, resulting in a more secure and more precise attack;

(3) it helps to give a clear *indication of the tempo* of the song.

In a song with a very fast tempo it would seem risky to let the initial beat also indicate the inhalation of breath. This would only result in a feverish snatching for breath, and would not allow time for a proper breath or a clean resilient attack. In such cases the singers should inhale before the cue beat, a process which can be regulated by a supporting gesture from the conductor. This gesture can be significant in unifying the choir, putting the singers at ease and at the same time heightening the concentration of the choir. Many directors reject this unified breathing before an attack, particularly because of an inability to negotiate this somewhat complex procedure, and partly because they feel convinced that such "prebreathing" can lead to cramped choral breathing. They assume that a sufficient amount of breath is always available for such quick attacks. By refusing to draw attention to the breathing process it is assumed that attacks will be relaxed and resilient. Now it is true that singers generally inhale far too much air, but without a conscious breath control it would appear that that which is regarded as a relaxed attack is in reality a flabby, indecisive attack. Relaxation in singing is not to be practiced for its own sake but as a sound physical basis for realizing and fulfilling the demands of the larger spans of tension in the music itself.

120

The person who approaches his work with a good knowledge of his craft, manual dexterity, and some caution will, by the use of this corporate breathing in preparation for an attack, gain an unusual advantage. In fact, it is questionable whether a good attack could be attained by any other means. (Compare with A III, p. 43 ff.) Through such a conscious corporate breath the choir director is assured that the choir is prepared for the attack — he knows that the bow is drawn and is ready to shoot the musical arrow. The director knows in advance whether the attack is going to "click" and whether or not the forthcoming tone is going to be sung with "abandonment." Since the attack is mutually prepared with his choir he can add or subtract from the energy and intensity of the choir in the moment preceding the attack as necessary.

If the attack does not occur on the main part of the beat but on the "and" as in Arnold Mendelssohn's "Thanksgiving Motet" (Augsburg 1223) (written in 2/4 time and begins on the second half of the second beat), the beat should come on "one" and the choir would come in on the rebound of the second beat. The precise moment of the attack can be indicated by a little extra lift of the hand on the "and" of two, or by dividing the second beat and cueing the choir in on the second of the divided beats, or he may help the choir by a slight movement of the head or glance of the eye. One could also beat two eighth beats in a straight down and up fashion whereby the choir would commence on the up stroke which corresponds to the end of two as for example in the anthem "All Lands and Peoples," by Austin Lovelace (Augsburg 1397).

In any case, it implies all movements must be discreet, meaningful, technically secure and precise. The far too prevalent haphazard moving about of the arms and any movements which resemble such activities as hanging clothes on a clothesline, catching mosquitoes, pumping up a tire, or however ironically one would wish to describe such directing, must certainly be eliminated in choral conducting.

The attack itself always requires a clear downward movement. If the attack occurs on the full part of the upbeat, the choir begins to sing on the rebound of that beat immediately following the downward movement. Meanwhile the director should keep his eyes on the entire choir. He should pay particular attention to the section which has the most difficult notes to sing, and which might require the most assistance.

The beat patterns should at first be strictly adhered to by the prospective choir director, and he should practice these faithfully (Figure 27 a/i). Even though these patterns are variously illustrated in different books on conducting, certain basic forms have nevertheless emerged which must be regarded as basic and essential. These basic forms are represented in the following figures (certain modifications naturally arise in actual practice).

121

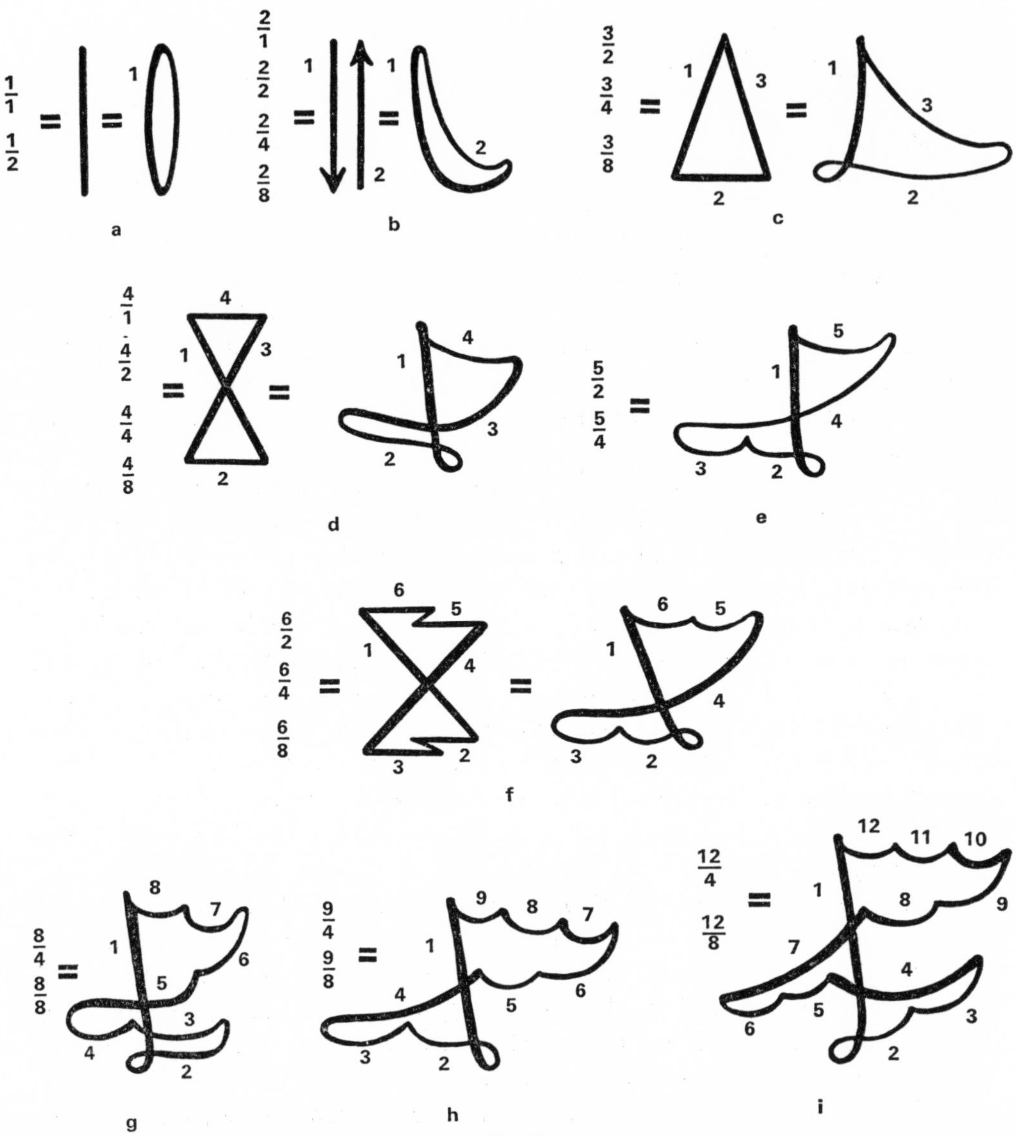

Fig. 27

The practice of the basic beat patterns should be preceded by a clear mental picture of the basic scheme (Fig. 27 a-e). The figures that follow illustrate the counterbalance or interception of the vertical movement of the beat (following the manner of orchestral conducting) with a horizontal movement (following the typical choral conducting practices). The downward beat must rebound, but in the sudden change of direction sharp corners must be avoided. The second, heaviest beat in 3/4 time should be beat toward the outside and not toward the inside as is frequently practiced. The reason for this is simply that the outward motion on the second beat conforms better with the physiology of the body and can be more readily seen

122

and followed by the choir than the other process. The same principle applies also to the third beat in a 4/4 time pattern. The stressed beat is represented in the diagrams by a thicker line.

For practicing these patterns one should choose folk songs in the various time signatures. To begin with one should use songs beginning on the beat. The song is hummed or sung to the beating of the time pattern. The song is practiced by conducting with the right, then the left arm, and finally with both arms. One should strive to maintain a very steady, even beat, particularly at the end of the phrases and during the rests. The beginning of new phrases can be indicated by an expansion of the movement, by a nod of the head, or with the eyes. At this point the novice is often quite helpless. To begin with, the beat patterns should be conducted as wide, swinging movements, but eventually these movements should be reduced to a carefully measured, smaller format. One should, as a matter of pedagogical principle, always proceed from the larger movements which encompass the full body dimensions to the very small movements, and not vice versa.

The first strong beat of each new measure must always be represented by a clear, downward movement. This principle is so self-evident that it ought to become second nature to the director, yet for many students of conducting it presents difficulties. As a preliminary exercise one might pull an imaginary bell rope and similar life-related activities which involve a downward pull (See A VIII, p. 118 ff.). To attain the precise format for duple time, one might draw an imaginary inverted walking cane in the air. To achieve close connection between tone and hand movement and to stimulate in the hand the necessary feeling of leading or controlling the tone, the student might pull an imaginary bell rope which moves the bells and produces a tone. At this point he should actively imagine that he "pulls" tones with each new pull of the bell rope. Other exercises of this nature could also be employed. The awareness of and feeling for tonal vibrations in the hand should be developed and maintained through every directional movement in each time pattern. The choir director must keep his hand close to the tone, so to speak, as if he were spinning a thread of tone, while holding it in his hand. The beat patterns can be performed altogether correctly and yet fail to evoke a good tonal response from the choir. In other words, the director conducts "beyond" the choir. The conducting motions of the director and the musical movement within the choir should mesh like gears. Many beginners have difficulty in achieving this kind of rapport. One can best help these people by introducing such concepts as pulling, stretching, spinning, catching, striking, and carrying tones. Naturally it is difficult with only private practice and without the opportunity of working with a group to develop conducting facility. It would therefore be best to assemble ten or fifteen students of conducting and engage a teacher to instruct them. The students themselves constitute the experimental choir which could be directed by each student in turn.

It would be helpful for such a class of conducting students to work through and expand as much as possible the exercises given in the preceding two chapters on body movement and rhythmic training. The rhythmic exercises of the Dalcroze school of eurythmics are particularly recommended. In any case one should always take advantage of any available activities which would be of positive and practical value. For example, the class may form a circle and then walk according to various meters. Meters could be emphasized by clapping or by varying the strength (stress) of the steps while walking, stopping at a given sign from the director and resuming the marching after a predetermined pause. The group could also walk and conduct while singing a song; the director may play pieces of different time signatures on the piano while the class identifies and conducts the appropriate beat patterns, responding instantly by changing to the right pattern whenever the director changes the song or meter. The author has observed how even the "hard core" cases in a conducting class finally respond through such an approach.

The concept of and feeling for the choric element can be supported and heightened by improvisational part singing. In conducting choral clinics and other conducting sessions, the author has successfully utilized multi-voiced improvisations to stimulate creativity among the participants and to free their faculties. These improvisations may be approached as follows: the class invents a suitable four or eight measure tune which is sung by several singers as a repeated "ostinato" while the rest of the singers improvise free contrapuntal parts above it. This may be sung to a one-tone syllable whereas the "ostinato" is sung to a dark, well-sustained syllable which sets it apart tonally from the contrapuntal parts above it. A conducting student directs such an improvisation, and to keep creativity alive, and to authenticate his own conducting, he may greatly vary the intensity, size, and character of his movements. (One may not want to caricaturize a well-known tune in this manner.)

According to the art and manner of his conducting, the student has the opportunity to stimulate, evoke, and guide the improvisational activity in his choir. This allows him to express himself freely in his movements and to test the effectiveness of his conducting gestures. These exercises also serve to further strengthen the feeling of "carrying" the tone.

The conducting beats are normally performed at chest level, and not at head or waist level. That most choir directors direct too high is due to nervousness or stiffness. The movements should normally not be expansive or sweeping, for the smaller and more economical the conducting motions are, the more attentive and alert the choir will be. Smaller motions also mean an economy of energy for the director. When working with an untrained or newly formed choir and when rehearsing a new work, the director will have to resort to larger movements. The conductor should economize his movements according to the extent to which the singers are vocally in rapport with each other and with the work. This applies in particular to the public performance of the work. A well-disciplined chamber choir can be directed with the eyes alone. In a larger performance where larger bodies of performers (singers, soloists, orchestra) have rehearsed together for only a very brief period prior to the performance, the director will frequently have to resort to large movements and gestures to draw out the optimum response. Generally speaking, the variation of the height and size of the conducting movements from the so-called normal level will be influenced to a large extent by the physique or physical build of the director, by the size and attention of the choir, by the level of difficulty and familiarity of the work, and by the tempo and dynamic level of the music.

The scheme of the various beat patterns may be modified in a variety of ways, and with further practice and experience each conductor will round out or tone down the basic patterns to a personal style. He should, however, conduct in such a way that the basic directions will always be clearly recognizable. The character of the music as well as the time in which it is written will influence the form and style of his movements. For example, in certain pronounced dance rhythms one would use sharply outlined patterns, while in a selection in an andante movement one would "lean into the beats" and in a free-flowing polyphonic piece one would modify or change the beat patterns to an almost fluid-like movement or pattern the entire phrase by an appropriate rising and falling movement.

Finally, the personal style of the individual composers and the prevalent style of a given era will significantly influence the conducting motions; the music of Handel feels different to conduct than the music of Palestrina which conducts itself, so to speak, while the music of the Renaissance feels different from a work of the Late Baroque or Romantic Era. Attempts have been made to represent the style of great composers in terms of curves of melodic motion. One could therefore postulate the theory that wherever the curves or motions of the conductor coincide with the curve of motion of the composer the result should be a satisfactory interpretation, particularly where both the composer and the interpreter have similar musical temperaments.

The movements of a conductor should not be ungainly as this might irritate the singers, nor should they be so "beautiful" as to evoke astonishment from singers and audience. All conducting motions must first of all be functional, i.e. they must serve the musical work.

The various beat patterns and all other conducting motions should be learned and practiced with both hands. Occasionally one meets a director

125

who believes in conducting with one hand only. This has the effect of "laming" the side of the inactive hand and this inertness of one side of the body greatly minimizes the animation and vitality of the choir. This also minimizes the director's control over the singers. The director should never hold the book in one hand and direct with the other because this again greatly reduces his effectiveness with the choir. If he doesn't have the score memorized, he should use a music stand. In advanced conducting practice the right hand is generally used to keep time, while the left hand remains free to mold the dynamics, to suggest accents, and for indicating every variety of shading. For this reason the right hand has been called the time-beating hand and the left hand the hand of the heart (i.e. the hand that controls those aspects of music which affect the feelings and emotions).

Since music has been conceived of and is identified with motion (See A VI, p. 78 ff.), the controlling gestures must also be in continuous motion. Each tone has its particular affinity for another note, and so the hand which guides the tone must never become inert. It must beat against the director's most primitive musical instinct to arrest motion in the process of music making. This applies above all to long notes, longer rests, fermatas, and cadences. At such points the knowledgeable and sensitive director will either make an expanded horizontal movement or a longer sustained vertical upward gesture. His hands should never come to a halt while the music is still sounding. This contradicts the activity of singing as a continuous inhalation and exhalation process, and the choir director who really identifies himself with this rhythmic wave will, if he resorts to "static motions," have the feeling that he is stemming the tide of the musical stream of sound. On the final chord it is best to sustain the sound with an upward movement of his hands. This suggests to the choir that the tone must be kept alive right to the end and the pulling, sustaining gesture prevents the choir from losing pitch on the final note. When the moment has come when the director wishes to cut off the music, the hands should have arrived to a height where they are clearly visible to all the singers.

In his conducting movements the director can at least attempt to approach the rhythm and movement of the dance, which is the most primitive form of all arts based on motion. Since music also belongs to the movement or motion arts the director should see his role as one in which he moves on behalf of the singers, who, because of their fixed position, could be thought of as "dancers on the spot." Next to moving, shaping and guiding the music, his conducting motions should also help to stimulate a sense of freedom and fluency within the choir. If a director uses only one kind of movement, or if he remains stuck with Lilliputian movements, the singers will become bored and the music will lose its resonance and flow.

126

The music should completely fill and inspire the conductor while he conducts. He should always anticipate the sound of the music, constantly keep an ideal tonal image before him, and try to realize this concept with the actual sound from his singers. He must continually think along with the music and always be slightly ahead of the choir in the giving of signals and of gestures; a director's movements should never have to follow the choir.

The time signature in modern notation is represented by a dividing line: 4/4, 6/8, in which the numerator indicates the number of beats per measure which the choir director must beat, i.e. 4/4 time — 4 beats; 6/8 time — 6 beats. It is wise that the conducting student at the outset of his training, adheres to this rule, particularly when studying a new work. In the process of his musical development he will deviate more and more from this mechanical treatment and simplify the conducting figures. In fast-moving music one might conduct only the stronger beats and would, for example, indicate only one beat in a fast 2/4 or 3/4 and only two beats in a fast 4/4 or 6/4.

It must be kept in mind, however, that in reducing 4/4 music to a two-beat pattern there will be the tendency to beat what was originally the third beat of the 4/4 pattern with the same degree of accentuation as the first beat. This must also be considered by amateur choir directors who do not follow a prescribed 4/4 beat pattern, but conduct most of their music in an up-and-down two-beat pattern. Such conductors can preserve the 4/4 meter in the music if they will beat the first beat deeper and heavier than the third beat. In this type of conducting it is always better to beat a secure and convincing duple beat than to flutter about with an insecure, poorly mastered 4/4 beat. Certain types of music in 6/4 can also be conducted in 3/4 patterns, i.e. 2 x 3/4 per measure (Example 36) and a 5/4 measure may be divided into one 3/4 plus one 2/4 beat pattern.

The conducting instructor will enlarge upon the suggestions given and with further illustrations and examples he can stimulate the pedagogical processes of teaching this to his students. The student who wishes to acquire the conducting techniques through self-study should begin with the most elementary songs. Children's songs are particularly commendable for such practice. Not only are these songs simple, but their gentle, swinging, cradle-like rhythms can help the student director to catch the concept of pulling and spinning tones and help him more quickly to gain the contact between the hand and tone, this being a difficult accomplishment for the beginning conducting student in particular.

In children's songs the rhythm moves regularly and uninterruptedly through the entire piece, without being halted at the end of phrases by pauses or fermatas.

The one-beat pattern is less frequently applied. A good example where such a pattern could be applied is the *allegro molto* section of p. 10 in Ralph Vaughan Williams' "O Clap Your Hands."

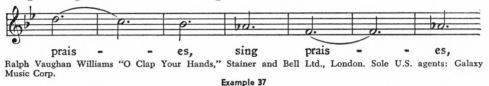

prais - - es, sing prais - es,

Ralph Vaughan Williams "O Clap Your Hands," Stainer and Bell Ltd., London. Sole U.S. agents: Galaxy Music Corp.

Example 37

The beat patterns should be smooth and rolling — elliptical shaped rather than too sharp and angular. At measures 5 and 6 the left hand may be used to sustain the B♭ major chord which is held for two measures, while the right hand continues to beat the one-beat pattern. To achieve a unified articulation and flow of words in all the voice parts the director may mouth the text during singing.

For practicing the duple beat pattern the following Bohemian spiritual folk song represents a good example.

Let our glad-ness know no end, Al - le - lu. - ia! Un-to earth did

Christ de- scend, Al - le - lu - ia! On this day God gave____ us

Christ, his Son, to save____ us, Gave us Christ, his Son, to save us.

Example 38

The beat pattern to be used here is Fig. 27 (b). The "blind" upbeat on two serves as the preliminary beat to the downbeat on one, on which the song begins. This is preceded of course by the "blind" preliminary upbeat on two. The director should strive to communicate to the singers the correct tempo and to have them take a breath during this preliminary beat. The hand motion should clearly express the musical motion in the first two measures. Each two notes in the first three beats receives one beat. The even, lilting motion which is established in these two measures should be maintained for the length of the entire stanza. There are no ritards or fermatas at the cadential points to stem the rhythmic flow. At the beginning of new phrases the pattern may be lengthened and heightened somewhat. The director can also give added clarity to the beginning of a new phrase or section by a light movement of the head, perhaps even with his upper body, or with his eyes and facial expression.

The release of the song on the last note is best achieved by conducting through the half note on "us" and then cutting off the "s" by a sharp down-

128

beat and rebound. This simple short tune hardly calls for the use of the hands to visually illustrate and portray the musical flow of the song. It is too elemental and straightforward for that. A chorale tune which would serve as a good example to practice conducting in duple time is the Christmas hymn "All my heart this night rejoices" (No. 26, SBH). It should be conducted in *alla breve* form. The second measure is conducted in a triple beat pattern, but the following measures — to the end of the first phrase — should be conducted in duple time. From the repertoire of choral music for mixed choirs, Johannes Riedel's four-voice setting of "O come and mourn with me awhile" by G. B. Pergolesi (Augsburg 1327) would serve as a good example for conducting in duple time. The simple vocal form and the *alla breve* notation allows this to be conducted much like the previous example. The quarter note after the dotted half at measure 20 could be indicated by sub-dividing the beat on two. On the final note it would be best to beat only the *one* and then to draw out the tone as long as required in the manner described earlier by a stronger and quicker rebound. Numerous English madrigals by Bennett, Morley, Weelkes, and others could serve as excellent examples of music in 2/2 time. (See A VIII, p. 137 ff.)

For practicing the *triple beat pattern* the following Swabian folk song might be used:

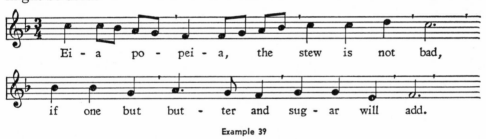

Example 39

Here one could apply Fig. 27c. The attack is to be given as in the examples in duple time, but with the third beat being the "blind" preparatory beat. The even and consistent movement of the music is conducted with both hands. On the last two notes of the first phrase, the left hand should be used in the form of a gesture to support and sustain the tone for the dotted half note values. At this point the right hand should beat through the triple pattern in regular fashion; on the downbeat of the next phrase the left hand should unhesitatingly join in.

The beat patterns reflect the particular shape and flow of the melodic line. For example, the first beats in the first two measures could be beat with a little more weight and depth while the second and third beats on the eighth notes that follow could be conducted with as much lightness and crispness as possible. The three successive quarter notes in the third measure should be conducted with a uniform beat, and the dotted half note at the end of the first line could be conducted with a more horizontal and widely expanded second beat to help sustain the note and maintain the alertness and concentration of the choir. A good example of a sacred song in triple time is the tune *Lasst uns erfreuen* to Paul Strodach's hymn text "Now let the vault of heaven resound" (No. 103, SBH). Here, too, the conducting motions should be quite uniform. At the same time the conductor must do justice to the joyous and triumphant character of this Easter hymn by employing an elastic, lilting beat. The cadences should be well supported and the beginnings of new phrases should always be approached with firmness and energy. On the final note the rebound of the last beat must move in an upward direction to sustain the tonal vitality and to prevent loss of intonation in the choir.

Madrigals in triple time furnish good material for practicing the triple beat pattern, e.g. the 3/4 "fa-la-la" refrain in Morley's "Now Is the Month of Maying." The first three quarter notes in the first measure again are conducted quite uniformly, but then the pattern of relative stress is modified to express the carefree dance-like character of this delightful refrain.

Among the many sacred choral compositions one might select "Jesu, Joy of Man's Desiring." The preparatory upbeat is indicated as described earlier even though the choral parts are preceded by a longer instrumental prelude which sets the tempo and flow of the piece. Here, too, the outward-swinging second beat of the triple-beat pattern is decisive in lending transparency, clarity, and flow to the choral parts. In the next to the last measures of the last two lines, the soprano voice has a quarter note followed by a half note. This change of rhythm and accent should be clearly shown by accenting the second beat and then widening the motion on the second and third beats to keep the tone alive and sustained.

The four-beat pattern can be practiced with the familiar French Canadian folk song "Alouette" (p. 46, *Let's All Sing*).

Example 40

130

The beat pattern in Figure 27d is used here. The beats should be somewhat bouncy and dance-like in character and should be conducted in a consistent manner throughout. In the last measure at *Fine,* the fourth beat need not be conducted, but on the third beat the hands should rebound in an upward direction, hold the tone for the duration of the fourth beat, and then make the final cutoff. At this point one might insert the tune "Neander" with the text "Open now thy gates of beauty" (No. 187, SBH). The four-beat pattern should be conducted with strong, resilient beats. The fourth beat on the final note should be brought down in preparation for the cutoff. As an example of a multivoiced a cappella composition one could make use of Orlando di Lasso's "Bon jour mon coeur" (Good-day, my heart) (p. 22, *European Madrigals).* This song can be conducted with the regular 4/4 beat pattern. The left hand can help prevent the pitch from sagging at the phrase endings. New phrases should be commenced with clear and intensive preparatory beats. In the second to the last measure special attention should be given to the syncopated alto part — not only because the rhythm is different from the other parts but also because it contains the leading tone (F♯) which moves into the tonic of the final chord. The fourth beat on this F♯ should be conducted with a stronger and deeper beat than usual. It is understood of course that the director faces the alto singers and gives all his attention to them during this measure. After advanced practice the conducting techniques could be modified so that the half-note sections could be conducted in 2/2 time. The 4/4 pattern may be used with phrases which begin on the second or fourth quarter note beat.

Heinrich Schuetz's "Jesus, our Lord and Savior" from the *St. Luke Passion* (No. 1438, Augsburg) is an example of short, sacred choral composition which could be used as a practice piece for conducting. The normal 4/4 beat pattern can again be used throughout with some modifications here and there.

Even on the successive entries "our Lord" and "our King forever" which commence on the second part of the beat, the pattern does not have to be altered from its basic format, although it should assume somewhat of a lilting, bouncy character wherever the note values are shorter than quarter notes. In the second to the last measure of the piece the right hand should lead the soprano through the syncopated quarter and half note rhythm while the left hand assists the tenors in their dotted quarter and two sixteenth notes. The final note (whole note) may be conducted through to four and then sustained *ad libitum* until the director wishes to cut off the sound.

The seldom used five-beat pattern can be practiced with the following excerpt from Benjamin Britten's *A Ceremony of Carols.*

Be-hold, a sil-ly ten-der babe, in freez-ing win-ter night, In

home-ly man-ger trem-bling lies A-las, a-pi-teous sight.

Example 41

Figure 27f is used here and the preliminary beat is conducted as described earlier. The beat pattern should be kept small and graceful. The student will need to practice until he is able to conduct this pattern in a light, playful manner while giving real impetus and direction to the melodic flow. Constant practice of singing while conducting is helpful and necessary for the conducting student. The first and third beats should be conducted with the necessary pull and depth while the beats in between should merely obtain a light, wave-like impetus.

A good hymn to use for practicing the six-beat pattern is "Lift up your heads, ye mighty gates" (No. 8, SBH, second tune). The J. S. Bach setting of *In dulci jubilo* could also be useful in cultivating a flowing 6/4 beat. While studying this four-part setting the student should also mentally sing the tune in the tenor. In this particular setting Bach gives the bass part some active eighth note movement at points where the tune and other parts have a half note. Naturally, the conducting student should direct his attention to the basses at this point and attempt with his gestures to bring these actively moving notes into greater prominence. In practice one would seldom conduct the six-beat pattern in a mechanical way or adhere slavishly to its format. The six-beat measure can be divided and organized in a variety of ways: into two 3/4 patterns; three 2/4 patterns; three 1/2 patterns; one 3/2 pattern in two beats, each of which contains a dotted half note. Certain 6/4 patterns can also be conducted with a four-beat pattern, using large, rather heavy motions for the first and fourth beats, and small, light beats for the second and sixth beats whereby the heavy beats receive the value of two quarter notes and the light beats one note each.

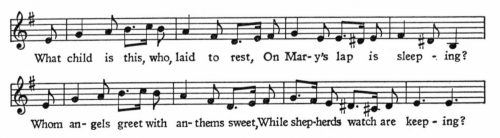

What child is this, who, laid to rest, On Mar-y's lap is sleep-ing?

Whom an-gels greet with an-thems sweet, While shep-herds watch are keep-ing?

Example 42

132

4/4 pattern	1	2	3	4
6/4 measure	(12)	3	(45)	6.

The choice of beat patterns should be determined by the melodic and harmonic structure, the rhythmic structure, the relationship of varying degrees of musical tensions within the piece, and finally by the degree of musical comprehension the choir has attained in connection with the music at hand.

(For further practice material see examples 46, 47, 48, 49, 51 and the instructions given.)

In polyphonic choral settings which are not based on a cantus firmus but where the voice parts are of equal importance, the regular beat patterns are inadequate. These are works in which the melodic treatment of the individual words and imitative treatment of the voice parts become prominent structural devices, particularly in all motet-like settings. Here the director must single out and direct specifically those voice parts which constitute the basic rhythmic and melodic structural elements of the music. The selection and joining together of these parts constitutes the conducting line. This conducting line (*Dirigierstimme*) is the red ribbon by means of which the director weaves and holds together, so to speak, the entire composition. Sometimes the director will give his close attention to selected imitative passages, at other times the rhythmic entities or the word accents. The combinations of the various areas of emphasis constitute the "conducting line." Here he must let his hands express the melodic line or let them follow the word accent, just as he has practiced in conducting an unharmonized melody. Frequently he may, even in motets and motet-like works, conduct longer passages in regular beat patterns. The director should carefully plan and thoroughly practice the various combinations and possibilities of conducting.

Examples of compositions where the use of a regular beat pattern is not adequate for their proper rendition are some settings of Heinrich Schuetz's metrical versions of the 150 Psalms, e.g. Psalm 57, "Have mercy now my God and Lord" (No. 57 in Henry Drinker's edition of *Schuetz's 150 Psalms*, Association of American Choruses, Choral Series No. 188). Here it is best to conduct the rhythm of the text according to its natural word accent. The syllables with half notes receive a strong half note beat while the syllables with quarter and eighth notes could be conveniently conducted in lighter quarter note beats.

The back-and-forth path of a conducting line is illustrated in a simple form in such two-part canons as Carl Schalk's setting of "Now sing we, now rejoice" (p. 8, *Two Part Canons*, 98-1764, Concordia Publishing House). The melodic high points are shifted from one voice to another in a regular recurring pattern, and so the conductor, in following the resultant conducting line, must address himself back and forth accordingly between the two voice

133

parts. The four-part introduction to Heinrich Schuetz's *St. Luke Passion*, edited by Maynard Klein (No. 16337, Boosey and Hawkes), is a good illustration of how the director can change freely from half note to quarter note beats as he follows the "conducting line." The motions of the director must follow the main word stresses and accents but at the same time he must always be ready to address himself to the various imitative parts of the different sections (as in measures 28-35).

In addition to this flexible manner of conducting, the return to regular beat patterns will always be necessary at various times in a given song. In doing so, two possibilities of directing a choral piece are combined. Thomas Weelkes' five-part madrigal "In Pride of May" (p. 61, *European Madrigals*) is an illustration of this. In the first twenty-four measures the director could most certainly use the regular 4/4 beat pattern (Fig. 27a), and from measures twenty-five to twenty-eight he could use the basic beat pattern. In the opening imitative parts a more intensive manner of communicating and bringing in the various parts through clear signs and gestures should be employed. The simpler entries which follow on the text "the fields are gay, the birds do sing" could be directed with a regular 4/4 beat pattern, while the "fa-la-la" section should be conducted with shorter, lighter, and bouncier beats. The following "so nature would that all things" could again be conducted with precise directions for imitative entries as suggested for the opening measures of the madrigal. The four measures in triple rhythm are conducted with a clean-cut three-beat pattern. The final measures of the madrigal should be conducted in strong, clear beats while the syncopated rhythm of the soprano in the second to the last measure should be "caught up" by a vigorous rebound from the second and the fourth beat of the measure. In the following example taken from the closing chorus of Heinrich Schuetz's setting of the *St. John Passion*, the path of the conducting line is illustrated by the dotted line.

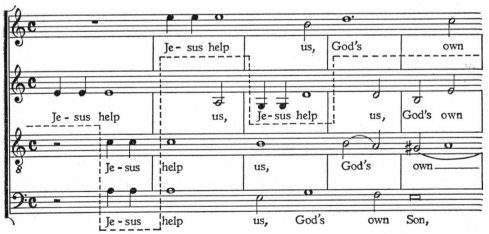

From *The Passion of Our Lord Jesus Christ According to the Gospel of St. John*, Heinrich Schuetz, edited Maynard Klein. Boosey & Hawkes, Inc., New York.

Example 43

The change of meter within a musical composition requires particularly clear and decisive conducting motions. Since some of the more recent editions of the vocal music of the sixteenth and seventeenth centuries use short lines between staffs instead of regular bar lines, a brief, temporary change of meter is usually somewhat difficult to recognize from this system of short measure lines. Such instances do not call for a change of time signature in the same way as is called for in much of our contemporary music, but simply a tentative alteration of the conducting pattern. The music of this era should not be tied up into separate little packages by rigid or mechanical changes of beat patterns.

The director, in using different modern beat patterns to indicate the temporary metrical changes of the music, should be careful not to impose such patterns mechanically, but let the characteristic movement and flow of the music be the guide. The singers should be able to negotiate the measures with the change of beat patterns in terms of the former or basic patterns, and so make a smooth transition back into the former pattern. If the choir is alert and responsive, the director may, in accordance with the historical example of the old cantors, retain the same regular down-and-up movement in the case of a transition through a triple beat passage from a duple beat movement. This approach gives the music clarity and ease of flow and could prevent it from becoming rigid or even brittle at such metrical transitions.

Such hemiola structures are illustrated in two examples found on p. 74 and p. 80, *European Madrigals*. Even with singers who are not good independent note readers the director may change his conducting patterns (in spite of the fact that the editors have consistently placed bar lines after every two half notes!) to render more clearly the rhythmic nature of these selections. In the first example, "Good health, all gathered here," a four-part setting by Erasmus Widmann, the first six measures could be conducted with a 2/2 or 4/4 beat pattern. The beginning of the second phrase in measure 7, "Be careful, gay," however, offers the possibility of using two 3/4 beat patterns preceded by an upbeat, after which the 4/4 beat is resumed for the rest of the song. Here all voice parts basically move in the same rhythmic pattern. A somewhat different rhythmic movement and structure exists in Heinrich Isaac's setting of "Innsbruck, I Now Must Leave Thee" (p. 74, *European Madrigals*). The basic rhythmic movement is centered in the tune which is in the uppermost voice. The accompanying voices move with the soprano in similar rhythmic and metrical motion. The director must then concentrate on directing the tune, but even here he should be prepared to use different beat patterns than those suggested by the metrical scheme supplied by the editors. A continuous four-beat pattern could be used for the entire song except for the last three measures on the words "scarce will stand," which would be more effective musically if directed with two 3/4 plus one 2/4 beat patterns.

The immediate perception and presentation of meter changes should first of all be thoroughly practiced in connection with folk songs and common hymn tunes like "Es ist ein Ros' entsprungen." (Lo, How a Rose E'er Blooming) Ex. 44. The time signatures have been given by the author to facilitate practice.

In carrying out the exercise according to the suggested time patterns, a precise time-beating technique must be combined with an artistic directing ability. One should not forget to give a preparatory upbeat for the initial entry. In the two 4/4 measures containing a quarter note rest on the third beat, the third beat in the pattern should be utilized as a preparatory beat for the beginning of the next phrase beginning on the fourth beat. The second beat on the word "sprung" at the end of the first line serves the same purpose. The use of the 3/2 beat is in keeping with the melodic structure, the flow as well as the verbal emphasis. The use of the 3/4 beat in the 6/4 measures generally proves to be more helpful than the use of the 6/4 beat. The syncopated second beat in these measures should be sufficiently stressed. The use of the *alla breve* beat for the 4/4 measures might lead to inaccuracy and hurrying of the tempo, and is therefore to be recommended for use with well-trained singing groups only. The final note receives only one downbeat from which the hands move upward in preparation for the cutoff. The left hand, opened with palms facing upward, supports the entries. At the phrase endings it sustains the tone while the right continues to conduct through the beat patterns. All movements must be flowing and as much as possible approach a horizontal direction. The preservation of the basic pulse throughout all the changes of varying beat patterns is of decisive importance.

Es ist ein Ros' entsprungen
Tr., Theodore Baker   M. Praetorius

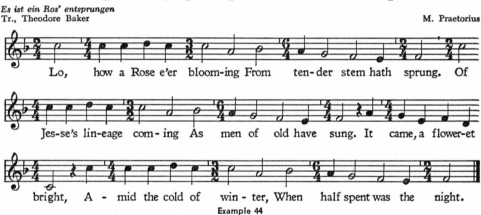

Example 44

The use of various time patterns should not be applied to such tunes in the same way as one would apply them in the type of contemporary music which is based on irregular meters. The motion in such older rhythmic tunes is governed by a steady pulse above which various undulating melodic movements take shape. This musical stream must not be fragmented by the mechanical application of changing beat patterns. Good direction of such music does not depend upon moving smoothly and gracefully from one beautifully worked-out mechanical beat pattern to another, but should be regarded as a proven and effective means to facilitate the directing of traditional music with irregular metrical stress. With this approach in mind these changing patterns can serve as a framework for conducting such music if the gestures and movements of the director are pertinent and meaningful. Otherwise the director's function is reduced to that of a metronome which at best indicates the change from one meter to another.

For further practice in changing from one meter to another the music of Example 49 may be used. (See instructions in B II, p. 164 ff.) For additional examples one could choose dances with a regularly recurring change of meter involving an entire change of body movement with each change of meter. Contemporary choral music makes extensive use of metrical changes to avoid the regularity of the classic meter and also to come much closer in expressing verbal meaning. The student must grasp such changes with decisiveness and intensity.

Copyright Baerenreiter Verlag, Kassel, Germany.

Example 45

138

The final note in a song should not be "beat out" for the full length of the note; only the first note receives a beat which is then sustained on its rebound for the length of the note at which point the cutoff signal is given. The director must conclude his conducting motions and the music with an unequivocally clear cutoff motion. For most directors the release presents a greater problem than the initial beat. Seldom does one see such disgusted faces in conducting classes as when the students are required to indicate clear cutoffs. Beginning students of conducting seem to have the same sensation as the inexperienced car driver who, after bringing his car into motion, does not quite know how to stop the vehicle. While the car is still in full momentum he suddenly brakes or veers off the road into the ditch! There are, no doubt, many effective signals to end a piece of music with clarity and precision. One should arrive at a mutual understanding with one's choir as to the kind of movements which best serve the purpose. In any case it would be wrong to use a horizontal or even a circular motion for a cutoff. The first type (side cutoff motion) is senseless and the second type is inexact. One must therefore literally "strike" off the tone, by lifting the hands to a height from where a vertical cutoff motion is possible. The lifting of the hands also heightens the attention of the singers which is so necessary in maintaining the pitch and vitality of the tone right to the moment when the music ceases. It is important that the rebound from the downward movement has a specific point in space in order to avoid any extraneous movements. The hands must bounce back easily and gently to this point in space. The height from which the cutoff is made and the depth to which the hands fall depend on the tonal strength and size of the choir. The angle of rebound of the hands is determined by the flowing, strongly accented, or dance-like character of the music. In choral music the particular structure of the word presents an added problem to the successful ending of the music, and so the director must take into consideration any peculiarity of pronunciation of the final word. Some kind of extra signal must be given with the cutoff motion to indicate precisely how and when such consonants as *n, t, p, z, s* are to be pronounced.

Since the effectiveness of such detailed signals depends so much on the sensitivity of the choir and its director, one should not try to systematize such hand and finger signals but let them be worked out in keeping with the individuality of the director. What really matters here is that the director give full consideration to particular needs of certain words and that he prevent "frayed" or untidy endings which are caused when individuals or groups of singers continue to hang on to the final note after the cutoff signal has been given. Some singers are slow in their reactions to the conductor's signals. The best results are obtained if the choir achieves a good ensemble sound from a close identity with the music. Such details as the clean and unified articulation of final consonants "come off" by themselves because

139

these technicalities have become an integral and culminative part of the organic flow of sound. Since highly trained choirs and vocal ensembles which have achieved a true ensemble of thought, feeling, and sound naturally negotiate final consonants with greater effectiveness, less trained vocal groups should be given special exercises and assistance in this.

The signifying of a final *m* or *n* by bringing together the thumb and index finger, or by indicating a final *t* with a finger or hand motion seems to be a useful practice for many directors. However, since such signaling can very easily appear artificial and somewhat foreign in relation to regular conducting movements and signaling, it is better to incorporate the signal for the final consonant right into the cutoff signal itself. The author will, for example, have his singers sound the final singing consonant (*m, n* or *ng*) the moment the cutoff beat commences on the rebound, maintaining the sound for the duration of the return of the rebound during which the hands are raised much more slowly of course than when cutting off a nonmusical consonant like *t* or *k*. At the conclusion of this rebound motion another small fingertip motion signaling the termination of the consonant will be necessary. Such final singing consonants are drawn out with the fingers so to speak. The cutoff of such consonants as *b, d, g,* at the end of a song may also commence right at the beginning of the rebound, and are articulated by the choir until the rebound motion comes to a stop. In the case of such consonants the rebound must occur with lightning speed!

By the use of this longer rebound motion to indicate the articulation and release of final consonants at the end of a song a more unified articulation is achieved and a too-sharp or over-articulated *t* or *p* is prevented.

While conducting the choir the director needs to be aware of a great many factors which he must constantly unify into a coordinated function. The beginner who has just emerged as a singer in the choir to the position of director will frequently catch himself singing along with the choir. This is often a reflection of his own insecurity. The director should not, however, sing while directing. He may of course occasionally help the basses, tenors, or altos in smaller inexperienced choirs, or he may be asked to lead in informal singing sessions in the traditional manner. Or he may sing a voice part in a small chamber choir, according to the practice of the old cantors who, while standing in the center of the choir, directed the singers with small, pertinent gestures and so kept the different parts closely unified. In regular professional choral groups, which require the director to face the choir, any singing on the part of the director while conducting can easily interfere with the performance in several ways:

(1) The isolated position of the director in relation to the choir prevents him from

blending his voice with the total choral sound. The listener hears the director's voice as a separate source of sound production and therefore it has a disrupting effect.

(2) Singing along with the choir prevents the director from blending his voice with changing tessituras at various points within the music.

(3) Most serious of all, the director's own singing prevents him from really hearing what the choir is doing. This means that he is not able to guide and shape the tonal forces of the choir, and consequently he loses musical control over his choir.

On the other hand, it can be a great help to the choir if the director occasionally mouths the words. In the singing of memorized or partially memorized pieces, this mouthing of the words can be a welcome reminder to the singers, and for the purpose of clear diction such soundless articulation can be a good incentive for the choir to respond to the efforts of the director with rich, resonant, cleanly articulated sounds. A choir should be so alert that it appears "to hang on the lips" of the director, proverbially speaking.

Directing from memory has become a universal practice since the astonishing memory feats of Hans von Buelow, and more recently, Arturo Toscanini. Since choral works are usually quite a bit shorter in duration than orchestral works, the conducting of choral works from memory should be just as easily achieved. However, relying on memorization can be risky in conducting longer choral works. The orchestral director may devote himself with great freedom and abandonment to his artistic intentions, and the professional player follows him closely with respect to his one part. The choir director, on the other hand, is much more tied down. In addition to working out his artistic intentions with his choir, which often comprises mostly amateurs, it is also his responsibility to give constant technical assistance with respect to breath control, clear diction, word coloring, etc. For this to happen the singers must be thoroughly familiar with their parts. Because of the continual surveillance which must be exercised over the vocal and musical progress of the singers, the choral director needs a much closer contact with the score than the orchestral director and should therefore think twice before he attempts to direct from memory. Furthermore, the sight of the music on the conductor's stand gives the singers a greater sense of security, even if the director is so free from the score that he refers to it only when turning the page.

A choral director who indicates every entry, spoils his singers by making them too dependent on the conductor and so weakens their independence and reliability. The singers should be "right there" at the right time. The director will indicate the most significant entries for reasons of interpretation as well as for assisting the singers. To help him to do this he could use gestures employing movement of the fingers, hands, arms, head, eyes, or articulate a word by mouthing.

It can become difficult if, during the singing, the director holds himself responsible for giving every possible technical help including the indication of virtually every entry. This approach to conducting so absorbs the conductor in the mechanical aspects of singing that he becomes a kind of musical "security police," hindering him from giving himself unreservedly and wholeheartedly to the guiding and shaping of the musical dynamic forces — which is really the artistic purpose and function of the director. Such "overcontrol" of technical aspects of singing hems the artistic activity of the director and tends to thwart his musicality. It requires much foresight and perhaps even more instinct on the part of the director to find the right synthesis between technical assistance and artistic guidance. The director who constantly works with the minute technical details is by no means always the greatest artist.

While singing, eye contact between the director and the singers must never be lost. The guidance and direction communicated by the eyes is at least as vital and important as the direction and gestures of the hands and arms. The director must jealously watch for complete and constant attention from every singer. By means of the eyes a close relationship is established between the choir and its director. The glances of the director are not only a technical means to secure the attention of the singers, but a vital means of communicating and sharing the artistic aspects of the music. During a performance, the eyes of the director should not be glued to the score nor to the floor — the first can happen for musical reasons, the second because of shyness or embarrassment. The attention should move from the score to a sphere encompassing the entire choir and the eyes of the director must be "speaking" eyes. Some singers are so hemmed in that they cannot withstand the steady look of the director and continually avoid catching his eyes, and yet most people will loosen up after a while. Even if singers are somewhat reluctant at first, the director must, with patience and tenacity, bid for the full attention of each singer.

During the entire time of a musical performance the director should, through the radiance and strength of his personality, through his poise, motions, signs, gestures, articulation, and eye contact, continuously transfer energies to the choir, for by so doing he greatly stimulates and multiplies the energies within the choir; it is a state of highest activity. The choir director must, so to speak, constantly pour oil on the fire, but at the same time retain the possibility of controlling the fire.

There are endless details which the director must keep in mind during singing, and before beginning to conduct, he should at some time bring each of these details to his attention. If, however, he wants to coordinate all these various details, then they must eventually become a self-evident part of the subconscious. The coordination of and control over infinite details during a performance can be developed to the point where it looks as easy as play and where it appears to be a spontaneous activity resulting from the conductor's immediate and lively response to the music. At best such conducting is a free and joyous release of musical energy. Such mastery, however, can be achieved only by conscious effort and patient practice which, with more talented directors, becomes second nature much more quickly than would ordinarily be the case. For supplementary reading compare the instructive courses on conducting technique in the conducting books by Kurt Thomas (English translation published by G. Schirmer).

Contemporary choral practices seek to develop a unified choral sound and style which would also influence the approach to and methods of choral training. We have not yet attained this new ideal of choral sound by any means. The difference between the traditional choral sound and the present sound ideal becomes particularly clear when one compares the sound of a mixed choir immediately with the sound of a modern organ which has been built in accordance with the principles of modern organ building trends and according to the sound ideal of the baroque organ. The incompatability of the two kinds of sound is disturbing and hinders real music making. Even though the nineteenth century renaissance of choral singing as well as the choral movements of the present day have contributed to a new outlook on music, we are still in need of a contemporary choral sound, and a systematic pedagogical approach for its achievement, which would conform to the present-day organ sound.

The old practice of "singing into the organ" must once more become a possibility. That this kind of choral sound which is compatible with the organ sound of present-day organs must become the accepted ideal for today goes without saying. Most of the prevalent choral practices — and this applies to England and North America as much as to Europe in general — are based upon the a cappella ideal of the Romantic Period. This sound conforms to the broad, soft, suave, affective, overtone-deficient, and harmony-saturated organ sound of that period, namely the Romantic French organ sound which sought to imitate the symphonic sound of the Romantic Period. For the achievement of a new contemporary choral sound the methods, aids, and techniques described in the first chapters of this book should be most helpful. A free choral sound which issues from a way of breathing which is developed on the basis of the organic relationship between the psychic and physical being prevents the choral tone from overpressure of breath. Intelligent and thorough work with the singing consonants instead of the one-sided preference of vowels with additional training and cultivation on the *oo, ay, ee,* instead of constant training on the *ah* vowel, gives the sound slenderness, clarity, brightness, richness of overtones, flexibility, substance, and transparency. Exercises for the body posture required to produce this sound enhance the resonance possibilities. Body and rhythmic exercises lend the sound transparency, breadth of resonance, precision, brilliance, and intensity and gives it basic core. Ear training helps to achieve good intonation and purity of sound and gives the choir the possibility for controlling the sound. Alertness to the text and intensification of articulation encourage plasticity and flexibility and sharpen up the rhythm. To achieve this kind of new and unified choral sound one must work systematically and with conviction. The different epochs in the history of music have derived their sound ideals not only from the instruments which were being currently used, but also from the sound of the prevalent practices and styles. Singing never needs to be the same from one epoch or situation to another. The sounds from one approach of singing to another can be as varied as the sounds of a Ruckers harpsichord and a Steinway grand!

Section B

Chapter I

The Preparation by the Choir Director

The conscientious preparation of the choir director for each rehearsal and for each performance is a prime prerequisite for his vocation. The most thorough preparation, however, is no sure guarantee for success. Every director knows of unsatisfactory or even unsuccessful rehearsals which had been planned with painstaking care. He also know of rehearsals for which he thought he was totally unprepared, which turned out unusually well because of his good humor; there was something "in the air" which made it click! The director should not, however, in any case, draw the conclusion that he can "take a chance" each time and hope for the best. This experience should teach him — and he should have this kind of insight at the outset of his career — that artistic and creative work with people is not subject to predetermined calculation and defining of situations, and that one must allow the creative energies and artistic powers to unfold freely in accordance with the inter-actionary forces between the music and the performers. The choir director must not only be capable of and prepared to respond to any new stimuli and thoughts which come to him beyond his anticipated reactions in the course of his preparation, but he must be ready to cast aside instantly even his best plans and procedures in order to follow the unanticipated but superior approach to his rehearsal. Like any pedagogical activity, choir directing is a creative activity — a creative work. Even though the unprepared rehearsals may occasionally turn out to be the better ones and even if the director must occasionally discard his carefully prepared plan, these unanticipated switches of events are exceptions. The director should, therefore, under all circum-stances, prepare himself thoroughly for each rehearsal, including the minut-est details — even if this does nothing more than give him the satisfaction and the secure feeling that he has done everything humanly possible to meet the requirements for a good rehearsal.

145

The preparation begins with the selection of the music. In setting up the criteria for selection the occasion or the specific purpose of the music should be kept clearly in mind. The music must first of all be suitable. In choosing the music for a special event such as a welcoming celebration, a memorial service, a general or religious festivity, or a regular worship service, the director must be very clear as to the essential nature of the occasion. The orchestral director — and frequently the organist — will, in such cases, have the easier choice, because he has more music to choose from since instrumental music is not bound to specific occasions. The choir director must therefore not select only according to agreeability or suitability of the music, but also according to the sense of the text, which he must carefully consider.

If the director is not bound to any specific event but is giving a concert of sacred music, he should still strive for some kind of unity and consistency of programming. The various short numbers in a concert program following as they usually do in close succession, are often in complete contradiction to text, music, style, and source. If our stomachs had to digest what we sometimes expect the ear to absorb, the listener would experience one physical catastrophe after another! The catastrophe of the ear may not be as readily obvious, but the aftereffects are as detrimental. Taking the church year into consideration could be helpful in more coherent programming of the numerous choral concerts presented annually. It is particularly suitable for a choir to sing spring songs during spring, and Christmas songs during the Christmas season. Many of the finer choral societies heed this principle, particularly by singing Bach's larger choral works at the appropriate season of the year.

The words, to put it mildly, should not stand in absolute contradiction to their *bearer*. Not every text is equally suited for mixed, treble, male, or children's voices, and if the composer should have made a wrong judgment in his choice of voice setting, the director always has the prerogative of looking for another selection! Some texts suggest that the songs be performed in settings which are not too dissimilar from the situations in which they originally were meant to be sung. For example, imagine a serious-faced, eighty-voice male choir singing a rollicking pleasure song in a four-to-eight-voice arrangement on a concert program and for their next song, from the same spot — the stage — singing a richly harmonized lullaby without as much as suggesting a rocking movement!

The director must also carefully consider the grade of difficulty of the work to be chosen. It is common (mainly because of a false ego) to select and attempt to sing music which is too difficult for the choir. One should make it a principle to perform the type of music which the choir can sing with the greatest amount of perfection. It is always better to perform simple music well than difficult works poorly. The greatness of a simple piece often

146

remains hidden to many people because of the director's misconceptions as to what consitutes true greatness in music.

In selecting his music the director must consider the level of the pedagogical and artistic development of the choir. He should be able to judge which work could at the moment further his choir both technically and musically. He should know how his choir could best move from one musical style to another, as for example, from a work of the Romantic Period like the *Liebesliederwalzer* (Love song waltzes) by Brahms to a work of the Baroque Period like the *Tageszeiten* (Times of Day) by Telemann, or from a work of the Renaissance like the *Missa Pange lingua* by Josquin de Pres to a contemporary work like Ralph Vaughan Williams' motet "O Clap Your Hands." He should take note as to what his choir still needs in order to do justice to the different styles represented in the repertoire of the choir, and which selections he should choose to bridge gaps between such strongly contrasted stylistic differences as between the music of the nineteenth and twentieth centuries.

The director must be clear in his own mind whether the size of the choir is commensurate with the sound required for a given work which he wishes to choose for his choir, since the tendency is to sing a cappella works with too thick a sound. In choosing a choral work with instrumental accompaniment, he needs to consider the availability of instruments required for the work, and if the instrumentation is flexible as in many of the late renaissance and early baroque works, he should decide how he can use available instruments to best advantage.

In working with a seasonal choir, like a choral society which gives regular musical concerts, the repertoire should be rounded out, balanced and continually expanded. For a choir which performs regularly for specific functions (e.g. a church choir) the director should choose music on the basis of frequency of use throughout the year. Even though the church choir is to a great extent bound to the main events of the church year, it would greatly facilitate and lighten the work of the choir and the director if the choir had in its repertoire music with the kind of text which appears more frequently in the liturgical church year — as for example a musical setting on "For God so loved the world" or settings of texts which fit many occasions, e.g. songs of praise.

If a choir sings on an occasion when an address or sermon is part of the program, the speaker should be consulted before choosing the musical numbers; in choosing the choral music for a church service, it should be understood (what in many situations is obligatory) that the director consults with the pastor. In any case there should obviously be a clear understanding between the speaker and the director.

The size and acoustical properties of the room can be a factor in the choice of choral music. A church sanctuary with several balconies would suggest the possibility of performing a polyphonic work with separated choirs. A large hall with overly strong acoustics would forbid the use of very fast tempos or the performance of works with a thick polyphonic texture. Out-of-door performances would also influence the choice of a work, in which case the harmonies should be relatively plain and simple.

For the serious and often difficult task of choosing the right choral pieces, the director should avail himself of the suitable music catalogues and sample materials which can be obtained from the various music publishing companies. Under no circumstances in any serious music making situation should one choose a choral work because of the "effect" which one hopes it may have on the listeners. The choosing of choral music for its immediate appeal only (this being understood and a temporary animating effect on the listener) is very questionable.

Once the choice has been made, the choir director must make a thorough study of the work from the tune to the sound image of the piece as a whole — as the singers will do later on. He should carefully sing through each of the voice parts until he can sing all of them fluently. Then he should try to "hear" all the voice parts together. For many directors this may at first seem difficult or impossible, but even here constant practice can lead to mastery.

Only after this preliminary work should the director play the music on a piano. Even though the cantors of the great choral epochs may never have used a keyboard instrument for their own preparation and rehearsal, the ability to play the vocal parts on the piano is almost a necessity for the modern choir director. First of all, the sound image of the selection should be clarified at the piano. The director can play the piece as he sings each of the voice parts. However, in doing this he must always keep in mind that the piano can never, as a harmonious percussive instrument, represent the aural image of a single melody wind instrument, which a choir of singers actually represents. It can, on the other hand, give a totally wrong impression of the actual sound image. It is therefore impossible to get a genuine aural impression of a choral work from the piano alone. If the director wishes to get the right aural image of the music prior to the choral rehearsals, he should select a few good singers and form a small choir to read the music. This would certainly be the ideal kind of preparation.

While studying the music the director should note those spots which may cause his choir some difficulties at the rehearsal. A good director will anticipate the difficult spots, e.g. unusual intervals or chords, complicated rhythms, unexpected entries, etc. He should carefully plan how he can best help his choir to overcome such difficulties.

Before rehearsing the music the director should become so familiar with it that he literally "lives in the music." If the composition is based on a sustaining tune (e.g. cantus firmus), he must at least know the tune by heart. In the case of a different type of composition, he should work out the "conducting line"(See A VIII, p. 132 ff.) and make sure that the line on the printed page has been transferred into his head! He should also take note of the pitch level of the entries and earmark them in his score.

Furthermore, the director ought to go through every part for the purpose of deciding where the choir should breathe. He should mark in signs which indicate a full (regular) or short (catch) breath and in this way help to clarify and develop the phrasing. (Compare with Fig. 5.)

In a similar manner the text of the work should be prepared by the director. Not only should he read it silently, but he should speak it repeatedly with flow and resonance, just as he will later expect his choir to do. (See B II, p. 156 ff.) He must have a clear understanding of the sense and meaning of the text. He should do some research on any unclear passages (e.g. old word forms, unusual imagery) or on texts taken out of their context as in selections taken from longer sections of poetry or Scripture passages.

It is most desirable that a director has enough knowledge of foreign languages so that he can translate, understand, and work through phonetically for example, a Latin mass, an Italian operatic chorus, a French chanson, or an English madrigal. This is necessary if his interpretation is to grow out of the spirit and peculiar feel for the various languages. A director will not always be required to be adept in several languages, but whenever he is responsible for directing a work in a foreign language he should consult a language expert.

Finally the director should define and analyze the technical speech problems and reflect carefully as to how he might best deal with them, as for example the difference between open and closed vowels, mastery of melismatic or florid passages, exposed entries beginning on vowels, formation of pharyngeal and labial consonants, treatment of adjacent consonants, etc.

As far as knowledge and information are available, the director should get a clear understanding of performance practices of the work to be performed, e.g. the number of instruments, types of instruments to be employed, the manner of playing these instruments, the physical arrangement of singers and players, tempos, dynamic level, the type of conducting, particular problems in giving the entries, the application of conducting techniques. With older music he should concern himself with such historical questions as the performing media for which the work was originally written, the original instrumentation, its occasion, in what kind of a performance hall it was to be performed. What connection did this music have with the life and thought of the people of that time? In what kind of environment did people originally hear the work? Personal thought and reflection, the reading of prefaces to performance editions of the work, consultation of music lexicons and historical books, and discussion with other musicians may give the necessary information. If the director cannot or will not consult historical sources for information about the work, he must have some very good reasons for not doing so!

It is essential that the director go carefully through all musical material before the rehearsal begins — breathing places must be marked, phrasing should be indicated and the relation of text to music should be checked. Sometimes it will be necessary to write in dynamic and tempo instructions as well as bar numberings. At other times it becomes necessary to revise overedited editions such as the Romantic editions of older works, etc. All this preparatory work saves time and energy at the rehearsal. The value and validity of this kind of preparation and research may not be realized until the actual rehearsals are in progress.

Finally the director should prepare a rehearsal plan. He should be very clear as to the procedures and methods he intends to use in studying the work, e.g. how should he divide a larger work into meaningful sections for rehearsal purposes? With what section should he commence the rehearsal (not necessarily the first, but usually with the easiest and most familiar)? How many rehearsals will be required for the preparation of the work? What kind of technical preparatory exercises are desirable? Should the choral selections be approached from the text or from the music? (See B IV, p. 181 ff.)

When the director is thoroughly prepared, the rehearsal will be better, the work will require less time to learn, and the result will be an artistic and secure performance. Remember that the choir must suffer the consequences of each sin of omission on the part of the director!

Chapter II

Artistic Unison Singing

Artistic unison singing of monodic music requires the same kind of thorough preparation as any other artistic achievement. The singing of monodic music is usually looked down upon by the people in many choral organizations because it is not regarded as artistic singing — artistic singing being associated with part singing, more specifically with four-part singing. Whoever has invented the dogma of four-part singing and wherein is it rooted? What is the basis for such a dogma? The history of artistic unison singing goes back much farther than the history of multivoiced singing. One needs only to think of Gregorian chant, which flowered centuries before the discovery of polyphony and which today enjoys an uninterrupted artistic cultivation and musical existence — an existence requiring the highest kind of musical artistry, knowledge, and ability. The choirs of the great epochs of choral composition differentiated between the *cantus planus* — the unison singing, and the *cantus figurativus* — that is, multivoiced, melismatic, and polyphonic singing. Frequently both types of music were performed by the same choir and because of this the singers developed the kind of artistic abilities which contemporary choristers, for the most part, have lost. One reason why the earlier choir could constantly perform great musical works with great understanding and artistry was that, in addition to mastering the *cantus figurativus,* they had also mastered the *cantus planus* singing and they knew how to transmit the spiritual energies and technical abilities from the latter to the former type of singing.

To the multivoiced choral culture of today we must add unison singing. A marvelous and special art lies hidden in unison singing, and most of our choirs today would fail if they were tested on their ability to sing monodic music. Unison singing is a true test of a choir's real ability. It serves as a good test of the choir's singing skill and artistry, and any time and effort spent in this area will improve multivoiced singing.

The most basic and vital aspects of the choral art are to be learned from unison singing. The choir singer, and particularly the bass, tenor, or alto, is forced to sing a melody, and cannot get away with merely producing musical blurs or filler parts; he must develop a feeling for his own musical line, for musical tension and relaxation, for ebb and flow of a phrase line, for varying mixtures and stratifications of vocal resonances, and for plasticity and flexibility of the vocal line. He will lose his feeling of dependence upon other singers and develop independence. A unified mental and artistic posture toward singing is activated in this way. Unison singing is the preparatory school for polyphonic singing and requires the ultimate in terms of freedom and relaxation. Such "looseness" and freedom can be achieved in unison singing. The choir also acquires the right kind of corporate feeling. In no other way can the choir learn such unified choral breathing as through unison singing. Singing the long melodic arches in one breath also trains the singer to phrase properly. Through unison singing in mixed choirs the singer is compelled to listen with great discernment; no harmonizing or "skipping over" difficulties can cover up a musical or vocal deficiency. Unison singing is an excellent training in musicianship. It requires a very close acquaintance with language. Each mispronunciation, any slovenliness of diction, becomes obvious. Nowhere else do the sense, meaning, and musical flow of the words present themselves with such immediacy and directness as in monodic music. Here a choir can learn about the very essence and technique of musical language.

Unison singing also has a symbolic significance. The singing of only one melodic line signifies unanimity of spirit and is the symbol of intimate fellowship. This symbolism has sometimes been applied to multivoiced singing as well. The singers are virtually carried along so to speak by this surge of energy of united activity resulting from unison singing. Unison singing is also an acid test with respect to the value or worth of a tune. A tune which can stand on its own merits without harmonic support or decoration of any kind must be regarded as a superior one. Unison singing is the essence of music making; it forms the bridge from improvised folk song singing to artistic choral singing.

In no way should the reader acquire the impression that entire choral concerts should be sung in unison or that such a concert would be desirable. However, the art of choral unison singing must be acquired once more and practiced wherever and whenever it is necessary and meaningful, e.g. when warming up the voices before a choir rehearsal; singing Gregorian chant in Protestant or Catholic confessions; singing hymns of the Protestant church (particularly the antiphonal singing between choir and congregation as practiced in European Protestant churches); singing folk songs; singing the theme of an instrumentally accompanied choral movement of a cantata, as a cantus firmus in an instrumental composition; and finally it would be of instructional value if, preceding the performance of a multivoiced instrumental composition, the tune itself is introduced without any accompaniment. Numerous unison anthems have been written for junior choirs in the last two decades and some have been composed for adult choirs as well, for example, the various types of hymn anthems (e.g. hymn anthem on the tune "Marion" by Healey Willan — of which three stanzas are sung in unison — Edition Peters 6065).

Not all tunes lend themselves to good unison singing, e.g. aria-like hymn tunes requiring harmonic support. Most appropriate are the modal and sacred tunes, pentatonic tunes, contemporary tunes based on the whole tone scale, very flowing tunes, tunes with strong rhythmic structural elements, and tunes in which the harmonic element recedes into the background and which are melodically rather than harmonically conceived.

Here are some suggestions for unison singing taken from several types of tunes. To start with, it is best to choose a tune which can be sung with ease and relaxation, one with descending, gentle melodic curves, e.g. "So did once three angels." One can approach the singing of this song either

Mainz, 1605

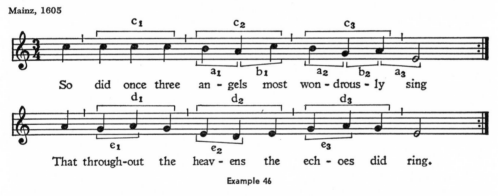

Example 46

from the text or from the tune because they are almost of equal importance for the artistic structure of the song. Let us start with the tune. The choir should, without any outside assistance, feel its way into the tune with its melodic motives, points of tension and relaxation, the rise and fall of the melodic line, the points of climax and repose. It requires a delicate and sensitive adjustment of the ear to anticipate the exact pitch and tone color of each new interval. The singer must, so to speak, use only a small flame. The choir hums the tune to *ng*. The *ng* permits a smooth gliding line required by this tune and yet does not fill the ear with an overabundance of sound which would hinder the individual singers in listening to each other. The *ng* sound also develops the high frequency head resonances, aids vocal train-

153

ing, and prepares the *ng* sound as it will appear in the text. The director should see to it that each singer opens his mouth sufficiently on the *ng* sound, that the back of the tongue is humped, its tip lightly touching the teeth that the breath is inhaled through the nose and that the individual tones are not divided from each other by a glottis stroke but that they glide smoothly in a portamento-like manner from one pitch to another. Even the first four notes on the same pitch should not be sung in a detached manner because of pressure on the larynx. When moving from one note to the next on repeated pitches, the tone should be focused in the head and the vibrations should be felt behind the upper part of the nose. If the choir has not yet mastered this somewhat difficult skill of smoothly separating repeated notes, it is better to sing the first four notes together as one whole note. As a change, the singing tone on *ng* could be alternated with the singing consonants *m* and *n*. These consonants fulfill the same vocal function as the *ng* and also serve to prepare for better singing of these consonants whenever they appear in the text which is to be sung. The facial muscles and lips must be kept as relaxed as possible in the humming of any of these consonants.

When humming on *m* the lips should never be drawn together in a tight, cramped manner, but one should rather project them slightly forward by a gentle breath pressure into a somewhat pointed formation. The lips must be so sensitive and the humming tone should vibrate so gently that the singer experiences tickling sensations between the lips. When singing on *n*, the tip of the tongue lies relaxed between the upper and lower front teeth. This position helps to keep a high focus of the tone. To give it more projection and intensity one might distend the nostrils somewhat and draw the upper lip slightly inward. In learning a new tune all three consonants should be utilized to full advantage to help achieve a smooth-flowing, closely-knit line when singing the text. For the transition from the humming consonants to the vowels, *oo* and *oh* should be used; these vowels produce less resonance, are easier to sing with glide-like smoothness, keep the larynx in a lower position for singing, and are a preparation, of course, for the *oo* and *oh* vowels in the text — these often being the most prominent vowels. The director should ask for a flat but slightly stretched out position of the tongue, for slightly protruded and rounded lips, for a relaxed and open pharynx, and a relaxed gliding from one note to another without any vocal breaks. An *m* or *n* may be used for the initial attack. Following this the singing consonants may be combined with *oo* and *oh* in *noo,noh,moo,moh,* whereby one tone syllable is given to each note, care being given to make each singing consonant as pliant and sonorous as possible so that they will not interrupt the stream of gliding vowel sounds but rather help to gently propel the vowel sound forward.

154

While the choir is feeling its way into the tune in the manner just described, and while the voice is conditioned for the eventual singing of the text, the director must help his singers to discover the unique characteristics of the melodic movement. This process is not achieved by many instructional words or theoretical explanations, but by meaningful repetition and directed effort. A conducting gesture or a brief, interjected comment can urge the singers onward in their task. After the choir has instinctively grasped the interrelationships of the formal aspects of the tune, the director should, if time permits, through pertinent explanations make the singers intellectually aware of the structural aspects. Normally the two types of learning experiences will blend and overlap. First of all, the singers will notice that the song is divided into two parts (A, B). The director separates the parts by a quick, light nasal breath. No breath is to be taken during the singing of either of these parts. Only two breaths are required — a breath preceding each of the two parts. This of course also clearly defines the phrase division. This division, however, should not leave a gap in the middle because both parts are like two parts of a hinge which come together at this point. The breath taken at the middle, while it separates the two parts, also binds them together. To strengthen this feeling for the unity of the parts, the choir may be divided into two equal sections, each section singing one of the parts. The point of this exercise is that the second group makes the right connection with the first line so that the music at this point will really be "handed over" to the next group!

The two parts may be analyzed and divided into a variety of ways. The choir will have noticed how each of the two parts is divided into easy descending sequences of melodic motives. The appropriate physiological and psychic span of tension must be sensed in the inhalation for each of the two parts. Each phrase contains definitely recognizable undulations of receding energies. The relaxation of the melodic curves in both of these lines culminates at the same note, e; the first line begins a minor sixth above the e, the second line a perfect fourth; the melody in the first section is spanned between e and c and the melody in the second section may be regarded as the lower floor of the two-floor e — a span of the first section.

According to Medieval theoretical teaching of melodic leading, the Phrygian mode of this tune uses the c in the first section as a kind of repercussive note, i.e. after commencing with four repeated c's the tune, after a brief melodic descent, comes back and reaffirms the c as the characteristic or central note of the first phrase. In a similar manner the a of the Hypophrygian mode becomes the repercussive note in the second phrase. The first line thus has the wider descent, the second line having a more flattened melodic arch. The melodic tensions and the melodic thrusts are inherent in the

155

first line on the words "angels sweetly did sing"; musically these words represent the sequence of a descending second, third, and fourth interval (a^1, a^2, a^3). The rising third and second intervals which follow immediately (a^1 and a^2) are "dead intervals" which provide the anacrusis to the descending melodic motive. To absorb the "feel" for this intervallic movement, the choir may make an appropriate body movement (c^2, c^3); each of the three motives could be represented by a unified movement, with an anacrustic momentum (c^1, c^2, c^3).

The second part (B) also contains three melodic motives of three notes each (d^1, d^2, d^3) of which d^1 and d^3 are completely identical. The second motive d^2 is an exact inversion of the other two. These gently swinging motives should also be transferred into a body movement by the choir. The intervals of a major second within these motives (e^1, e^2, e^3) must be executed quite deliberately. The thirds between each of the melodic groups should not be sung in the sense that the second intervals were sung — the singers merely alight on them gently without a trace of portamento or glissando after making a very slight tenuto on the last note of the three-note motive. The motion of the melodic motives of the second part of the tune may be regarded as a contrary motion to the motives of the first part; c^2 and c^3 form an inverted melodic arc; the motives d^1 and d^3 form a rising melodic curve.

When the melodic energy and the structural relationship of the motives to each other have been consciously examined by the singer, the entire tune should be sung to the syllables *noo, noh, moo, moh*, in a smooth, uninterrupted flow of sound, using relaxed jaw and opened pharynx. The choir should have a feeling of light buoyancy and should swing into the melodic undulations and permit itself to be carried forward to the melodic climaxes as a swimmer would catch the rising wave and let himself be carried by the propelling and lifting force of the wave to its crest. In this kind of melodic singing the quarter notes should not receive the same rigid quarter note values: the heavier notes will probably be somewhat elongated and the lighter ones be measured somewhat shorter. The time value of the notes is conditioned by their relative importance within the linear dynamics. The unison tune moves back and forth like a wave and like a full waving flag that keeps up its own undulating movement. The tonal stream, however, should maintain a uniform thickness. In other words, the tune should be prevented from bulging out at any point.

After the choir has fully mastered the tune in all its musical and dynamic vitality, the director proceeds to the text (compare with A IV, p. 48 ff.). To begin with, the director reads the text — perhaps only the first stanza — and the singers speak it after him. On the first try the choir may speak too loudly, the women with a slightly strained and too high pitch, while the men may tend to spoil the opportunity for good articulation by speaking too low — "in the cellar" as it were. One should establish a comfortable middle-range pitch so that every singer can speak in a relaxed, easy manner with medium voice strength. The rigid and, figuratively speaking, "frozen" words must be thawed out and blended into a flowing stream of sound — into a kind of textual conveyor belt. This process of melting rigid word blocks (hard diction problems) often gives the director great difficulty. General instructions are helpful only up to a point. Such instruction will have to be augmented with specific aids and exercises.

The average lay singer, by and large, is lazy with respect to clear enunciation. He hardly modifies his speech mechanism even in the speaking of entirely opposite sounds. Everything is spoken into the same mold or dye. To activate the speech apparatus and to intensify the speech process, one might have the choir whisper the text. Each singer acts like a prompter in a drama and with utmost clarity and intensity whispers the words to the director who purposely has moved a considerable distance from the choir. The choir might then attempt to speak the words without any tone or noise whatsoever, mouthing the words like a person who is deaf and dumb. The director first "speaks" the text in this manner and the choir is expected to lip-read it in the same manner. Individual singers may then select different texts and speak them in the same manner while the rest of the singers try to catch the meaning and mouth the words with such clarity that they become visual. This activity can easily be turned into a social game. Lip reading and imitating soundless speech is a very helpful means of intensifying and clarifying diction.

To test the degree of unanimity the singers have achieved in thinking and reading the text at a given speed, they may merely think the text and, at a signal from the director, speak it. All singers are expected, of course, to come in on the same word. The same exercise can be applied to soundless singing. It may also prove to be helpful to conduct an imaginary soundless "deaf and dumb" choir.

Next, the director selects all the words containing the same consonants and has the choir speak them after him. Meanwhile the director checks the technical aspects of consonant formation and pronunciation. For example, he might single out the s's in "most sweetly did sing" and illustrate how they should sound in the context of each word and in the context of the phrase as a whole. (Compare with A IV, p. 49 ff.)

To give the words a dynamic, propelling force and color, the director could choose those words that correspond to the note of the melodic motives which propel the music forward. These words then become the pivot points of the text. The director speaks these words and has the choir speak them after him. In doing so the director proceeds entirely from the concept or meaning of the word, and makes it clear to the choir that the very essence of what the word is to communicate is actually present in the word itself. It remains only for the singer to invest the word with full meaning both technically (i.e. correct pronunciation and clear enunciation) and conceptually, namely, a clear, vivid concept and imaginative thought. If, for example, the word "sky" is correctly and imaginatively spoken by the choir, the singers should see the sky in all its glory of blue expanse and fleecy clouds or stars; or if the choir speaks the word "music" with a feeling of being inwardly filled with it, then the air should seem literally charged with beautiful sounds (compare with A IV, p. 46 ff.). The predicative words should also be singled out, and the characteristic energy of the activity which they describe, i.e. its onomatopoetic effect must become clear to the choir — e.g. singing, ringing.

After the choir has mastered the technical aspects of enunciation, after it has learned to sing every word with imagination and vitality, and when both the flow and plasticity have been achieved, we must once more turn our attention to the flow of speech. Like the singers pictured in old paintings and drawings, so each choral singer has, as it were, a waving scroll in front of his mouth. The song (Example 46) which we have been discussing is a good illustration of how tremendously important the singing consonants *m, n, ng* are for the achievement and maintenance of a smooth, connected flow of the text. These consonants must glide from one word or syllable into the next with pliancy and resonance. They are the bridges between words and syllables, the wheels on which the vehicle of the textual structure can roll; they give to the total sound a dynamic and vibrant quality. Words and syllables are directly and sonorously bound together except where two vowels, one at the end and the other at the beginning of a word are adjacent to each other. Here one must separate the words slightly to preserve the clarity and intelligibility of the text and to prevent the words from liquefying and dissolving into an unintelligible melliferous succession of vowels and consonants. In speaking, such words would be separated by a stroke of the glottis and in singing by the insertion of an *imaginary* "h" sound between the two vowels (compare A IV, p. 54 ff.). For example, "three angels" would be sung "three (h)angels." The textual "conveyor belt" could then be illustrated as follows: "A songthe three (h)angelsmostsweetlydidsing." "That(h)inhighheaventhe (h)echoesdidring."

Many of the same aspects of rhythmic propulsion, accent, stress, relaxation, etc. which were singled out and examined in the music may also be found in the text, e.g. the breath pause in the middle of the song, the upbeatish rhythm, the distribution of the strong and weak accents into a dactylic rhythm, the light triple pulsation, the movement of the first line toward the last two words "did sing" while in the second line the energy culminates in the word "echoes." With longer texts the phrase marks, the breath marks, climax points, spans of tension, and the balancing and comparison of parts should be ascertained and clearly indicated.

After the text has been worked through in this manner and has become a part of the singers, there follows the task of fusing text and music into an integrated whole. In this song the structure of the text and the music is almost completely identical. The problem now is to blend the heretofore separately prepared tune and text without having the words disrupt the easy flow and without letting the sonority of the tune overshadow or dissolve the clarity and sense of the word. To avoid this danger it is best not to proceed directly from the text back to the tune but to merge text and tune in a gradual manner. One could proceed as follows:

. . . Speak the text in a normal tone of voice.

. . . Recite the text in the rhythm of the music on a single comfortable pitch.

. . . Recite the text at the interval of a fifth or on a triad (in our example the recitation in the two sections at the interval of a sixth and a fourth signifying the melodic span of the two sections would be significant).

One should always take care that the clarity and flow of speech is not disturbed by sheer musical sound, but that the words unfold from the moving stream of sound as flowers emerge after a rain. The singers should always "sing with their ears," so to speak, and consciously make themselves aware of the intervallic tensions and the extent of the spaciousness of the different tones. They should be aware that when text and tune are combined, the "spinning" of tones is particularly brought into play and that one syllable emerges from the other syllable as it were. The singing consonants assume their full function of binding the syllables and words together; in singing they should be more prominent than in speaking. Each singer in the choir should slightly exaggerate his mental image of the verbal stream, so that the tonal image will be forceful enough.

Finally, the choir must get caught up in the pulse and movement of the tune and discover the unity of text and tune — how the text enhances the tune and how the tune in turn enhances the text. The singer will realize how much art lies concealed in this short space of a two-line Phrygian tune — particularly because it is sung in unison. The clean singing of this pentatonic-like tune is dependent on the singers clearly hearing the sixth and fourth intervals, the rising major seconds being approached high enough, the thirds not being sung too low, the same pitch sounding exactly as high on the darker *aw* sound as on the brighter *ee* sound, and the ascending minor third (Ex. 46 -b[1]) achieving the same pitch as the four previously repeated notes.

159

The conducting movements may be reduced to a simple, flowing triple-beat pattern. The beat preparatory to the upbeat must not be forgotten. The entire movement of the tune has a somewhat "upbeatish" feeling, and the third beat should be executed very deliberately. To prevent any bulging of the flowing melodic stream the first beat should not be brought down too low, but rather be drawn slightly inward at an angle to the left to allow the second beat plenty of room for a longer, horizontal, outward motion. The first and second beats should be conducted in a close-knit fashion, since these beats constitute the wave-like motion as indicated by the brackets $a^{1,2,3}$ and $e^{1,2,3}$. Since the first two notes of each measure are so closely united in their melodic function, one could also use the triple pattern sometimes used in conducting dance music, in which the first and second beat are combined into one large outward curve — the third beat is conducted like the upbeat in a regular duple beat pattern. The bracketed two notes at a and e must then be directed with sureness and clarity. In any case, the directing of this tune must be smooth and pressureless, with an emphasis on the horizontal directions of the patterns.

Another tune in which the flow is characterized by a series of descending motives and which lends itself particularly to unison singing is the old twelfth-century German Easter carol tune *Christ ist erstanden* (No. 107, SBH). Further examples are *Christi sanctorum* (No. 204, SBH) and *Verbum supernum"* (No. 277, SBH).

Following a study of tunes with descending melodic arches and "drooping" melodic motives one should proceed to analyze a tune with a descending melodic movement. A simple tune which might serve as an example for such a study is the short, two-line tune, "O Christmas tree, you bear a green small branch."

German folksong

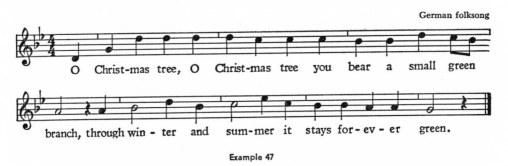

O Christ-mas tree, O Christ-mas tree you bear a small green branch, through win - ter and sum-mer it stays for- ev - er green.

Example 47

The discussion need not be as thorough or detailed as in the first example. The suggestions given there may be adapted and applied to this example as well as to some of the larger melodic forms which will follow later. In the Westphalian Christmas tree song, text and tune must once more be regarded

160

as an entity. The isolated work in the tune and text will, however, in the long run save time and strength and will more readily reveal the essential character of the song. A few suggestions should suffice. The singers must first of all become very much aware of the span of the interval of the fifth in which the entire tune, with the exception of the first note, is contained. In the attempt to fill out the ascending melodic arch with sound and musical intensity, one must be careful not to let the singers make "cramped" efforts. One should not suddenly "stir up" the choir in an effort to incite more energetic singing. The concentration and energy prior to the attack need not be greater than in Example 46. From a state of maximum relaxation, ease and looseness the necessary sustained effort should emerge naturally. The tone syllable which is used in rehearsing the tune should be formed in such a way as to allow the tone to expand with the expansion of the melodic arch. It is best to use the singing consonants *m* and *n* with such syllables as *don, dan, ban, bom*, since they have such a prominent function in this text. When sustaining and expanding the syllables in the word "win(ter)" and "sum(mer)" care must be taken not to let the closed vowel sounds turn to open vowels. Approximately the second half of the half note must be sung on the singing consonants *n* and *m*. The word builds up the tune stone upon stone, so to speak.

In conducting the tune the four-beat .pattern is used. The "up-beatish" character is noticeable throughout the tune. This needs to be taken into consideration while conducting. The left hand, for example, will be used to sustain the tone on "branch," but it should participate with the right hand in giving the new upbeat to the next phrase. Here too, as in the previous example, the movements should be kept flowing and horizontal. The half notes in the second phrase might give occasion for the entire tune to be conducted with a larger swinging 2/2 beat pattern. This is possible if the choir has been warmed up to the piece sufficiently and if it has a good grasp of the music. The upbeats to both phrases would, however, be conducted in quarter note beats.

As other examples of tunes with an ascending melodic arch one could mention the tune "Hamburg" (No. 513, SBH), "St. Theodolph" (No. 11, SBH), "Wachet auf" (No. 7, SBH), *In dulci jubilo* (No. 39, SBH) and the tune A *solis ortus cardine* (No. 20, SBH). When learning tunes which have a more decisive rhythm, as for example, *In dulci jubilo*, sharper tone syllables like *sum, tan, too*, should be used. When the text has been rehearsed to the point where it has attained an easy flow, it should also be spoken to the sharply accented rhythm of the tune. While singing, the words must serve to rhythmicize the tune. Even simple folk songs from the eighteenth and nineteenth centuries may be treated according to the principles of artistic unison singing which we have been discussing.

With respect to the formal structure and the melodic course of a tune, its rhythmic character, and the relationship between text and tune, one must make a clear distinction between tunes which originate from Gregorian chant — or which have a close resemblance to it — and those tunes which have a definite metrical character. Among the longer, larger structured tunes which have developed from Gregorian chant, one could mention the old German *Leise,** Media vita morte sumus.* This tune was used by Luther for the hymn text, *Mitten wir im Leben sind* (In the midst of earthly life) and so has found its way into the stream of modern hymnody.

Martin Luther, 1524
Tr., composite

Words from *The Lutheran Hymnary* published by Concordia Publishing House. Reprinted by permission.

Example 48

The tune may be rehearsed on singing consonants, and on tone syllables with and/or without closed singing consonants. The singers should become conscious of the intervallic spans $e - a$ and $e - c$ which characterize the Phrygian mode in which most of the tune happens to be written. The target notes "T" must also be deliberately approached. The first lines of section B begin either on a shortened or lengthened note. Both types of beginnings produce a

162

strong forward surge of musical energy in the various musical phrases. With the eighth note at B and A one leaps into the already established momentum of the music and on the half note gets a firm footing for a good forward thrust like the competitive runner who gets a good footing from his starting line. The momentum or thrust must be renewed for each phrase regardless of the kind of beginning notes it may have.

The cadences on the other hand must be deliberately expanded. This is demanded not only by the characteristic Phrygian cadence, but occasionally by three extra melismatic notes. The text is of assistance here because of the presence of round vowels and pliable consonants — e.g. "surround," "only." The individual lines form an artistic, larger musical form: AABACC-DEA^{1}E. The longest lines A constitute the larger superstructure and the shorter lines BCDE undergird this structure. A^1 can be regarded as a variation of A. The symmetrical structure at the beginning and at the end make the shorter lines CCD the core. It is these shorter lines that carry the litany-like invocations. The melody lines in these follow a descending pattern. The singers must become aware of the conformity between words and music, in order to present and balance the various parts of the total structure effectively.

In these musical pieces which originated in Gregorian chant, text and tune are coalesced. In this *Leise* it is true both in a symbolical and in a technical sense. The "target notes" of the melody correspond with the "target words" of the text, so that important words seem to be emphasized musically, e.g. death, foe, Lord, etc. After the Mixolydian introduction the tune stays mostly in the Phrygian mode, which for centuries symbolized man's suppressed existence. The saving redemptive answer to the sorrow-pressed question of the A section and the invocations of the sections that follow are completely removed from the Phrygian tonal plane (B). Thus the affirmation "Thou only, Lord, Thou only" stands apart, musically, from the realm of human suppression. This phenomenon is present in all stanzas. It has already been observed that the three litany-like invocations constitute the very center of the tune. Even technically one cannot separate text and tune since they are amalgamated into each other. A different text for this tune is hardly imaginable in the sense that many tunes of secular or sacred nature which do not have their origin in Gregorian chant have for centuries been wedded to various texts (e.g. the use of one choral tune for several chorale texts). While singing, one feels and hears the tune with the text and vice versa. In the singing of this old *Leise* one must proceed both from the meaning and flow of the words, and from the vitality and flow of the music. The rhythm emerges from the natural accent and stress of the word and from the sonority and vibrations of the musical line. Choirs with community singing or choral society backgrounds will have a difficult time discovering this style. Such a choir will put rigid blocks into the music where it should produce a flexible, moving flow of sound. In the attempt to attain this flowing, singing line, for which the director will have to employ all types of teaching aids, the pendulum can easily swing too far in the opposite direction; singing can become furtive, lose its substance, and forfeit the intellectual, aesthetic, and spiritual stability and consistency. Younger choirs can easily get worked up into a kind of "Neo-Gothic" ecstasy, which only too easily leads to inner and outer rigidity. In spite of all the textual and musical activity and the dangers that are present in any musical activity, one must constantly seek to achieve an animated restfulness, a feeling of being carried by the music and a kind of dynamic, flowing objectivity. These are objectives which must not be confused with the average lay singer's self-confidence and will to succeed. What has been said so far about nonmetrical tunes applies not only to the German songs which have been adapted from Gregorian chant, but in particular to Gregorian chant itself. Other types of tunes which should be approached in a similar manner are the medieval tunes, numerous chorale tunes which were used in Luther's time, tunes from Johann Walther's hymnal of chorale tunes and, to some extent, some of the more recent tunes.

The conducting pattern to be used here is the 4/4 beat pattern. To prevent the interruption of the linear flow of the music, the first beat in the measure should not be conducted too low or too heavily. The second and third beats should be conducted more horizontally than usual to promote the smooth linear flow of the melody. The eighth note upbeats should also be cued in as eighth notes, which necessitates the subdivision of the fourth beat. The left hand supports the half notes at the beginning of the phrases at C; it could also, by means of appropriate gestures, delineate the larger melodic arches, freeing itself from slavishly copying the movements of the right hand. Furthermore, both hands must reflect the rise and fall of the natural word accent by making motions which "speak."

An illustration of a tune which originates from measured music is *Herzlich, tut mich erfreuen die froehlich Sommerzeit* (Now fain my joyous heart would sing). This tune, which was first printed in the sixteenth century (Rhaws Bicinium, 1545), is given here with "O Jesus, King of Glory," a translation of the hymn *O König aller Ehren* by Martin Behm.

The chief difference between the two previous tunes and this tune is that the intervallic relationships of the church modes are melodically filled out with a predominance of consecutive seconds, while the intervallic space between the tones of the overtone series in the present example are frequently arrived at with wider intervallic jumps. In the previous examples the rhythmic form was derived entirely from the natural word accent, while the tune in the above example has its own mensural character which does not grow out of the word accent, but can stand even in contrast to the verbal inflections. Tunes of this category thereby achieve a strong feeling

164

of melodic drive, a spacious melodic structure, a greater degree of potential energy within the melodic line, and a kind of musical autocracy with respect to the relationship of the tune to the words. However, here too the separate study of text and music is in order, and it would be best to begin with the tune because of its obvious predominance. The division into the four complete phrases (cp) is made by taking full breaths at these points (ABCD), the breath taken during the rest between BC being the deepest and most relaxed. Breathing in the middle of the longer phrases (h) becomes a little more difficult. A short snatch breath has to suffice here but this short breath must furnish the momentum to reach or achieve the climax of the next part of the phrase and at the same time serve to bind these two lines into one close-knit musical unit. This somewhat many-sided, complex, difficult matter of "snatch breathing," which is of such decisive importance in so many songs, should be especially practiced in connection with the first phrase of our present example. To gain a clear understanding of the relationship between the musical movement of the first and second part of the phrase one must first clearly grasp the difference between the character of the quarter notes and half notes. In rehearsing this phrase, tone syllables may be used according to the general principles for the other examples quoted above. One might sing the quarter notes to a short, crisp *don* and the half notes to a flowing *doh*. Rhythmic aids and exercises may also be

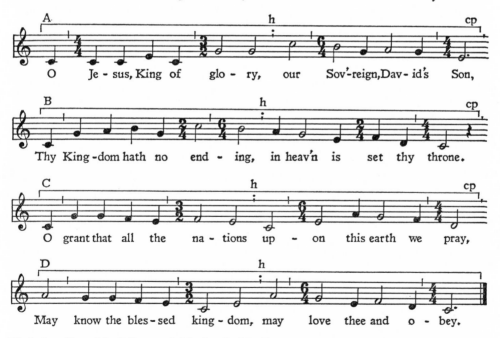

Words from *Hymnal for Colleges and Schools*, edited by E. Harold Geer, Yale University Press, New Haven.

Example 49

165

applied here (see A VII, p. 107 ff.) by clapping the rhythm of all the phrases and then by clapping only the first five notes and stamping the rest with the feet and vice versa. Through such activities it should become obvious that the first five notes of each phrase constitute a kind of running start for a wide leap into the next span which consists mostly of half notes.

The text is worked through as described earlier in connection with Examples 47 and 48 except that the gradual return of text to tune is not possible here as it was with the nonmensural tunes. As the last prerequisite to combining text and tune, the words are first spoken in the rhythm of the tune and then on a single pitch. Only when the choir has mastered this exercise so well that the words flow with ease and the rise and fall of the phrase, as well as the relationship of the sections of the phrase, are keenly sensed should the text and music be freely combined. The momentum-giving quarter notes at the beginning of each phrase should be sung with a dominant emphasis on the consonants so that they almost sound over-crisp, while the vowels of the longer half notes should be sustained in a facile, elastic manner. The long notes may well remain unemphasized so that the emphasis of the words "kingdom," "may know," naturally falls on the under-lined syllables and notes. It is in particular this gentle surge through these longer unstressed syllables which imparts a song-like charm and excitement to such points and which invests the song with its own kind of unique beauty. Praetorius, in his setting of this song, uses a text which has the word "nightingale" as the final word; he uses a half note on "ing," the second to the last note, instead of the quarter note as given here. This allows a stream of relaxed vocal sound to move freely and smoothly right into the final note. The director must be careful that the highest notes (target notes) of a phrase are not emphasized so much that they are pushed out of context (e.g. in the first line, "Our Sovereign David's Son"). The vowel should retain the right mouth formation. In the structure of this larger melodic form one must bear in mind that although A and B are contrasted musically they nevertheless constitute two branches of a continuous musical span (i.e. the *Stollen* of the bar-form). The musical climax comes very early (in other tunes it is arrived at in the third to the last section) and must be achieved in the first line by a rapid surge of energy from the five quarter notes which emphasize the tonic c, followed by the sudden leap of the half note on g. One must be aware that the division between the *Stollen** and *Abgesang** (C and D) comes after "set Thy throne," and that the entire *Abgesang* constitutes a kind of relaxation — an ebbing away of the musical wave which was formed in A and B, and that the melodic turn to the span of a fifth from a to d in the third line "this earth we pray" becomes an integral and symbolic characteristic of this ebbing process.

The conducting technique must not interfere with the larger spans of musical tension. Yet it is necessary to decide beforehand the conducting patterns to be used and to bring to this musical example all the conducting technique and ability which the director has at his disposal. Even if singers and director have thoroughly mastered the song and have achieved a degree of ensemble and musical unity, it is still advisable to stay with definite beat patterns. The arch-like structure of the tune must, however, be maintained, and it is here that the left hand in particular must fully participate.

The tune may be divided into measures with varying time signatures as illustrated in Example 49. This results in a continual change of conducting patterns and so affords a perfect example for practice in conducting polymetrical music (See A VIII, p. 135 ff.). The 6/4 measures can be conducted as two 3/4 measures. The movement from one meter to another must occur so easily and effortlessly that the singers never sense an abrupt division but feel carried securely along on an unending stream. Frequently the choir is required to breathe before the last beat in the conducting pattern. This could be indicated by a slight, extra outward movement. In the artistic formation and direction of the song, the light attacks on the quarter notes in the 4/4 measures must be indicated by small, lilting gestures; the more sustained 3/2 measures must be expressed in larger, more sustained movements with a strong outward and sideward pull. In the 6/4 measures the first and second and the fourth and fifth beats may be united into a heavier, somewhat rounded and outward moving beat while the third and sixth beats are conducted with a light, precise, more "upbeatish" motion. By fitting the conducting patterns to the measure and by modifying them to fit the dynamic relationships and the structure and rhythm of the text, the movements of the conductor can actually control and shape the artistic development of the song.

Similar principles and observations could be illustrated particularly from the numerous sacred and secular cantus firmi of the sixteenth century as well as in many tunes of the Baroque Period (as for example the musical settings of Johann Crüger to the lyrics of Paul Gerhardt) and in various more recent vocal forms — e.g. hymn tunes of Ralph Vaughan Williams.

The development of unison singing has since earliest times been aided by antiphonal singing. The historically proven examples of this practice can be profitably expanded in the cultivation of artistic singing. The division of the choir may take place between groups of the same vocal tessitura, between men and ladies, boys and men, precentor and choir, solo quartet or ensemble and the larger choral body, and others e.g.:

(1) changing the vocal group with each stanza: as in "Come, O Come, Emmanuel" (No. 2, SBH):

Stanza 1 — everybody; Stanza 2 — men;
Stanza 4 — ladies; Stanza 5 — everybody;

(2) changing the verse or alternate lines in keeping with the structure of the song — e.g. the Epiphany hymn, "Watchman, tell us of the night" (No. 525, SBH):

1st line — ladies; 2nd line — men; 3rd line — ladies; 4th line — men.

The interesting Christmas carol, "Sir Christmas" (No. 21, *Oxford Book of Carols*), calls for the alternate use of solo voice, small SATB group, unison group, ladies' voices, full chorus. When the opening lines are repeated at the close as in "O Jesu so meek" (No. 501, SBH) the choir may be divided into two groups, which alternate on each line but sing together on the last. A further division can be effective in the first line in which the first group sings the first part of the line "O Jesu so meek," and the second group immediately responds with "O Jesu so kind." Other illustrations of this form can be found in the large repertoire of carols.

Specific invocations or expressions of praise are effective when sung responsively, such as the resplendent Easter hymn "Jesus Christ is risen today" (No. 92, SBH). If this song is sung in unison, the opening line may be sung by the ladies' voices and the "Alleluia" by the men; the second line, "Our triumphant holy day," could be sung by the men while the ensuing "Alleluia" is sung by the ladies. The "Alleluias" could also be sung by the combined ladies' and men's voices.

Responsive singing between precentor and choir may be practiced with songs like "Winter's Snow," a Christmas Carol by R. O. Morris (No. 190, *Oxford Book of Carols*). The solo voice sings the short four-line stanza while the entire choir answers in the refrain. In Martin Shaw's setting of "Kings in Glory" (No. 194, *Oxford Book of Carols*), the solo voice sings the first line and the choir continues the narrative in the second line. The pattern of alternating each line between solo and chorus continues throughout the eight-line stanzas.

The alternation between solo and chorus singing can be arranged in accordance with the sense of the spoken dialogue, as for example in the familiar and beautiful "Cherry Tree Carol" (No. 66, *Oxford Book of Carols*). The narrative part which does not contain dialogue can be sung by the entire choir, while the dialogue between Joseph and Mary is assigned to male and female solo voices, respectively. Other examples of "conversational" carols which could be treated in this way are "Mary's Wanderings" (No. 93, *Oxford Book of Carols*) and "Joseph, dearest, Joseph mine" (No. 77, *Oxford Book of Carols*).

The conducting motions used in directing unison singing should help to show the direction and shape of the musical line, to set and keep the music in motion, to clarify enunciation, to assist the singers in breathing, to delineate the phrases, and to build and relax spans of musical tension. In unison singing, the "deep" downbeat should be avoided even more than in linear music in four-part harmony. The conducting patterns should continually assume a more horizontal direction. Here again one might strive to imitate or achieve the old traditional modeling of a melodic line (chironomy). The director must nevertheless guard against a disorderly free-lance style of conducting. He can be instrumental in assisting the singers to enunciate clearly by occasionally mouthing the words, by illustrating mouth formations for various vowels, and by clarifying the singing consonants with hand gestures (e.g. wide mouth position — spread fingers; O formation — forming a circle with thumb and forefinger; m, n, ng — lightly pressing two fingers together, etc.). Aids to breathing can be given by breathing with the singers at the breathing points, by using a sustaining hand in a "palms up" position, by pointing one's hand to the midriff, the area of support and by allowing sufficient time to inhale between phrases. The termination of one phrase and the beginning of the next can be indicated by appropriate hand signals (compare with A II, p. 25 ff.).

Leise—p. 162: Medieval congregational hymns in the German tongue, so-called because of their refrain: *Kyrie eleis(on)* which was abbreviated into *kirleis* or *leis*.

Abgesang and *Stollen* p. 166: from the term "Barform," which is used frequently in modern German studies to denote one of the oldest and most important musical forms, that is the form with the basic scheme aab. The name is derived from the Medieval German term for this form, namely *Bar*. This consisted of two *Stollen* (section a) and the *Abgesang* (section b). (Definitions from *Harvard Dictionary of Music*, Willi Apel, Harvard University Press.)

Chapter III

Artistic Canon Singing

The distinction between artistic canon singing and informal (social) canon singing is the same as that between artistic and informal unison singing. We will consider only the singing of canons which does not involve the active participation of the listening audience. (See B II, 151 ff.) The singing of canons is less suited for a performance since the musical character of canons renders them more suitable for singing by an entire audience. The canon by its very form and nature is more suitable as a performing than as a listening medium. Even so the use of the canon in artistic performances has played an important and expansive role in the development of European music. In this context the symbolic possibilities of the canon are of particular importance. For example, in his *Mass in B minor,* Bach symbolically represents the trinity of God by a three-voice canon, and in his treatment of the cantus firmus in his organ chorale *Dies sind die heil'gen zehn Gebot* (These are the Ten Holy Commandments) he has one canon voice obediently follow the contour and musical structure of the tune.

On a coat of arms the ornamental symbols and epigrams symbolize a rank, a city, or some important family. One might draw an analogy here by saying that canons are epigrams or aphorisms set to music. They constitute a musical coat of arms and a symbol of music making. The various aphorisms and the famous literary expressions or biblical verses when set to music in canon form (with its terse and precise melodic structure, its systematic, predetermined overlapping of one melodic part over another and reduction to a forceful, simple, but most basic form) attain, in the continual repetition of the same melodic and rhythmic elements, something of an abstract, symbolic, and mythical significance. The canon becomes a musical symbol of the meaning and content of the verse or epigram. Since the end of a canon flows again into its own beginning, this unceasing sphere of musical motion has been looked upon as the symbol of lasting worth, of loyalty, fidelity, and eternity. The various singing schools also looked upon canon singing, in which all participants sing the same parts, as a symbol of the choral fellowship.

170

This symbolical character of the canon limits the possibilities of its use. It will seldom have a place on an all choral concert, unless it is used to open the concert as a kind of musical fanfare as is customary among some male choruses. The symbol-laden canonic settings of the text of the mass (e.g. Palestrina and more recently O. Heinemann) and the "Ten Commandments" by Haydn are seldom encountered in choral performances of today. On festive occasions it would be meaningful and desirable to express musically the central thought or purpose of the occasion by an appropriate verse set to a canon. This could be sung at the very beginning of the program as a kind of announcement or at the end of such festivities as school concerts, graduations, anniversaries, birthdays, weddings, etc. Poets and composers should exploit the possibilities of the canon much more for such uses. After a long era of musical composition which was based predominantly on harmonic principles, many listeners will no doubt have some difficulty in realizing and grasping the various overlapping and intertwining voice parts of a "musical coat of arms" upon the first hearing. Some training in this respect is necessary. Nothing should hinder a choir from occasionally singing a canon of an entertaining nature, especially in the context of music making at a house party; and why shouldn't a choir, after a gay evening of music making, bid their listeners a jovial "Good Night" while singing the Mozart "Bona-nox canon"! (For utilizing the canon as a medium of choral training, see A V, p. 71 ff.; A VI, p. 91 ff.; and A VII, p. 103 ff.)

The first step in learning a canon is to sing it in unison in an artistic choral manner. (Compare B II, p. 151 ff.) After the canon tune has been thoroughly mastered according to the suggestions given for unison singing in the previous chapter, the director must divide his choir into the necessary number of sections and assign to them the different canonic voice parts. In informal singing situations, the different canonic parts may sometimes be left to the choice of the individual singer, but in artistic choral singing the division of the choir into sections and the assignment of parts must be carefully determined in advance. As a matter of principle, one should avoid the unjudicious mixing of male and female voices, which unfortunately, happens so often. This results in indistinct sonorities and such clashing of timbres that the individual voice parts are often unrecognizable. Artistic and musically satisfying canon singing is, to a great extent, dependent upon clear delineation of voice parts and voice textures. The mixture of deep male voices with high female voices on the same part sounds as if a sixteen foot organ pipe were coupled to each treble voice.

To obtain the necessary contrast of sound and color from the different canonic parts, the voices should be divided not only according to sex but also according to weight and color. When using male voices for a two-voiced

171

canon the tenors could sing against the basses and when the same canon is sung by a ladies', girls' or boys' choir, the sopranos could sing their part against that of the altos. If the canon has more than two parts, the choir may be further divided according to the vocal character of the voices, as for example — a three-voice canon could be sung by the tenors, baritones, and basses respectively. In a canon with a wide range of pitches singers will have some difficulty in reaching the right pitches. This is true especially of the more harmonically structured canons of the Classic and Romantic Periods in which a four-voiced canon represents four-part harmony, in which a bass singer would be required to sing some notes belonging to the range of the first and second tenor voices. It is best in such cases to combine higher and lower voices in such a way that a low voice in the tenor group can supply the low notes and a higher voice in the bass group the higher notes.

In a mixed choir it is of course easier to obtain the necessary tonal contrast between voices. In a two-voice canon the female voices sing against the male voices even if this results in a "canon to the octave." In a three-voice canon the sequence of voices for the different parts could be sopranos, male voices, altos or tenors, ladies' voices, basses. In a canon of four or more parts the entries of the various voice parts can simply alternate between male and female groups, e.g. sopranos, tenors, altos, basses. It is inadvisable to enter all the ladies' voices first, followed by the men's voices or vice versa because of the lack of tonal balance that this creates. In canons with uneven-numbered voice parts one should, whenever possible, for the sake of clearer melodic delineation, give the largest number of parts to the ladies' voices. In a five-voice canon, for example, one would have three groups of ladies' voices and two groups of male voices. The proper arrangement of voices in the final chord of the canon must also be taken into consideration. If the final chord contains an additional lower octave or a lower fifth, the ladies' voices should not be permitted to sing the top voice while the men sing the lowest part, for this would increase the distance between them by another octave. Here it would be best for each voice part to sing the same ending, as for example in Gebhardt's four-part canon, "Give to our God immortal praise" (No. 299, *The Youth Hymnary*). One must also watch the relationship of treble voices to male voices in double, triple, or quadruple canons, as for example in Mozart's canon, "Light from above," for three groups of four voices each (No. 295, *The Youth Hymnary*).

Even after the canon has been rehearsed in unison and the voices satisfactorily grouped for their various canonic parts, one should not proceed directly from unison singing to the prescribed multivoiced canonic setting. For example, in a four-voice canon one could move progressively from unison singing to a two-voice, from two-voice to a three-voice, and finally to the full four-voice singing of the canonic setting. This would give the director the opportunity to check each voice carefully as it is fitted into the overlapping canonic structure. In this way the singer also experiences with growing interest the "birth" of a canon. To achieve a secure rhythm the words could be spoken to the rhythm of the music, first in unison and then in canon. Before singing the canon to the text it could be hummed on singing consonants and sung on tonal syllables. This enables the singer to sing the vocal line with greater ease, helps to establish the finely meshed vocal web, and encourages keener listening. All this results in better control of the vocal and musical processes. The various voice groups can now, in turn, sing the text to the music while the other three groups hum their parts. Then two groups sing the text and the remaining two groups hum, etc. This method of exposing each voice group by alternate singing of the text, forces the singers to listen to themselves more critically and helps them to blend their enunciation of words more completely into the linear flow produced by the parts that are hummed or sung to tonal syllables.

The voice group which begins the canon must sing with clarity and confidence since this voice part is most exposed. One might strengthen the leading group accordingly by selecting stronger, better, or simply more voices.

When singing canons informally the director may allow the canonic cycle to continue indefinitely according to the interest and participation of the singers and bring the canon to a close at his own discretion. In artistic canon singing, however, the exact place for concluding a canon must be determined at the outset. The canonic orbit must not whirl too long. In the performance of longer canons one could follow the approximate rule that the canon is concluded when the last voice part has been sung through once. In shorter canons the last voice part might be sung through twice. A canon may easily get into a rut if prolonged by too many repetitions, and it becomes increasingly more difficult to bring it to a satisfactory conclusion. It is better and more interesting to conclude the canon somewhat early and then repeat the performance since the regular entries and gradual buildup of the several voices constitute the essential musical nature of the canon. In the performance of canons it has become a practice to first sing it in unison. In proceeding from unison to multivoiced singing of the canon one should not come to a full stop after the unison singing and then start over again. The various parts should enter as soon as the unison singing is completed. In the performance of a six-voice canon (as in rehearsal) it has been proved effective to postpone the transition from the unison to the full six-part singing by first presenting the canon in three parts. When singing it in three parts it is best to sing the first, third and fifth voice parts. The full six-voice setting of it can be introduced by further dividing the parts and having the respec-

173

tive groups come in on the unsung entries after the second round of the canonic circle. Many solutions are possible.

The harmonic progressions play an important role in concluding a canon. The closing cadence must conform to principles of good voice leading. In a canon in which the musical movement is governed by harmonic progressions, as in certain types of three- and four-voice canons, the lowest available voice group, possibly the bass group, should conclude the canon at the lowest canonic branch while the soprano sings the highest voice part. To have the desired voice groups appear in the right place of the final chord, one must enter the voices accordingly, in the sequence indicated at the outset. When deciding upon the sequence of the entries of the voice groups the director must arrange the sequence of voice groups so that the deepest voices will conclude with the typical V — I or IV — V — I chordal progression with the other groups overlapping in their proper place of the chordal structure. In the four-part canon "Alleluia" by Phillip Hayes (Augsburg 1332), the various entries can be arranged in such a sequence that the bass sings "le-lu-ia" on the notes *c, d* and *g* (Part I) while the soprano sings *e, e d c b* (Part II). The alto and tenor parts fit in as shown in the example (See Ex. 50). The cadences do not always work out so smoothly, nor do canons usually happen to end on the same word or even on a rhyming word. Where necessary, the director should rewrite some notes to allow for a satisfactory cadence.

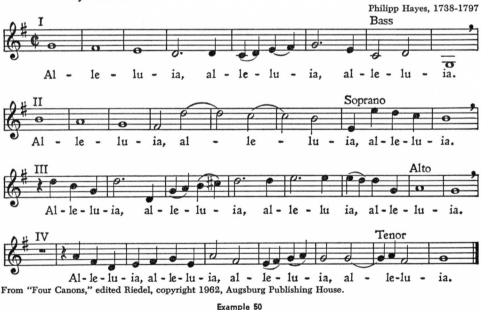

From "Four Canons," edited Riedel, copyright 1962, Augsburg Publishing House.

Example 50

When a canon is sung by a mixed group the director should conclude the music on a chord where the lowest voice comes to rest on the tonic;

otherwise the music might end on a first or even on a second inversion chord. For example, in Joseph Haydn's three-part canon, "The King Shall Come" (*Nine Easy Canons,* Augsburg 1333) the lowest part of the final chord must come to rest on *g* and not on *b*. In Phillip Hayes's six-part canon, "Where Is Joyfulness" (Augsburg 1333), the bass voice should end on *c,* the last note of the canon, and since the last two measures contain the highest notes of the canon, it would be in order and even necessary to transpose the entire two measures down an octave on the last round. The structure of many canons does not allow all the voices to close simultaneously on the same part of the measure, or on the same fermata, with the result that some voices keep on moving for a beat or two. Parts with such undulating "after-movement" should be assigned to the upper voices. Both director and singers should be unequivocally clear about who sings which part and where. This can be quickly determined by observing the character and relative pitch of the voice parts in the music. A simple but good illustration of this is Phillip Hayes's "Where Is Joyfulness" just referred to. This simultaneous and anticlimactic stopping of the voice parts could frequently result in a truncation and mutilation of words. Here the director should decide beforehand where he can draw important words together or further sustain the music on a key word of the verbal phrase. A good example of this is Gebhardt's "Glory to God in the highest" (No. 276, *The Youth Hymnary*). The group which concludes the canon on the second entry could sustain "men" on the Bb for two more beats while the singers at the end of the third entry should sing the words "and goodwill t'wards men" with the last five notes by allowing one syllable to each note. The low Bb should be extended to four beats (from a half to a whole note). If the voices in a canon do not stop together, the voices which come to a close should sing with particular clarity and firmness so that the music doesn't just seep away, e.g. in Carl Schalk's two-part canonic setting of "All praise to God who reigns above" by Melchior Vulpius (Concordia 98-1763).

The addition of instruments can substantially enrich the serious artistic performance of canons. Instruments may be freely employed, but the combinations used should be decided upon in advance on the basis of sound musical and acoustical principles. Generally speaking, one would give preference to brass instruments (See B IV, p. 182 ff.) since the nature of their tonal production comes closest to that of the production of the singing voice. Furthermore, the concise and terse musical form of the canon can be realized with great sharpness and clarity by a wind instrument and conforms better to the more objective musical expression of the canon. Recorders may also be used in a variety of ways, but they should not be used with a male voice choir since the cool, impersonal sound and the high frequency vibrations of this instrument do not blend well with male voices. Recorders best lend

175

themselves to the long, spun-out linear canons of the sixteenth century, as in the *Agnus Dei* by A. Gumpelzhaimer. String instruments, on the other hand, lend themselves best to the performance of the harmonically orientated canons of the Classic and Romantic Eras, e.g. "The King Shall Come" by Haydn or "Light From Above," by Mozart.

In using instruments with the singing of canons it seems best to couple them with voices. They help to clarify, enhance, and support the vocal lines. Each vocal part is combined with an instrument whose timbre is best suited to the vocal sound of the group. The balance between voices and instruments must be carefully adjusted so that the instruments will never overshadow the singers or the text. Recorders may be used with boys' and ladies' choirs as a higher octave part.

The canonic parts may also be divided between singers and players, in accordance with the available instruments, the size and strength of the choir, and the structure of the music. In two-voice canons it seems best to let the singers begin, as in "Suffering Son of Man" by Melchior Vulpius (Augsburg 1332). It is particularly advantageous to have the second voice played by an instrument if it follows the first voice at a fifth instead of at the octave or unison. In the two-voice canon setting by Carl Schalk on the chorale tune, "Now thank we all our God" (Concordia 98-1762), the instruments could play both parts at a fifth below the singers' parts. In a three-part canon two instrumentalists could take the middle part while the first and third could be taken by the singers, or vice versa, e.g. *Dona Nobis Pacem* by an unknown composer (No. 281, *The Youth Hymnary*). In canons for four or more parts the entries should be alternately taken up by singers and instrumentalists. A unique and favorable combination for the four-voice canon "Give to our God immortal praise" by Gebhardt (No. 299, *The Youth Hymnary*) would be as follows: first part — women's voices; second part — trumpet; third part — male voices; fourth part — trombone. Such regular change between voices and instruments in canons of more than four voices produces its own unique tonal architecture. In the eight-part canon "He Who Music Despiseth" by J. Staden, the following scheme of voices and instruments could be used: the fouth and fifth parts form the center or core and are sung, while the first, second, and third parts form one flank and the sixth, seventh, and eighth parts the other flank of the core and are played with instruments. The seven-voice canon "With Instrument and Violins" by E. Sartorius could be similarly performed by having the middle (fourth) part sung by a solo voice which is accompanied on each side by instruments. The same architectural principle should be observed when using a mixture of string, brass, and woodwind instruments.

The vocal canon form may be expanded by the instruments, using the actual music of the canon as a short prelude and postlude. The music between this musical introduction and conclusion might be performed with voices only or with a mixture of voices and instruments in the manner suggested. After the instrumental introduction and just before the instrumental conclusion the music could come to a complete temporary stop. This provides two more opportunities for setting the canonic wheel into motion. Another variation would be the withdrawal of voices for one complete round and then re-entering them — which could produce an effect similar to that achieved by an organist when he adds a Vox Humana stop to the registration. The voices are successively withdrawn, allowing the instruments to play the postlude by following the canonic course until the director gives the release.

In many cases a soloistic setting or presentation proves to be most effective, particularly for two- and three-part canons. For example in the "Alleluia," a three-part canon by Mozart (No. 292, *The Youth Hymnary*), a soloist leads and is followed by a solo string instrument on each of the two remaining parts. The two-part canonic settings of traditional choral tunes by Carl Schalk could be treated similarly, except that some of the chorales, like "All praise to God" (Concordia 98-1763), could use a light trumpet instead of a violin for the second part.

The conducting signals and beat patterns used in directing canons are similar to those required for unison singing. While rehearsing the canon in unison the director may proceed according to the principles and procedures described in the previous chapter in connection with unison singing. However, as soon as the canon is sung in all its parts, it becomes almost impossible for the director to control the musical movement of each part. Even if he could simultaneously use both of his elbows, his shoulders, head, eyes, and mouth for conducting, it still would not be advisable to attempt to direct each section! Therefore, above all he must direct his attention to the giving of clear entries and cutoffs and maintaining a clear, steady flowing beat throughout the singing of the canon. Every director should seek to attain a complete mastery and security in this regard. He should trace the conducting line of the canon and in performance address himself successively to each new group at the moment of entry by giving as clear a cue beat as possible. The conducting line for the opening four measures of Christoph Praetorius' four-part canon "O Trinity Most Blest" (Augsburg 1333) would appear thus:

From "Nine Easy Canons," edited Riedel, copyright 1962, Augsburg Publishing House.

Example 51

177

The half note units of time measurement in this canon should be beat most decisively and should be conducted with a "deeper" beat than one would use when conducting unison music, or for that matter, any other type of choral music. The suggestive gesture of supporting and holding the voices together at the conclusion of a canon is most important. The notion of many soloists and choir members that one should automatically ritard the final phrase of a song must in the case of singing canons be strictly avoided, for if one section is sustaining the final note in the canon, the other singers will find themselves near the beginning or in the middle, and (as a result) the entire musical framework will begin to waver. Dynamic shadings are also contrary to the nature of canon singing because the melodic and textual section which would invite dynamic differentiation are constantly coupled with parts of the canon which might not require such dynamic treatment. Each canonic voice must follow its own path of musical motion and should strive to unite the various spans of tension of the canon into a unified whole. For this reason the canon remains one of the surest means of preventing the choir from false musical interpretation and of guarding the singers against excessive individualistic expression which might be quite unrelated to the nature and structure of the music. The singers are required to base their musical and artistic expression on that which is happening musically while the canon is being performed.

Generally the entries should be accented more strongly than the rest of the music in the canon. Even if the procedure for the conclusion has been agreed upon in advance so that the bass singers, for example, know that on the repeat of the first round they must stop exactly in the middle of the canon, the director must still, when approaching the cutoff, give some warning signal which is visible to all. This signal is preferably given by raising the left hand, this being a clear indication to all musicians that a fermata and cutoff is to take place at the end of the phrase which is being sung. The cutoff signal must, especially in canon singing, be given with energy and clarity and with a gradual enlargement of movements as the final cutoff is approached. If the different parts do not conclude simultaneously but rather successively, as happens in so many canons, the termination of each voice part must be clearly indicated. The final part particularly should be conducted and released with care.

Although the director may give much attention to entries and cutoffs, it is still also possible to hinder the musical process and turn it into a rigid, dull affair by becoming too enslaved by the mechanical aspects of conducting. Canon singing offers the finest opportunity for developing a choral autonomy, and so the director should, whenever it is feasible, withdraw or reduce his conducting motions. In the exercising of such independence, however, every singer must always remain flexible in his singing and keep his ear open to what is going on in the other parts throughout the entire canon. Only too frequently one encounters groups of singers who try to sing through difficult musical passages with great determination and vocal gusto without the slightest attempt to listen and relate to each other.

If a semicircular formation is generally recommended for choirs, it is even more valid for canon singing. The circling, soaring canonic voices constitute a dense, spherical mesh of musical sound. The symbol for the canon is the circle, and since the music and the choral formation should comprise a unity, the circle is the most desirable formation, even if it cannot always be maintained when performing for an audience. The various groups of voices should be arranged in the order of the entries, but in semicircular formations these groups should not be visibly separated from each other. Instrumental groups may be set up in the same manner. Both the musical form and the symbolic meaning of the canon suggest the encompassing sphere or circle of people. For this reason it has proved meaningful for festive or informal social occasions to have a four-part canon sung by the four singing groups located in the four corners of the hall. The intertwining strands of musical sounds emitted from the different parts of the room encompass, allegorically speaking, the entire room and unite all the people who are present. A particularly good possibility for this kind of physical arrangement is the multigrouped sixteen-voice canon "Light From Above" by W. A. Mozart (No. 295, *The Youth Hymnary*). Such space-encompassing and symbolical music making is of course also possible with two-voice canonic settings, by placing the two groups at some distance from each other, e.g. from two opposite balconies. The effectiveness of the canon as a symbol of an all-embracing fellowship can be further heightened by the addition of movement. For instance, a cast of actors on their way to the stage could sing a three-part canon while moving through the audience in three separate aisles, unite on stage, complete the canon, and then proceed with their play or drama. A choir might follow a similar procedure at the outset of an informal but festive musical evening. Youth groups and glee clubs could liven up some of their cultural and social activities by commencing their performances with this kind of canon singing. Such singing could be the "upbeat" to the occasion by setting the tempo and spirit of the entire performance or social function.

The procession is an ancient tradition which grew out of the introductory ceremonies of the old cultic rites. Canons used in connection with processions link us with the historic past and become a symbol of the ongoing cycle of life. The space, size, and architecture of the building must of course be appropriate to such processional use of canons. The church at one time also made more use of such symbolical creative media. These should be reinvestigated and made accessible once more for use in our time. The use of music with processions is still practiced in some churches today. In many churches, confirmands proceed into the sanctuary to the singing of hymns. This would indeed be a good starting point for exploring and further developing the possibilities of music in combination with processions.

Chapter IV

Multivoiced Choral Singing:

The Method of Rehearsing

The question of the use of piano in rehearsal is raised whenever the method of rehearsing new choral works is discussed. The association of the piano with rehearsals is close in the minds of the average choir director and singer. Many directors hardly ever leave the piano or organ during the rehearsal, and only too frequently the method of literally hammering out every note for each voice part — even in octaves — is resorted to. This procedure should by all means be discouraged and can be eliminated in all types of choirs whether large or small, amateur or professional. Such an approach to learning new music is both mechanical and unmusical, and contradicts the unique and peculiar character of choral singing which stems and develops from the combined functions of the breath and the voice in the process or reproducing the word-bound musical line. The use of the piano in duplicating the voice part brings together two phenomena which are foreign to each other — the piano which is basically a chordal instrument, and the voice which has to do with the linear aspect, i.e. the single melodic line. The nature of the tone production of the larynx and of the piano are entirely opposed to each other; the piano tone resounds from the action of the hammer on the strings. Old historic books on musical instruments classify all keyboard instruments as *Schlaginstrumente* (German term for percussion instruments), and the earlier traditional term for organ playing was *Orgelschlagen* which literally means "striking the organ keys"! Even today one speaks about *Anschlag* (German term for attack) in connection with keyboard instruments. The larynx, however, fulfills its singing function by means of the air which rushes past and activates the vocal cords. For this reason it can be classified as a wind instrument. The tone of a harmonium (reed organ) is produced by blowing air through the pipes and into the reed column. By constantly pounding the piano during rehearsal the director actually breaks up and destroys the true songful elements in his choir, both with regard to the production of the tone as well as the realization of the structural elements of the music. The choral tone becomes tight and rigid, the choir tends to lose pitch more easily and is being taught to move in a mechanical fashion from one pitch to the next. Because the piano at one time was classified with the percussion group of instruments, one might therefore quite justifiably speak about "drumming in the music" when using a piano for teaching the singers their notes. Choirs and their directors usually deceive themselves by assuming that the use of the piano saves rehearsal time. Generally speaking, the opposite is true because the choir director becomes accustomed to leaning on the instrument as a crutch. When one finally removes the crutch, which is inevitable in the preparation of a cappella works, the choir is helpless and much of the early training will need to be repeated. The choir, chained to the sounds from the hammered tone, cannot find itself, aurally speaking. The author has met with choirs which were so slavishly tied to the piano that they could not repeat a single pitch which was sung to them, whereas, on the other hand, they had no trouble repeating a pitch which was struck on the piano. A further consideration is that good a cappella choir singing requires the singing of pure intervals as opposed to the well-tempered intervals of the piano.

It is therefore in the interest of best choral singing that the choir director works without a keyboard instrument. The human voice must be set alongside, or in proximity to another voice, and the singer must learn to listen to the singing voice, learn from it, and adjust to it. In a cappella choral singing, voices must adjust and relate to each other. As early as 1528, M. Agricola required of a certain cantor "that he work with his singers according to artistic principles and not with the lute." What he really meant was that choirs were to sing artistically while learning their parts by solmization. The assistance of the lute, which at that time frequently assumed the same role in rehearsal as the piano does today, and which was also struck (the old expression for playing the lute was "striking the lute"), would tend to negate these artistic principles. The great era of choral music took a critical attitude toward the use of all percussion instruments in connection with choral training. In rehearsing and training his choir, the director should develop his own pedagogical skills based on, and originating in the unique nature of choral singing itself. This requires the most thorough preparation on the part of the director. Furthermore, he must know how to use his own voice to illustrate both technical and artistic musical aspects, for everything which he wants to illustrate and communicate musically to the choir is dependent to a great extent on that which he can suggest and pattern with his own voice. The director must save his voice as much as possible at times when rehearsals become more frequent and more intensive, in modest choral situations in which there are few readers in the choir, and in activities outside of the rehearsal which require a great deal of speaking. Rather than resorting to a keyboard instrument when giving illustrations, he should choose a melodic wind instrument, preferably one in which the origin and production of the tone most closely resembles the production of the singer's vocal tone. According to this point of view the order of preference for using instruments as an aid to teaching music in a rehearsal, could be stated as follows: (1) brass instruments (trumpet family – horn family); (2) reed instruments (oboes – clarinets); (3) flutes (recorders – traverse flutes); (4) string instruments (viol family – violin family); (5) keyboard instruments (cembalo and spinets – piano). The author has experimented with the use of these various instruments in choral work and has found that the generally accepted order of rank and preference as given here is quite valid. As indicated, the piano, which today is chosen and used more frequently than any other instrument, is placed last in the group of the least preferred instruments. This fact should be carefully considered when music teachers and conducting students choose an instrument for their minor study in the performance field. The same consideration should also be made when volunteer choirs and directors choose an instrument.

Even the more preferred melody instruments should not be used for note drilling purposes. To "blow in" the notes with a wind instrument appears to be little better than to "hammer them in" with a piano. An instrument should not be used as a constant pulling device to which one hitches the voices, but it should be used between periods of singing and therefore not in a simultaneous singing and playing activity, but as an alternative activity to singing. Otherwise it hampers the singer's listening, spoils his ear, and hinders him in developing independence as a singer. When properly blown, a trumpet can imitate the vocal tones of a singer. A given phrase which is to be learned by the singers is played with the same tonal character, the same breath control, the same phrasing, the same tonal strength, and with the same span of musical tension as is expected from the singers. The singers are then asked to sing the phrase. When the singers can sing the phrase correctly, the director (or instrumentalist) plays the nearest contrapuntal part to the sung phrase and vice versa. In this way the entire tune is played and sung in its various sections in a continuous cycle from instrumental player to choir. The instrument is therefore not used to drill or hammer in the notes, but as a means of illustration and as an adjunct to the music produced by the choir. The pipe organ which is used to accompany the choir is in a more unique position. It combines many advantages of the woodwind instruments with the fingering possibilities for the multipart playing which characterizes the piano and harpsichord. It therefore remains a very useful instrument for choral work, even though the wind-produced tones are mechanically produced.

Even when rehearsing a work which requires instrumental accompaniment for its performance, it is better to rehearse the work without instruments in the earlier stages of preparation. The instruments are added later at a suitable stage in the progress of the work. For a musical work which requires a full orchestra and possibly also continuo accompaniment, one should employ a keyboard instrument which can reproduce the orchestral parts well in advance of the dress rehearsal and performance. The choir has an opportunity to get used to singing tempered pitches, becomes acquainted with the instrumental interludes, and gains more security in singing its entries. The keyboard instrument represents the instrumental counterpart and helps round out the music with melodic and harmonic details. In rehearsing larger choral works the director should have an accompanist or a vocal coach at the piano so that he has greater freedom to work with the choir and to work out his musical intentions. Even though the use of the piano at rehearsals (as stated earlier) is limited to certain types of works, it should nevertheless be strongly restated that the contemporary choral director should possess the ability to play the choral parts on the keyboard.

Some choral directors, who use the piano to assist the note learning process, justify their practice by maintaining that the music of the late sixteenth century, and particularly the music of Bach, was "instrumentally conceived," even to the point where these people understand exactly the opposite of what is really meant by it. Neither the practical musicians nor the learned musicologists are agreed which music was traditionally performed vocally or instrumentally, let alone which music was chorally or instrumentally conceived. The justifications for such assertions by choral directors are often flimsy and threadbare, and serve to cover up a lack of knowledge and ability. One thing, however, is certain — namely that Senfl, as well as Bach, never used a piano in their choral work, simply because the piano in its modern form did not yet exist!

The task of rehearsing a new choral work should commence with an introduction to the work. Such an introduction should be the occasion for throwing some light on the work with regard to the period of its composition, its composer, style, disposition, and degree of difficulty. It can also help the choir to identify more quickly with the work. Such introductions must always be terse and to the point. A long written dissertation has no place here. Both the choir and its director must allow themselves to be gripped by the creative breadth of the work. The musical sounds and not the words must inspire the performers. When the work has been mastered, and when the singers have been gripped by its artistic essence, it might be in order to deepen the understanding and appreciation of the choir by giving a well-prepared lecture on the music. This could be done on such occasions as an evening devoted to contemporary music, or an occasion when a historical cyclical work is being performed. Too many explanations and too much lecturing during a choir rehearsal is always wrought with some problems. As a matter of principle in musical organizations of lay people, very little is said about the music which is being rehearsed, whereas in some more sophisticated choral circles the informative lectures of the director occasionally take up more time than the actual music making. Here one should heed the words of Goethe, "Build artists, don't talk." It is always a valid criteria of the quality of a musical composition whether it can capture the attention and interest of its listeners on its own merits and then continue to influence them in a positive, wholesome manner. Every additional word during rehearsal must serve the music. Words are used to give practical instructions, to provide the key for unlocking difficult spots, and to shed light on the background of the work insofar as is required for its understanding and mastery. An occasional word thrown in for no particular musical purpose may have its own immediate purpose and value. Any further explanation, if necessary, should be reserved for a special presentation.

For further familiarization with the work it is often quite meaningful to read the text as a work of art. In a strophic text one should present at least all those stanzas which are to be sung, whereas in a longer work, one might refer only to the most crucial sections, or, the particular section which is to be rehearsed next.* The text does not always have to be read by the conductor, for often it is of greater benefit to engage one of the members of the choir to do this. If the meaning of the text is not clear upon the first reading, a short, clear explanation of the sense of the text, its difficult grammatical structures, and its farfetched imageries from folklore or the Bible is in order. One might draw attention to any phenomena or circumstances which influenced the work in any significant manner, particularly if this makes it easier for the choir to grasp and appreciate the meaning of the text. In any case there should be no obstacle which would hinder the singers from receiving and understanding the sense and meaning of the text. After such introductions to and clarifications of the text, the music may be played on a keyboard instrument insofar as this is not incompatible with the style and spirit of the music. In an ideal situation the work could be introduced by a group of selected singers who have previously sung it, or a group of first-rate note readers could be asked to sing it at sight. With larger works one would have these singers sing only the highlights of the work or the particular passages which are to be practiced at the rehearsal. In this way the other singers can catch a glimpse of the artistic nature of the work and an atmosphere is created in which the pedagogical work can proceed according to definite musical and artistic principles.

Such creative and stimulating introductions to the words and music should be followed by the actual singing and rehearsing of the music. With

*Translator's note: The translator recalls the first rehearsal of the *St. Matthew Passion* in which Dr. Ehmann, who had completed a new English translation, took an hour to read the entire text. This set the tone and created the right *niveau* for the daily rehearsals in the following six weeks of preparation for the performance.

a fairly well-trained choir, or with a choir in which there are several good singers and readers in each section, one should begin by having the entire choir carefully read through the selection. This helps to awaken the choir's perception of the music, gives the singers the feel of the musical terrain, quickens their incentive and wakens their musical powers and joy of singing. Ofter directors do not trust their choirs enough in this respect and thereby dampen the musicality of the singers instead of awakening it. This is also a good practice in sight singing. It has been the author's experience that ordinary rural choirs in which the largest number of singers were unable to read notes, could, after a few helpful instructions, sight read even a Bach choral composition!

If the harmonic structure of a composition is bound to a melody, the entire choir should first sing the tune until it is thoroughly familiar to everyone. In addition to the fine pedagogical training values of unison singing (See Chapter B II), the following observations could be made with regard to the singing of multivoiced compositions:

(1) All singers, including the singers in the less important parts should first become familiar with the musical framework upon which the entire composition with its several voices is based — they should be completely familiar with the melodic reservoir from which their particular voice part has its origin and its roots;

(2) All singers should work through the text simultaneously; it is not necessary to repeat the same text with each section;

(3) All singers are drawn into the movement of the music, and if they happen to be singing homophonic or chordal music, they can apply the breathing places and phrase divisions of the tune to their own voice parts;

(4) The tune becomes the musical and spiritual possession of the singers. If a bass singer, for example, never learns the tune, it is possible for him to attend all the weekly rehearsals of his choral society faithfully, and throughout his life to sing his part in hundreds of songs, and yet not even be able to sing any of the songs with his friends or family since he knows nothing but his own part, which in many instances, is only of relative significance to the whole song! Perhaps he can only sing the song if all the members of his section are present at the rehearsal!

When the tune is to be sung by the entire choir, it should be done in a key which will have the most comfortable range for all voices. This procedure of having everyone first learn the tune can become a problem with unmusical singers or with singers who cannot read. It is possible, for instance, that the singers on the accompanying voice parts may lose track of their voice part and quite obliviously drift into the tune, with the result that eventually a large part of the choir would actually be singing the tune. (This happened one time to the author in his first performance with a male voice choir!)

186

If the music offers special rhythmic, melodic, or harmonic difficulties, it is advisable to remove them before the choir attempts to sing through the music in all its parts. It might even be well to work out these difficulties before the singers pick up their music, since the holding of music may be a hindrance to certain types of rhythmic activity. The director devises a short, unified exercise which he writes on the board, or which he sings, plays, or rhythmicizes or which he visualizes and illustrates with his hands and fingers, for instance the use of hand positions to indicate different intervals. For a more thorough work-out, the exercise is performed by the entire choir and not only by the singers in whose voice part the difficulty occurs. In this way the choir can be prevented from making similar mistakes or even from becoming so confused that they are unable to continue, which would of course only increase the difficulty of solving the problem.

In moving from the unison singing of the tune to the simultaneous singing of all the parts, it may be helpful to exploit the possibilities of choral improvisation to stimulate interest and creativity. The melody singers sing the tune, while the others seek to invent a suitable second voice from the disposition and character of the tune. With simpler songs this is possible and has proved helpful. A choir may practice this kind of improvisation a great deal, provided some specific instructions and guide lines are given. This helps to stimulate the desire for music making within the choir, prevents it from getting into the rut of note drilling, encourages the singers to listen to the tune and to anticipate some of the possibilities for its vocal accompaniment. Choral improvisation can also be a kind of touchstone for the further working out of the various parts of the entire musical compostion.

When the singers have been variously exposed to the music through listening, explanations and clarifications, by unison singing of the tune, and by improvisational singing around the tune, they must proceed to the work of learning the other voice parts. It certainly would not be necessary to take up all of these various intermediary steps in each case; this would vary from one situation to another according to the nature and length of the work, the make-up and musical qualifications of the choir, and the disposition and ability of the choir director. The occasional criticism that such a procedure is a waste of time is simply not valid. Experience has shown that such seemingly roundabout ways are in reality the shortest and most logical ways, since they appeal to the choir and stimulate its musical growth, allow the singers to participate mentally, and permit them to experience the process of achieving a musical and artistic result — something they would not experience by sheer drill. The singers are drawn into the activity of independent music making from the very outset of the learning process.

The procedure for further rehearsal should grow out of the dominant musical phenomenon. A director who starts out from this premise is thrust directly into the creative and artistic *niveau* of the music, and the singers have the opportunity of taking hold of the essential nature of the work — a hold which they will not have to relinquish as they continue their work. The solution to technical problems will also be easier from here on. In compositions with strongly pronounced styles, there are three basic elements, any one of which can become the decisive dominant musical phenomenon.

(1) the text as the seed of musical inspiration and growth and as the embodiment of the music;

(2) the melodic musical element in which there is a free interplay of melodic parts above and beyond the text;

(3) the musical rhythm which includes and assimilates the other phenomena and becomes their servant.

In the following pages a selection of easy musical examples illustrating each of these types will be discussed. It is true, of course, that all of these phenomena occur in every choral composition, but in the more clearly pronounced styles, one of these phenomena usually dominates. The choral director begins to work with the dominant characteristics and then proceeds to the less pronounced musical aspects. What will follow now is a discussion of the choral treatment of a selection of musical examples illustrating each one of the musical styles. The application to larger and more expansive choral works can be made without any further explanation.

The short four-voice setting of Heinrich Schuetz's *Aller Augen warten auf dich, Herr* (All our eyes now wait upon Thee, O Lord) undoubtedly grows out of the text (*Gesellige Zeit*, Baerenreiter 615). A preliminary literary appreciation study of the text and the playing of the music at the keyboard would be desirable. The pronunciation and enunciation of the text should be worked out by the entire choir. Because the soprano voice does not constitute the melody in the usual restricted sense of the term (even though it is melodically more prominent than the other parts), it would not make too much sense to have the entire choir learn it. One should simply sing the setting at first sight in all of its four parts. At any rate, the choir should attempt to approach it in this way. Any difficult or uncertain places could be worked out separately later on. If this is not possible then the sopranos should learn their part first. The director then lets each voice section find its way through its particular voice part. Where the singers deviate from the right notes, the director injects the corrections with his own singing. If the choir is too slow and unwieldy, the director should assist by singing the individual parts of the entire setting, and then if necessary, each individual phrase as well. These are repeated by the individual section, whereupon the individual voice parts are combined and sung by the entire choir. The voice of the director (or the instrument) should not have to become the locomotive of a lethargic "vocal train"! Singers in each section should listen very carefully to the director as he sings their part and then should attempt to sing it accurately after him. As a transition to singing their parts unaided, it might be permissible to have the singers lightly hum their part while the director sings it. One should avoid the commonly practiced method of rehearsing the voice parts in the mechanical order in which they appear in the score, i.e. soprano to alto to tenor to bass. Nor should one proceed systematically from the most to the least difficult parts for no apparent musical or pedagogical reason. This is illustrated in a situation in which the director, in an effort to appear clever, with great deliberation begins to work with the altos as the first step in rehearsing a new piece of music. Instead, the learning process of a new work should follow the musical progress and structure of the composition by choosing the parts in the order in which the composer most probably wrote them. In our example, which is a harmonically conceived setting, the bass voice seems to be next in importance to the soprano. When proceeding to the inner voices one should not sing them to the text, for the frequent repetitions result in a loss of vitality and enunciation of the words, which, at this point may have been carefully worked out while rehearsing the sopranos and basses. The too frequent repetition of a text also tends to weaken its sense and meaning — it deteriorates and becomes ineffective. In rehearsing a strophic song one could prevent this by singing a different stanza to each voice part, which would of course also help the singers to become acquainted with the rest of the text to be sung. (The stanzas following the first stanza are usually beneath the musical score and so require considerable familiarization if they are to be sung in parts.) It is better to sing the music to tone syllables which reflect the verbal character of the text, and which can help clarify and further develop its lyrical and melodic aspects. At the same time the tone syllables should contain those vowels and consonants which are predominant in the particular text at hand, and which would further help to improve the enunciation. Finally the tone syllable should also serve the voice training processes by focusing the voice upward and forward through the use of suitably chosen singing consonants. The passage containing higher pitches should be practiced in connection with *ee, oo,* and the umlaut *ü,* while the lower passages could be practiced with syllables using *oh* and the umlaut *ö.* Here is an English translation of the German text:

> All our eyes now wait upon Thee, O Lord,
> And Thou givest them their daily meat in due season,
> Thou openest up Thy hand, and Thou satisfiest
> Everything which liveth with your good pleasure.

The predominance of *ee, e(den), i(in),* and the diphthong *ah-ah-ah-oo* (as in Thou), could suggest the following sequence of syllables to be used in working for pure vowels and good tone: *nee, zea, din, vow, hahn.* When singing on syllables one should strive for a smooth, flowing stream of sound, spinning out the syllables as it were.

When the sopranos and basses have mastered their parts, one should combine them in singing, for they actually consitute a complete bicinium. This also brings the sopranos, who have been rehearsed earlier, back into the process of music making and so prevents them from becoming lethargic. The soprano and bass parts form the outer musical framework, and their basic relation to each other is clarified when they are sung together. These parts should then be sung to the words while the two inner voices, the alto and tenor parts, are hummed or sung to a tone syllable. Since at this stage it is only a matter of filling in the harmonies which have been determined by the bass and soprano, the inner voices usually master their parts fairly quickly — the total result being quite satisfactory. The middle voice section which learns its part with the most ease is worked out first to syllables, and then sung to the text. It is then sung with the two outside voices as a self-contained tricinium. When these three voices have been fitted and blended with each other, the remaining fourth voice is also fitted in to complete the musical and tonal picture.

Before beginning with the final artistic polishing of the music, the words should once more be thoroughly rehearsed by speaking them to the rhythm of the music. While performing this exercise it should again become clear that the musical rhythm not only proceeds entirely from the textual rhythm, but that the inner motion of the words fully corresponds to the inner motion of the music. These two motions must unite in an interplay of moving energy in which the ultimate in ease, smoothness, and transparent lightness is achieved. For this reason any mere strict beat-conducting must be avoided, for the music of this delightful little composition should emerge from the verbal stream of the text. Heinrich Schuetz himself has this fitting comment in his preface to the Becker Psalter: "melodies which do not have a text can be sung with even more grace and charm when they are joined to words."

In the artistic perfection of this little choral setting, breaths should be taken only during the rests and after "raised hand" signals indicating snatch breaths — e.g. one should snatch a breath after the word "liveth" in the final phrase to produce a little indentation before approaching the slightly broadened ending. The half notes in the cadence should be antici-pated as musical and verbal culmination points, the final syllables and chords of each phrase should remain unaccented, and the sound should be sustained in an easy, gentle manner. The contrary movement between the outside voices at "everything which liveth" should be intensified, the alto should lead in the final cadence, and finally the entire tone production should be easy and relaxed so that the music gives the words a kind of transparent quality.

In choral settings of this type, the rests should not be observed by mechanically marking time. Their function is to delineate clearly the textual and musical phrasing and to give the choir the opportunity for taking a breath. Heinrich Schuetz himself maintains that "in such genre of compositions the rests aren't actually observed." Their relative duration is essentially determined by the quantity and intensity of breath which the choir must take. Rests or pauses must never become "dead" moments.

The conducting motions used here must be freed from a rigid, schematic beat pattern. In music of this style one should follow the natural rise and fall of the verbal inflections and conduct it according to the rhythm of the words in a free "up and down" manner, so to speak. At "and Thou givest them their daily meat," one should conduct two eighth notes to one beat. Each new phrase should begin with a clear, light cue beat and conclude with a clear cutoff signal with a similar light touch. The dominant voice part and note movement at the cadences should be conducted with clear, firm beats as, for example, the alto passage of the final cadence. The word "with" which follows the snatch breath in the final phrase should be cued in with a quick, precise, separate upbeat. The left hand can sustain the final unaccented syllables of each concluding phrase and also indicate the broadening effect in the final line from "and satisfiest" to the end with a large, sweeping linear gesture. The mouthing of words by the choir director can often be helpful in this kind of "word-music."

The various principles, procedures, and suggestions that have been given could be elaborated and illustrated in other works of Heinrich Schuetz, insofar as they do not fall into the class of polyphonic works. Similar works representing the kind of relationship between text and music as was noted in Schuetz's "All our eyes now wait upon Thee," have been produced by composers like H. Isaac, L. Senfl, J. Eccard, B. Gesius, or the numerous simple note against note *cantiones sacrae* settings of L. Osiander, H. L. Hassler, M. Praetorius, J. H. Schein, M. Vulpius, J. Crueger, and in the many sixteenth and seventeenth century Italian and English madrigals. One could also cite examples of simpler settings from the Classic and Romantic Periods by composers like J. F. Reichardt, Johannes Brahms, as well as easier examples of numerous contemporary musical settings. The beginning of a mixture of note against note and florid polyphony can be seen in settings like, "Innsbruck, I Now Must Leave Thee" by H. Isaac (p. 74, *European Madrigals*). In learning the music of this setting one could follow the suggestion given earlier that all singers first sing the tune. In the final phrase the words dissolve into pure linear polyphony. This section should first be sung to short syllables (*dahn, tahn, bahm*). The soprano part should be followed by the parallel moving alto, then the tenor, and the bass. Clapping the rhythm can be an effective means to clarify the rhythmic structure of this closing section.

The musical interest of the German choral setting, *Wach auf, wach auf, du deutsches Land* (Awake, awake O German land ([people]), Ex. 52, by J. Walther, grows predominantly from the melodic musical tensions and the sounds resulting from the linear polyphonic texture. It obviously makes little sense to work through the text first, since the body of the text, i.e. its verbal essence, is not embodied in the music. One must therefore first be familiar with the linear web of the different melodic parts to know how the

Ein neues Christliches Lied,
dadurch Deutschland zur Busse vermanet

Johann Walter

192

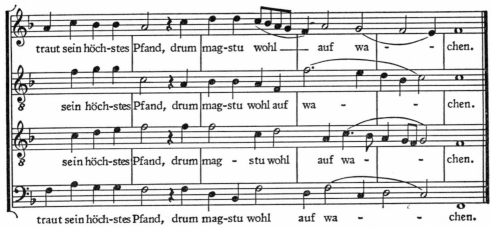

traut sein höch-stes Pfand, drum mag-stu wohl ___ auf wa - - chen.

sein höch-stes Pfand, drum mag-stu wohl auf wa - - chen.

sein höch-stes Pfand, drum mag - stu wohl auf wa - - chen.

traut sein höch-stes Pfand, drum mag-stu wohl auf wa - - chen.

From *Gesellige Zeit*, copyright Baerenreiter Verlag, Kassel, Germany.

Example 52

Literal Translation: Awake, awake oh (you) German land
enough you have been sleeping;
Recall (Think) what God for you has done,
for what (purpose) He you created.
Recall what God to you has given,
And you entrusted with his greatest pledge,
Then might you well awaken.

words fit in. In spite of this, the text of the poem as a whole should be read or otherwise presented in an artistic manner prior to the working with the music. The entire choir then proceeds to learn the tune which is in the tenor voice. One need not sing the tune in the key in which it is written but transpose it down so that the highest notes could easily be reached by all voices; the key of D might be quite suitable here. One should sing the tune (cantus firmus) to short tone syllables and to the text without working it through in detail at this point. The approach whereby all singers first learn the tune gives them a firmer grasp of the backbone and framework of the music. An exploratory sight reading of the entire four-voice setting should be made sometime during this stage of rehearsal. After the cantus firmus, the sopranos learn their part (discantus) in the original key. The discantus is then coupled with the melody (cantus firmus). These two voices actually form a complete bicinium and have been published in this special form. The next voice to be learned and sung with the tenor is the contra-tenor-bassus (i.e. the contrapuntal voice to the tenor). It is further sung with the combined cantus firmus and discantus. Finally the contra-tenor-altus (i.e. the high contrapuntal voice to the tenor) is practiced and fitted in with the other voice parts. Originally this voice was sung by male voices,

193

which explains why some of the lower tessitura parts seem somewhat low for the altos in our mixed choral situations.

The contra-tenor parts should be practiced on short tone syllables like *dahn, bahm, tahn, ding* in an easy, relaxed manner, or with a completely covered tone on syllables like *bim, boom*, etc., guided by a very keen listening ear. The consonants of the tone syllables should be attacked firmly and energetically and be sung with a clear, intensive tone. The singing consonants following vowels should be sounded as soon as possible so that the actual tone appears to begin on the consonants themselves. The choral tone should, as it were, flow through the singing consonants in an unceasing stream of sound which is interrupted only for very brief moments by the vowel sounds like a series of ignited sparks. To show clearly the importance of the supporting function of the cantus firmus, and to isolate its sound from the other parts, one could have the tenor sung to brighter syllables (e.g. *bahm* or *dain*), or to the text, while the other parts would be sung with a darker sound in a bouncy, almost plucked manner to such darker-sounding syllables as *boom* or *doan*. To begin with, each note receives one syllable, but after the lines have been clearly pegged down, each syllable should be sung to as many notes as there will be to each syllable of the words when the music is sung to the text. In the newer editions the groupings of series of notes which are to be sung to one syllable are usually clearly indicated by the curved phrase lines. One must therefore be careful to preserve the clarity and the contour of the individual line. In all voice parts there are significant kinds of tonal movement and expression: the pull toward the heavier accents and musical centers of gravity, the lightness and clarity of the runs, the easy, relaxed, playful movement of the little flourishes, as in the second to the last measure of the tenor, the driving energy of the syncopated note groups, the unritarded, relaxed note movement at the cadences and the sustained energy in the larger melodic curves which permit no intermittent breathing as in the first phrase of the second part. The recognition of all these tonal and dynamic variations is of decisive importance to the performance of the music. The parallel movement between tenor and alto, bass and soprano at *und dir vertraut* should be brought to the attention of the singers and rehearsed separately. The heightened and compacted movement of the weblike texture of the voices at *Bedenk, was Gott dir* must be thoroughly rehearsed by first working with the two outside voices until they, in their displaced positions, can be sung with ease and fluency. By separate practice one should at this point also seek to achieve the same kind of fluency and compatibility with the two inner voices, particularly in the singing of the identical rhythmic figure at the cadence on *hat gesandt*.

The rhythmic clapping of the entire setting would also be valuable — particularly the first and last phrases of the second portion. Here the rhythm of the tenor could be stepped while the contrapuntal parts could be clapped. The higher notes could be clapped with a brighter sound (flat hands) and the lower notes with a darker sound (cupped hands). (Compare with A VII, p. 102 ff.)

The rhythmization of the music should be followed by specialized work with the text (See B II, p. 157 ff.). In this process the words are increasingly absorbed into the rhythm and the melodic flow of the music until the text has been fully comprehended within the context of the rhythm of the music. Rhythmically it is very beneficial for the singers on the two inner voices to speak the words in the rhythm of their own parts. To begin with, every section can practice this exercise separately. This must then be followed up by an intensive simultaneous enunciation of all voice parts, resulting in a kind of polyphonic speech choir. Each person should speak softly, meanwhile listening to the entire speech choir and striving for absolute rhythmic clarity of the rhythmic sequences. This kind of practice removes all difficulties of fitting the syllables with the right note groups, even in polyphonic settings with less flowing and more jagged and irregular melodic lines. The singing of the text now succeeds with sureness and clarity. Inasmuch as the words, on the one hand, help to determine the musical character of the tune (e.g. *Bedenk was Gott dir hat getan*), the entire musical structure, on the other hand, is governed by inherent musical and structural principles. This holds true even more for the interlacing polyphonic parts. Frequently the words are only a means of supporting a passage or movement which is symbolically or musically self-sufficient. Words can give impetus to musical movement, produce little musical eddies and rapids within the larger tonal stream. There is also the kind of music in which the syllables, almost like ships on a sea, float along on the musical stream.

In conducting the example, the director should use the four-beat pattern. The left hand should sustain, without the slightest hesitation, the important moments of musical tension at the phrase endings, while the right hand conducts the beats of the measure. The upbeat which follows is given with both hands simultaneously, with an intensive rebounding motion as if the director were throwing an object at something. Particular attention should be given to the slur in the tenor at the end of the first and second sections, and the fourth beat following the cadential half tone of the soprano should receive a separate, clearly marked beat. Meanwhile the left hand supports the three lower voices. The final chord is cued in and sustained with both hands. The more expansive melodic line of the middle part,

Bedenk was Gott, should be animated by using larger and more sweeping gestures, and here the left hand could trace the wide musical arch of the tenor. From "und dir vertraut" the director should, if he wants to adhere consistently to the four-beat pattern, conduct the outside voices with smoother, more fluid movements in keeping with the more flowing quality of the basic duple rhythm of the entire piece. In order, however, to direct the cantus firmus with greater care and intensity for the purpose of exposing the textual and musical structure with greater clarity, the director can reflect in his conducting the sudden changes of melodic movement and musical tensions of the main voice which also gives him more effective control of the total musical happenings. (See A VIII, p. 135 ff.) It would be senseless to try to follow every little melodic curve or directional pull of the other voices.

The imitative musical writing of this type of composition can be further illustrated with "April Is in My Mistress' Face" by Thomas Morley (p. 8, *The A cappella Singer,* E. C. Schirmer, Boston). Each section will be better prepared to sing its own part if everyone first sings the tune and the melodic elements from which the imitative parts are derived. If a polyphonic setting contains canonic parts in addition to other free polyphonic parts, all singers should first sing the canonic voices, e.g. *Entlaubet ist der Wald* (The Forest leaves have fallen) by Ludwig Senfl (No. 98, *Gesellige Zeit,* Baerenreiter). Voice parts which are placed against each other in parallel or contrary motion require special clarification and security. By singing the parts in isolation, their relationship to each other becomes clear. The conclusion of the three-voice polyphonic chorale setting of "To Thee Alone, Lord Jesus Christ" by M. Praetorius serves as an example of this.

Example 53

Here is an excerpt from J. Burgstaller's setting of Psalm 100.

196

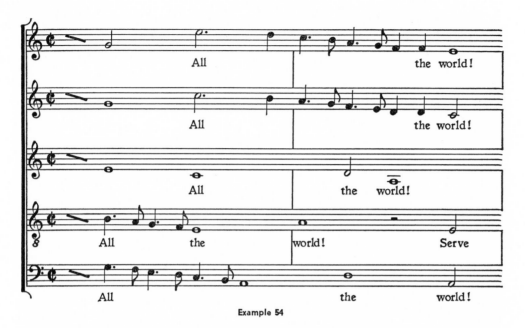

Example 54

A further example is the final (double) phrase of the four-voice madrigal, "Darling, You Have Me Captured" by Hans Leo Hassler (No. 82, *Gesellige Zeit*).

From *Gesellige Zeit*, copyright Baerenreiter Verlag, Kassel, Germany.

Example 55

These voice parts are rehearsed individually, sung together with short tone syllables, and rhythmicized by clapping. To strengthen the interrelationship of the parts, the singers should be seated in such a formation that they can see one another. Refer to what has been said earlier in regard to translating such musical sections into bodily movements. (A VI, p. 91 ff.)

Polyphonic cantus firmus compositions and polyphonic motets should generally be worked out according to these principles and suggestions, the approach being varied by condensing or expanding them as required in each case. This would include the sacred and secular cantus firmus works of the sixteenth century, the motets and masses of the Netherlanders and their successors, the polyphonic music of Heinrich Schuetz and J. S. Bach, and the contemporary choral works of Hugo Distler and Ernst Pepping. In this kind of study the many differences and varieties of word-tone relationships should be a determining factor in approaching the rehearsal of each composition. In the motet works of Melchior Franck, J. H. Schein, and Schuetz, for example, one should first analyze the form and study the sense of the text (by a sensible application of the above-mentioned principles of studying a new work) in order to discover how the dramatic truth of this type of polyphonic music is constantly affected in myriads of ways by the inspiration and vitality of the text, and how the long, expansive musical lines are always bound to the concrete word. In the choral works of J. S. Bach, on the other hand, the music, though inspired and ignited by the word, departs from a close dependence on the textual body for detailed musical and spiritual expression; instead, it achieves its inherent musical symbolism with its own musical and spiritual qualities. When working with the choral music of Bach it is therefore more sensible to isolate the musical web from the text (after the sense of the text has been clarified), and to rehearse the music until it is quite secure before singing it with the text. At another session the text can be fitted to the music — not for its potential for verbal expressiveness or "word-coloring," but to give orientation and meaning to the interpretative and spiritual qualities of the music. In combining words and music in the choral works of Bach one must not develop the text from its natural organism according to methods suggested for music of the early and pre-baroque period, but one must discover and elicit the particular phenomena which are required by Bach's musical intentions and creative will. For example, in the fugal theme of "Cum Sancto Spiritu in Gloria" in the *Mass in B minor,* the syllables "ri-tu-in" require a light and rhythmic martellato-like enunciation and a long, joyous, and rhythmic melismatic singing of the syllable "glo" in "gloria." The light, rhythmic, florid music on the word "gloria" is a musical representation (spiritualization) of the spiritual joy and richness associated with the meaning of this word. To sing the text as in natural, flexible speech, i.e. with the intent of making the words expressive in their own right, too easily gives the choral music of Bach a foreign, sensuous character. The word then merely hangs heavily into the web of voices and does not achieve the necessary musical spiritualization.

The well-known and delightful five-voice Italian villanella, "A lieta vita" by G. Gastoldi (p. 69, *Gesellige Zeit*), derives its musical life and interest from the rhythm. This dance-like pastoral song is written in binary form (*Aufgesang* and *Abgesang*) with a double bar at the end of the first section. The two-measure rhythmic entity is stated twice in the first section and four times in the second section. The basic rhythmic form of this madrigal is as follows:

First section   2 × ♩ ♩ ♩ | 𝅗𝅥   ♩ |
Second section   4 × ♩ ♩ ♩ | 𝅗𝅥   ♩ | 𝅗𝅥   ♩ | 𝅗𝅥. ♪♩ | 𝅗𝅥   ♩ | 𝅗𝅥. ‖

Example 56

In approaching the study of this song through rhythmic clapping, the choir should be divided into four groups. The director claps the rhythm of the "fa-la-la" refrain which the choir immediately claps after him several times in succession. The two-measure rhythmic pattern of the first and second sections is clapped in the same manner. The whole song is now clapped in rondo fashion with the first and second groups successively clapping the two-measure rhythms of the first section and with all four groups coming in on the refrain. In the second section, each of the four groups clap this pattern successively with all the groups clapping simultaneously on the second refrain. To keep the clapping lively and meaningful, the exercises should be varied in different ways. The first and third groups could clap with a lighter and brighter sound (flat hand), while the second and fourth groups clap with a darker sound (cupped hand), or the two-measure rhythmic pattern could be stepped while the refrain is clapped, etc.

When the choir is securely established in the rhythmic gait of the music the tune is practiced on tonal syllables which are chosen in keeping with the character of the music and the sound of the words, which in this case would be short, bright syllables like *deng, peng, vain, tahn, bahm, bahl.* It would be well for all singers to learn the tune, which incidentally has been adopted as a cantus firmus in German church music and as a hymn tune in a few English hymnals. Again, as in many previous examples, the outside voices constitute the melodic and harmonic structure and support for the total composition. In spite of this the filler voices must also, vocally speaking, be clearly defined. The first three notes of each rhythmic entity should be felt as an upbeat whereby the actual stress falls on the half note only. The phrases should be clearly delineated from the refrain by means of a catch breath. A clear differentiation should be made between F and F#. The overlapping thirds of the second soprano should be sung with a high focus and with as bright a sound as possible. Singers and director must listen carefully and deliberately to the frequent parallel third passages of the two soprano parts and rehearse them separately.

The tone syllables can be the bridge in making the transition from the

199

rhythm to the words. The rhythmic speaking of the text should receive a thorough-going treatment whereby the vowels are produced as brightly as possible and the consonants are articulated with great intensity as a further means of sharpening up and energizing the rhythm. The "fa-la-la" of the refrain should be pronounced with a short "a" and a long "l" and should actually be pronounced as "fal-lal-lal-lal-lal-lal-la." The breaking up of the half notes into quarter notes in the second refrain is not a problem since the rhythm grows out of the natural, rhythmic flow of the "fa-la-la" syllable.

There are three basic possibilities for conducting this uniformly flowing, dance-like music:

(1) each measure can be conducted with a regular three-beat pattern;

(2) one horizontally directed beat is given on the first beat of each measure, resulting in a back and forth pendulum-like movement; and

(3) the first and second beats of the measure are combined into one downbeat with a quick return motion on the third beat.

In the earlier stages of rehearsing, the author would choose the first form, i.e. the regular three-beat pattern. In working out the interpretative and artistic aspects, however, the director should free himself from such mechanical conducting of one basic pattern and seek to combine all three possibilities in accordance with the course and progress of the music. The regular pattern (first) should be used in the first measure to indicate the tempo as clearly as possible while the swing-like movement in the refrain would best be represented by one beat to the measure, particularly in the first refrain. In between these parts the possibilities of the second basic pattern should be used to full advantage with an occasional use of the third type of pattern. Besides the judicious combination of the various beat patterns, the director must also be ready to assimilate in his conducting movements the impulses and inspiration which the words give to the music. The various patterns and movements, however, must be instinctively combined into a unified whole.

The director can proceed in a similar way with different madrigals, traditional or more recent arrangements of dance songs, hunting choruses, sea chanteys, and other jovial and humorous choral music which is characterized by a strong, rhythmic interest. In this process the choir should enter immediately and without hesitation into the rhythmic momentum which constitutes the musical essence of such songs. All subsequent work proceeds from this rhythmic basis, and it is in this easy and play-like manner that the choir arrives at the true artistic core of the music, which would have been almost or completely inaccessible by the round-about way of separate practice of text and tune.

In studying the differently structured musical forms, it might be particularly helpful to have the singers think, i.e. mentally sing, their parts. For instance, while the sopranos (or tenors as the case may be) sing the melody, the other singers think their parts. This helps to strengthen both the rhythmic sense and the tonal imagery of the choir. The mental singing of a voice part should always serve as a preliminary step to the actual singing of the part. If one is rehearsing with two parts, the third part can be supplied mentally; this prevents the singers of the third voice from interfering with the practice of the other two parts. Meanwhile they have been actively involved in the rehearsal.

The approach of allowing the essential style and character of the musical work to determine the method of practicing the parts in the order in which they probably were composed, of taking note of the musical structure, and of using the suggested rehearsal aids, turns the whole learning process into a musical experience. This approach provides a sound way of arriving at the musical essence of the particular setting, it saves time and nervous energy, and is conducive to a more comprehensive and musical development of the choir. At one time choirs possessed these methods and rehearsal aids (which today are acquired artificially) as natural skills and techniques developed as a matter of course through everyday activities. These included the recitation of psalm tones (chant) and the unison singing of psalm tunes in the daily services in which even the children participated, the use of tonal syllables while yodelling, countless refrains, additions, and interludes to madrigals, villanellas and other songs of a gay and jovial nature. Folk dances and dancing games furnished natural rhythmic practice. To this kind of subconscious, play-like training, musical social games could be added, like the identification of a song by its rhythm, tongue twisters, song medleys, recognizing the words and meaning of songs with misplaced verbal accents, and quizzes like "Fractured Phrases."

The questions of performance practices that have to do with the dynamics and the use of instruments with the choir must be dealt with later. It may suffice to say here that the manner of music making must not be geared to the whims of the listeners but to the musical work itself; it must not seek only to produce effects but must be genuine in its artistic presentation. If it is the purpose to realize the inner form and structure of a work through the movement and flow of the music, then the dynamics, in order to serve this structure, must evolve from the opposing tensions created by the different forces of musical energy. Otherwise the music could be likened to a wall which has been outwardly decorated with wall paper. In many of our current editions we must frequently relinquish our dependence on the dynamic labels which have been "pasted on" to the music. A good way of testing the real worth of a musical work is to sing it without any dynamic swells for the purpose of discovering whether its musical substance is so genuine and strong that it won't collapse when singing it in this way. The director must also be clear in his own mind with regard to the use of instruments with the choir. He should realize that the so-called pure a cappella ideal originated during the Classical and Romantic Periods, and that during the great epochs of European choral music the method of freely combining and interchanging voices and instruments was regarded as a normal procedure.*

---

*Translator's note: Dr. Ehmann has written a discourse on this called *Der Thibault-Behaghel Kreis* for the *Archiv fuer Musikforschung* (Archive of Musicology) in 1938 and 1939.

Chapter V

The Choral Evening:

Rehearsal and Performance

According to familiar concepts a choir lives its life in a steady alternation from rehearsal to performance. One cannot deny that this kind of life includes a certain amount of mechanical routine. With the large musical societies devoted to the task of performing the larger choral works like the oratorios of Handel and Haydn, such a routine of rehearsal and performance cannot be avoided and is in fact desirable and sensible. Since such larger choral societies are largely comprised of specially selected and talented singers, one may assume that their musical ability is not exhausted by their participation in the rehearsals and concerts, but that their contribution to this climactic, concerted effort has a wide and sustaining basis in various types of their own chosen, creative musical endeavors in the form of social music making, singing and playing in chamber groups, singing in church choirs, solo singing and playing, etc. With this kind of background and preparation their participation in concert choirs should not be limited to tedious note drilling or the presentation of a sophisticated, unintelligible verbal and musical utterance, but it should rather be a festive and exciting experience and should represent a crowning effort of their previous individual musical experiences within the present context of a larger body of performers. This concept of the value of various previous musical experiences to the singing of larger choral works can be denied only by people who have never participated in such choral ventures under expert leadership. It can be denied only by those for whom rehearsals have had a relative value only, namely, the preparation for the final performance.

In terms of concerted effort, involvement, concentration, and musical growth, there are important ethical values which come to the singer through the careful, systematic preparation of a large choral work. It also provides the opportunity for a particularly intensive encounter with the spirit of the work and its composer. This, of course, requires some well-planned rehearsals for individual singers and special sectional rehearsals for the various voice sections. Such special rehearsals are a great time saver and prevent unnecessary fatigue. The coupling of voices for special rehearsals should be planned according to the structure of the music — e.g. adjacent voices in a canon or a fugue; the voice on the main melody with the voices on a part that moves in contrary motion to it. In multichoir works the individual choirs should first rehearse separately.

A larger musical society (e.g. oratorio choir) which must spend considerable time in rehearsing a work can, under competent direction and with a large proportion of active and enthusiastic members, overcome and rise above the routine of the incessant cycle of rehearsal and performance. This is achieved by keeping rehearsals interesting, informative, and creative through such innovations as the interpolation of appropriate vocal and ear-training exercises, by explanatory comments, by appropriate lectures and by "internal" musical events performed by smaller musical groups drawn from the choral membership, by social gatherings and other social and musical events.

Choirs with less ambitious musical aims, but which nevertheless would like to appear in a public performance, should make it their special concern and aim, before they begin to concertize publicly, to first become a community of singers by experiencing something of the stimulating, creative, and formative forces of music, and by realizing how music can personally influence and shape one's thinking and life. A rehearsal should not be a painful experience endured for the sake of a final glorious purpose. Ideally, a choir should find its own purpose and reason for existence quite apart from its obligations to a few public performances. It would therefore be more sensible to speak about a "choir night" or a "choral evening" instead of rehearsals and performances. Rather, one might simply differentiate between "internal" and "official" music making. Many well-known designations for serious music groups reflect the meaning of this type of a choral community: society of singers, singing circle, musical guild, Bach-Schuetz-Handel Choir or Society, collegium musicum, pro musica, etc. It is also common for many smaller choirs to adopt the outward mannerisms or behaviorisms of the larger choral societies, without possessing the necessary musical and social substructure, and for this reason become stereotyped instead of allowing themselves to be formed into a unique musical community which could be the basis for the superstructure — the repertoire performed at public concerts. Even the male voice choirs (more prominent in Germany, Wales and other parts of Europe than in North America), which today constitute a weak imitation of larger and stronger concertizing musical organizations, originally functioned as small musical societies (guilds) whose members often possessed a high degree of literary and musical training.

When such groups gathered for social and informal music making, they had to draw upon their own occupational backgrounds and existential roots, particularly if their choirs represented the music department of a certain trade or vocational organization, in which case they were entrusted with the task of influencing the larger society musically. A church choir should also go beyond the rehearsal of its anthems and responses. It too should become a singing community, the singing, musical core of the congregation, and carry forward the musical aspects of the worship service. The process of becoming a singing community applies equally to chamber choirs, school choirs, and to singing groups sponsored by, or growing out of, all types of organizations.

Such choirs should not expend themselves in the paralyzing cycle between rehearsal and performance, but preserve some time and opportunity to discover and develop their own quality and way of life which would enable them to express and fulfill musically a segment of life. To achieve this the rehearsal must, in addition to its relative and immediate value, be invested with an absolute worth by using it as a time of singing and music making for its own sake, as a creative activity in which the internal purpose supersedes the official purpose. It then becomes a meaningful life-giving and life-shaping force with its own unique form, from which every singer can obtain something positive and of lasting value for his own personal life. In striving for this the approach must be varied, of course, according to the type of choir, the age and social background of its members, its purpose and function, the size and nature of the rehearsal room.

In structuring and developing a rehearsal, the following general principles may be observed:

. . . The rehearsal begins with a unison song or with a song improvised in several voices; this encourages lively participation for the new singers as well as for the less musical. This kind of singing at the beginning of a rehearsal helps to relax the singers and also provides the opportunity of combining the choral evening with something seasonal (e.g. singing of a nature song in spring) or with some important event which can further help the singers to become attuned to the evening. The singing of an easier, folk-like selection at the beginning of the rehearsal also expresses the idea of corporate unity and activity and so forms the necessary prerequisite for artistic singing. Church choirs and other religious singing groups might use a hymn to introduce the rehearsal.

. . . Next, one might choose a canon either in place of or as the next musical selection. In addition to the values mentioned, a canon can stimulate and sharpen both ear and musical memory. It also furthers self-reliance and independence, linear thinking and rhythmic ability. Canon singing is the best preparation for polyphonic singing. It also offers various interesting and lively voice-training exercises by singing the music to various tone syllables. For example, in the canon "A Ram Sam Sam" (p. 30, *Let's All Sing*, American Camping Association), which contains a series of musical syllables in the Morocco tongue, one could substitute this syllable with any suitable syllables for vocalization purposes, particularly with such syllables as occur in the musical selection which is to be sung right after the canon. Such easy unison canons should be chosen in accordance with the time and season of the year, their inherent musical and teaching value, and the sentiments and aspirations of the group. When the interest of the choir has been roused and the singers have caught the mood of the evening, the director may introduce a few breathing and loosening-up exercises if such exercises have not already been used.

Following this the rehearsal of the main work of the evening begins. Rhythmic, ear, voice, and speech training exercises would normally not be practiced beforehand, but should be developed from the musical work itself and introduced during the course of the rehearsal (See A III, p. 32 ff.). In this way the relevance of these exercises to the work remains clear; they will not bore the choir as readily and they can help to loosen up the choir both physically and mentally in the course of a strenuous rehearsal.

After completing the rehearsing of the major work assignment, one or several familiar and more easily sung choral selections could be repeated. This keeps the choir musically flexible, helps to preserve the joy of singing, and is of course the best way of keeping the repertoire of the choir fresh and ready for use. At this point in the rehearsal one might occasionally consider some of the wishes of the singers with regard to the choice of music.

To conclude the rehearsal, a unison or multivoiced improvised evening song, a choral epigram, or an evening canon could be sung. The reasons for choosing this type of song are similar to those mentioned above in connection with the beginning of the rehearsal. A church choir might conclude with a short evening meditation.

The interpolation of technical exercises and the setting up of a meaningful rehearsal procedure is closely related to the question of handling the singers in a tactful manner. Large choirs and oratorio societies, which are composed of capable singers with a good musical background, are usually captivated and motivated by the power and greatness of the musical work itself. For this reason such singers can be confronted directly with technical aspects of the work. Here it would be advisable to begin the rehearsal with loosening up, breathing, and voice-training exercises and then refer back to these matters from time to time as necessary during the course of the rehearsal. One should also conclude the rehearsal in a meaningful way —

it should never be terminated suddenly and mechanically by stopping a chorus in a selection which still requires a great deal of study and rehearsal. Rather, one should select and review a familiar piece — or at least review the main work of the evening in order to experience it as a consistent and coherent entity. In such choirs the technical exercises can be offered to form a systematic course of instruction. For example, the chapters on voice training, rhythmic training, etc., could be divided into several parts and could be taken up in a systematic sequence at the beginning of the rehearsals. Whenever the intonation of the choir begins to suffer from a lack of concentrated listening on the part of the singers, the director should from time to time introduce ear training exercises taken from a short ear training course. Over a period of time an entire course could be completed in this manner.

In working with a youth choir, on the other hand, the director will want to lay a greater emphasis on the experiential side of music making, in which the evening of corporate singing would be conceived more in terms of an extended "music in the home" experience, or it could be treated as a friendly social gathering in which singing is the unifying factor. Technical exercises should be introduced in a more casual, perhaps somewhat play-like manner. It would also be quite in order to have an appropriate reading, or to play or sing something for the choir. The entire evening as such should take on a creative shape and should acquire a sense and meaning of its own quite apart from the learning and acquisition of certain prescribed musical numbers.

Inasmuch as it belongs to the essential nature of informal and social singing that the introduction of new tunes and the employment of the necessary technical exercises occur in a casual, play-like manner, insofar it is also a mark of artistic and creative music making if the director works consciously and seriously with the music itself. Even in artistic choral singing one should fully utilize the approaches and techniques of the entertainment world to lend freshness and imagination to artistic singing, and to provide enjoyment, amusement, and a positive and personal relationship with the singers. The technical work including specialized and detailed work which is necessary beyond this kind of informal treatment should always occur as music making. Every rehearsal or choral evening should be a time of music making, and only when it becomes this can a choir fulfill its true obligations. Only as the participants sing their way into a musical work can their creative powers unfold and blossom forth. This requires the constant active participation of every singer. Even if most members read notes well, the responsible director should not shun thorough, detailed work with each separate section. While listening to one section rehearse, the others should sing their parts mentally, and where appropriate, hum lightly. Everyone must be constantly "in the music" and the choir director should develop a special ability to draw all the singers back into the total musical event. He can achieve this by his own personal manner and procedure, by combining the voice parts in various ways, and by his criticisms, questions, and teaching. With well-trained and flexible singers one might occasionally have all the singers sing each voice part. This would, in addition to a more complete involvement of all the singers, help the singers to receive better understanding of the score and would make for more intelligent singing and music making. Dry, empty drills should be avoided at all times, for whenever note poking begins, music making ceases! Now this does not mean that the entire choral evening has to proceed in the spirit of fun and play. On the contrary, the true serious-ness of faithful, artistic labor should constitute the basis of the musical experience, and the director should, in his effort to unfold the meaning of the work, learn to put forth a holy zeal which is "worth the sweat of a nobleman."

The making of musical sounds should not cease until the next rehearsal the following week. A rehearsal is to be considered successful only if the music continues to sound in the singer's ear. The choir should experience the joy that comes from the transforming and creative energies of artistic activity, and this joy should not leave the singers when they leave the re-hearsal room but should continue to motivate and shape their entire lives. The responsibility of the choir director towards his singers therefore does not stop with the conclusion of the weekly rehearsal (choral evening) for whatever the singers sing, whistle, or play on their way home, at home, and at work is of concern to him. If the music continues to sound in the ear of the singer after the rehearsal, the director may consider this an indication of good, honest work on his part.

If a male choir, for example, according to traditional custom, gathers together for a party after a rehearsal, the choir director even as a professional or semiprofessional musician, should not exclude himself from their company. Whatever is sung at the table also belongs to his realm of responsibility and the fact that there is any singing at all on this occasion, and that the life-enriching powers of music may here also be in evidence is reason enough to be concerned, vocationally or otherwise that the singing on such occasions should not deteriorate into thoughtless, gleeful singing and stupefying rev-elry. So the rehearsal must authenticate itself not only at the concert per-formance but also at informal parties — for here the true worth of the re-hearsal is put on trial. The traditional collegium musicums, conviviums, and madrigal groups offer rich historical illustrations of the carry-over potential of a high level of music making at social functions. In the final analysis, even the quality of home life of the individual singers should be affected by the inspiration and import of the rehearsals.

The deportment of the choir director during a choral evening is to a great extent determined and conditioned by the musical work itself and by his choir. With a choir of laymen one would communicate in a different manner than to an academic musical organization. The director will conduct himself differently when rehearsing secular music than during the rehearsal of a passion oratorio. Even the inflection and modulation of his voice can help to create atmosphere. The director should express himself with brevity, clarity, and logic and always direct the attention toward essential matters. He should not shout or give verbal directions while the singers are singing, nor should he count audibly with the singers. Such shouting does more harm than good since the singers are too absorbed with their task of reading, watching the director, and listening to each other. A brief, appropriate instruction thrown in during a breathing pause at the end of a phrase is much more helpful. The director should always give a brief justification or rationale for his directions to the choir. This makes for a better understanding of the director's intentions and helps to dispel any unwillingness or hesitancy on the part of the singers. Unfortunately, the domineering temperament and rudeness of many directors in many instances have almost become legendary. Every fit of anger and harsh scolding harms not only the atmosphere for good singing but the voices themselves. If the tempers are too warm at a rehearsal, a good fire and thunder session, if justified, can on occasion certainly help to clear the air!

All singing should take place in an atmosphere and attitude of freedom and enjoyment, which is the best preparation for soul, body, and larynx (See A II, p. 19 ff.). Genuine authority, skill, and tact in dealing with contrary elements, a ready humor and a patience always ready to assume the task of dealing with musical and human elements, will always insure the director of a good response from the singers. The kind of temperament which sweeps the singers along and which has become an almost legendary prerequisite of the director, can be a great asset, particularly for his interpretative work. On the other hand, such a temperament should not lead to a continual shaking up of the elements, nor should it lead to the kind of ecstatic experience which leaves the body and particularly the larynx in a cramped, overexcited state. As valuable and necessary as the outgoing animation and enthusiasm of the director may be, so valuable and necessary is also his relaxed composure which bans all nervousness and personal distractions. He should not have to shout when calling for the attention of the choir. To the extent to which the choir becomes louder and more restless, the director should speak with softness and composure, for this is always the best way to establish a good contact with the choir. He should speak in a natural manner on a medium-pitch level. In everything which the director does, whether actively or passively, he should always bear in mind that there is hardly another life situation in which the example of the leader has such an all-inclusive and shaping influence as in a choral situation. This influence affects the voice production, tone color, the diction and breathing to the point where the music derives its own life and substance from the director who, of course, has first transmitted it to the singers.

In repeating isolated passages the director should have a comprehensive and a rather concrete goal in mind as to what he wants to achieve, and he should explain his intentions to the singers. He should not proceed mechanically with an instruction like, "Let's begin at measure 10," but should divide the composition up into meaningful phrases, motives, and other musical relationships within the work. Rehearsal practice in this respect ought also to be musical!

From the very outset the director should encourage his singers to sing as much as possible by memory. The printed music can set up unnecessary barriers between the choir and its director and also between the singers themselves. The traditional choristers (Kantoreien) stood around one large music stand and everyone sang from one large musical score. One can imagine the freedom, flexibility, and concentration which this gave to their singing. The lay singer today usually does not possess the capacity to watch the director, his music, and the other singers in the choir simultaneously as do professional instrumentalists. In order to devote himself entirely to the unified music making of the group, and to be alert to the impulses of the director, the singer should at least know half of the music by memory. So many singers are only too ready to hide themselves behind their music, and the director must use a large portion of his energy and efforts to bring these wayward and unalert people out of their hiding. Frequently singers stare into their books from sheer habit, and if they are occasionally forced to put their music away, one may observe, to the surprise of everyone, that they can actually do without it! Furthermore, there is a close relationship between memory singing and "inner" singing. One could almost conclude that the more a choir sings from memory the more "inward" it sounds. Many choirs are asked to sing for various occasions for which it is not always possible or feasible to use scores — e.g. an evening serenade or other occasions where there is insufficient light for reading. Every choir should have a repertoire of songs which can be sung at any time without the use of music.

The seating arrangement of the choir during rehearsal should follow the same principles as the recommended circular or semicircular formations for performance (See A I, p. 7 ff.). Even if the standing position is much more conducive to good singing, it nevertheless seems advisable to set up chairs for the rehearsal to permit the singers who are engaged in strenuous daytime occupations to sit down at least periodically during the rehearsal. This does not mean that they are to use their chairs as a reclining comfort by stretching the body between the edge of the chair and the upper part of the back support, leisurely crossing one leg over the other. During active singing the singer should sit in a natural and upright position with both feet solidly on the floor so that he can, with a slight motion, raise himself to a standing position. It would be mentally and physically refreshing to have the various sections vary somewhat frequently between sitting and standing positions. Normally one would rehearse the sections in a sitting position and after the parts are more secure they would be sung in a standing position. The director should stand as much as possible during rehearsal for this allows his physical motions and the radiant energies of his entire body to be unleashed and transmitted to the choir with the greatest freedom, thus greatly undergirding and supporting the entire work. Furthermore, the working out of the technical and musical task occurs almost by itself, so to speak.

For tardiness of singers at rehearsals there is only one remedy: start on time. This means that the director himself must be present on time and begin right on time with those singers who are present, even if there are only three. All other devices, like scolding, rewards for punctuality, verbal and written admonishments, prove to be ineffective in the long run. The rehearsal must stop as punctually as it started. If the spirit and enthusiasm of a choir is particularly high, one could of course on occasion take advantage of this by extending the length of the rehearsal and advance the work of the choir to a new level of achievement. However, such extension of rehearsal time must be regarded as an exceptional event. Whatever the situation, the director must know how to use the rehearsal time at his disposal to full advantage, for the creative opportunities of the rehearsal period can never be precalculated since they are conditioned by a hundred human and artistic factors. It is particularly in connection with creative, artistic work that one cannot produce results by coercion. The choir director must have the patience, the humility, and the ability to wait. In the life of the average choir the director encounters times of low productivity or "dead" periods, but once the iron in the fire is hot, he must not lose any time in doing some first-rate forging.

The final rehearsal (also known in America as the "dress" rehearsal) must be held in the hall in which the performance is to be given. The purpose of this rehearsal is to adjust the music making and the formation of the performers to the acoustical and physical properties of the room. At this rehearsal one should not have to work at the music itself. The singers take their places and the director should once more check the formation (See A I, p. 7 ff.) and decide when and how the choir enters and leaves. The lighting should also be checked. It should not be too dark, but neither so bright that the singer is blinded when looking at his music or when watching the director. Most important of all is the testing of the acoustical properties of the room. If the concert is to take place in a church sanctuary, it becomes a question whether to sing from the chancel or from the balcony. If the choir is to perform in a hall or an auditorium, the backward and forward shifting of the choir by one yard on the stage can greatly influence the acoustics. The use of curtains or partitions should be carefully looked into since curtains tend to absorb sound. In rooms with over-live acoustics the tempo should be reduced somewhat and the enunciation intensified. In rooms with poor acoustics and little resonance, the tempo should be appropriately increased and by careful and skillful utilization of the singing consonants the music can still be made to sound well. In an empty hall it is always a problem to predict the acoustical properties after it is filled with people. The director can develop a "feel" for this change in acoustics, but he must nevertheless be prepared during performances to cancel his previous approach for dealing with the acoustical situation. The choir might use a wooden wall, ceiling, or acoustical shell, to good advantage as a resonating surface.

The final rehearsals should not diminish the anticipation of the performance. The director should consciously allow for the possibility of a greater, more heightened experience than the dress rehearsal itself. He should be particularly careful not to exhaust his singers mentally or physically. It is here that directors in their well-meant zeal so often sin. It is better, at the final rehearsal, to ignore an imperfection in a certain passage and keep the singers mentally and physically alert and happy, than to dwell on details until the last moment and then have to drag the weary and nervous performers to the concert. An overexcited and overly tense dress rehearsal can easily result in a meek, lustreless performance. Perhaps this is where the commonly held idea originated that a dress rehearsal must of necessity go badly. This, no doubt, is an erroneous notion when considering that all musical and technical aspects should by this time have been thoroughly rehearsed and brought under control.

At a specific time prior to the performance, the members of the choir should assemble in a special room, not only to collect their thoughts and to prepare themselves inwardly and outwardly for their task, but also for a short vocal warmup. The author regards this as an indispensable prerequisite for a good performance. If this vocal conditioning is carried out with patience and a good knowledge of the processes involved, then a good deal of the performance has already been made secure. It is self-evident that a violin player tunes his instrument before a concert and that he practices until he feels that he is in good playing form. How much more should the choir member (usually a lay singer) whose instrument (larynx and body) cannot be put into a protective case during the day, be concerned about freeing his instrument from the activities and tensions which are in opposition to music making. He needs to condition the voice properly for music making. A choir of lay singers must also warm up mentally and emotionally before it is capable of its best production.

In these warming-up exercises one should certainly include a few calisthenics, loosening-up exercises (compare A I, p. 3 ff.), as well as a few breathing and voice-training exercises in the course of which the voice must be brought to its proper focus (compare with A III, p. 33 ff.). It might also be well to sing one of the choral selections, perhaps the first one on the program or the most difficult one, with an easy, light tone. This singing should never be an all-out effort; as soon as the choir has achieved the desired readiness the exercises should be discontinued. The director should use this opportunity to draw the attention of his choir to the particular character or mood of the music which is to follow. This is done, not by an appeal or general instruction, but perhaps by a casual word, and above all by the attitude and manner with which he relates to his choir. Some church choirs assemble for prayer before proceeding to their place of musical service.

During the performance the director should demand unqualified attention and dedication to the task at hand. Any casting of furtive glances into the audience, particularly during active music making, should be strictly forbidden. Thorough preparatory training must be the basis for the inner security and confidence of a choir as it appears before the public. Yet, in spite of such reassuring preparation, the singers should maintain the readiness and the capacity to rise triumphantly beyond the musical achievements and experiences of the rehearsal, to give the director the opportunity to elicit all the vocal and musical ability which they possess and to keep themselves open for a creative and musically formative experience which might never have been achieved during rehearsals. Nervousness and fidgeting should be overcome by the director's own tranquility and poise and not through reprimanding words.

If other artists (e.g. soloists and instrumentalists) are to make separate appearances during the concert, the cabaret-like on and off movement to and from the stage should be studiously avoided. One could seat the choir on a suitably prearranged formation of chairs, so that the choir need only to quietly rise to sing from where they are seated.

If the choir is to participate on a festive occasion, the director should be instructed in advance with regard to the entire procedure and his particular assignment within the context of the festivity. He should be in contact with the other artistic groups and performers, and with the particular speaker or master of ceremonies, well in advance, so that he has a clear idea of the kind of contribution his choir is expected to make in the course of the evening. Even if on such occasions the choir is required to contribute only one selection, it should participate wholeheartedly, inwardly and outwardly in the entire festivity. If the choir's collaboration could grow out of united effort at the point of its participation, this would further the course and movement of the festivity in a meaningful way. Appearing late on the stage or leaving it before the festivity is over not only disturbs in a technical way but disrupts the atmosphere and sense of a genuine festive celebration. This applies particularly to a worship service.

If the singer in his personal and everyday life must give heed to his body which is his instrument not only for singing, but of life itself, such care applies to an even greater measure during the frequent irregularities of a choir tour. Many other factors can be decisive in the success of a concert tour: the avoidance of celebrations extending into the wee hours of the morning, the use of the morning hours for traveling, refraining from much speaking while traveling in noisy vehicles, adequate sleep and necessary bed rest before performances, setting aside one free day each week, occasional change of program, careful choice of choir members in accordance with their ability to get along with each other, success in performances, and many other factors.